CUTTING LIFE SHORT

Cutting Life Short

Dan Fetsco

A SECOND LOOK AT LIFE SENTENCES

Foreword by

JAMES M. BINNALL

University of Wyoming Press
LARAMIE

Published by University of Wyoming Press
An imprint of University Press of Colorado
1580 North Logan Street, Suite 660
PMB 39883
Denver, Colorado 80203-1942

Printed in the United States of America

The University Press of Colorado is a proud member of
Association of University Presses.

The University Press of Colorado is a cooperative publishing enterprise supported, in part, by Adams State University, Colorado School of Mines, Colorado State University, Fort Lewis College, Metropolitan State University of Denver, University of Alaska Fairbanks, University of Colorado, University of Northern Colorado, University of Wyoming, Utah State University, and Western Colorado University.

∞ This paper meets the requirements of the ANSI/NISO Z39.48-1992 (Permanence of Paper).

ISBN: 978-1-64642-854-0 (hardcover)
ISBN: 978-1-64642-855-7 (ebook)
https://doi.org/10.5876/9781646428557

Library of Congress Cataloging-in-Publication Data

Names: Fetsco, Daniel author | Binnall, James M. (James Michael), 1976– writer of foreword
Title: Cutting life short : a second look at life sentences / Daniel Fetsco ; Foreword by James M. Binnall, University of Wyoming, Laramie.
Description: First. | Laramie : University of Wyoming Press, 2026. | Includes bibliographical references and index.
Identifiers: LCCN 2026008346 (print) | LCCN 2026008347 (ebook) | ISBN 9781646428540 hardcover | ISBN 9781646428557 ebook
Subjects: LCSH: Imprisonment—Wyoming | Life imprisonment—Wyoming | Sentences (Criminal procedure)—Wyoming | Prisoners—Legal status, laws, etc.—Wyoming | Prosecutorial misconduct—Wyoming | Clemency—Wyoming | Criminal justice, Administration of—Wyoming | Criminal justice, Administration of—United States | LCGFT: Case studies
Classification: LCC KFW4788 .F48 2026 (print) | LCC KFW4788 (ebook)
LC record available at https://lccn.loc.gov/2026008346
LC ebook record available at https://lccn.loc.gov/2026008347

Cover art: Unidentified artist, *Untitled*, ink on cotton. Courtesy National Hispanic Cultural Center Art Museum. Accession # 2019.30.47

To those imprisoned and deserving of a second chance, and to my father, who spent time in the Wyoming State Penitentiary and taught me that greatness exists behind the walls

Contents

Figures

Foreword

In 1999, I was the driver in a fatal DUI wreck that claimed the life of my passenger, a close friend and a college wrestling teammate. A year later, I was convicted for that crime and sentenced to three-and-a-half to seven years in a Pennsylvania state prison. I began my term of incarceration in 2000 and was released on parole on June 21, 2004.

The first stop in my incarceration was the State Correctional Institute, Graterford, a maximum-security state prison in the Philadelphia area that was featured in Victor Hassine's prison memoir *Life Without Parole: Living in Prison Today*. When I arrived at Graterford, I was wholly unfamiliar with how to navigate life inside prison. For months, I struggled to get "dug in." I was wary of making friends but even warier of trying to do time alone and isolated.

It was then, a few months into my sentence, that I met several fellow inmates who took me on as a sort of mentee; all of them were inmates serving life sentences. They schooled me on the "convict code," which demanded that I comply with rules and regulations promulgated by prisoners but not

https://doi.org/10.5876/9781646428557.c000a

found in the inmate handbook. They explained that while an administrative rule violation brought the threat of solitary confinement in "the hole," noncompliance with the convict code created the real possibility of immediate injury or death at the hands of another inmate. These "lifers" emphasized the importance of having a trusted group of people with whom to associate in prison and how a regular routine could help pass time. Above all else, they noted that prison is home for however long one is there and ought to be respected as such, because for them, it was the only home they would ever know. In those early days of my imprisonment, the men who protected and guided me (without recompense) were all lifers who, in the end, ensured that I understood the incarceration assignment and eventually made it out even when they never would.

Prior to prison, I had views of lifers that were largely shaped by movies and media accounts that depicted them as monsters forever locked in the dungeons of our nation's "correctional facilities." Folklore held that they had "nothing to lose" and would uniformly respond to any overture with aggression. Lifers were not amenable to friendships, I assumed, and did not possess normal feelings of empathy or compassion. Rather, they were the quintessential "criminals," confined for life because they simply could not walk free without repeatedly and severely victimizing the weaker and unsuspecting among us.

After my quarantine time at Graterford ended, I was moved to Pennsylvania's central classification center—the State Correctional Institute, Camp Hill. The site of a bloody riot in 1989, Camp Hill housed roughly 4,000 inmates when I arrived, a large percentage of whom were serving life sentences. Again, my time at Camp Hill was made easier by the men around me who were lifers. The men who called Camp Hill their permanent home helped me secure a work assignment, got my phone/visit list approved, and arranged my living situation such that I had a safe existence when I was in my cell. They also encouraged me to take advantage of the time I was inside, explaining often that they lived vicariously through the men who did their time and went home to experience and accomplish amazing things. In response, I promised them I would take their advice to heart and that I would work to get better while I was confined.

Along those lines, in 2001, I petitioned the superintendent of Camp Hill for permission to take my Law School Admission Test (LSAT) while incarcerated. Though my request was initially denied, the superintendent later relented after strong lobbying from my prison supervisor, the Vocational Guidance director at the prison school. Then, in October 2001, I took my LSAT in my supervisor's office on a Saturday morning under the watchful eye of two correctional officers assigned to help proctor my exam. In the end, I scored well and was accepted to ten of the eleven law schools to which I applied while in prison, but nine of the ten who offered me admission made enrollment contingent on successfully completing my term of parole. At the time, I estimated that if I were released near my minimum sentence, I would still have roughly three years to "walk off" on parole once I came home. I felt behind in life and did not want to wait to start my legal studies after release. So, I took a full scholarship offer from the only law school to which I was accepted that would allow me to attend on active supervision—Thomas Jefferson School of Law in San Diego, California.

When I matriculated at law school in January 2005, I took my first class that touched on the criminal law. And while my professor took great pains to speak about criminal defendants and those who have been convicted in humanizing terms, most of my future colleagues took no such precautions. I heard weekly about "those people" and "criminals" and "convicts." As I listened to otherwise rational people deny the humanness of those inside, my mind took me back to those lifers who—again without any benefit—looked after me and helped me navigate my incarceration experience.

What Professor Dan Fetsco has done with this book is to breathe a measure of humanity into a body of research focused on those whom many consider "irredeemable" by drawing on historical accounts, legislative histories, policy debates, and his own experience working in Wyoming's criminal legal system for over twenty years. But his book is far from a detached analysis. Fetsco focuses on the individual cases of several lifers with whom he has built a relationship, providing context to crimes and individuals most often viewed in a vacuum. The book challenges prevailing narratives about those serving life sentences using data and firsthand victim accounts that suggest strongly that redeemability is possible. He surmises that many of the individuals detailed in his book ought to have been released years prior, offering recommendations (both policy and moral) for addressing the issue of long-term confinement and reentry both in Wyoming, the focus of the book, and nationally.

As someone who now uses empirical research to inform policy debates around juror eligibility for those with serious criminal convictions, I find

Fetsco's approach familiar and welcome it. While criminal legal issues like life sentences and reentry typically stir intense emotions for many, we ought to continue to eschew those emotive concerns in favor of objectively verifiable data. In *Cutting Life Short*, Fetsco has done just that and offers a powerful critique of our collective use of life sentences, humanizing the men and women who receive them while thoughtfully sketching out alternatives to perpetual incarceration.

I am honored to write this foreword for my friend and fellow academic, and I congratulate him on confronting a controversial topic in a measured, thoughtful, detailed way. It is what lifers deserve as they wait in concrete and steel cells for the second chance they so desperately seek. Thank you, Dan. Your work will undoubtedly change the lives of the men and women all over the country who have very rarely had such a passionate and competent advocate.

James M. Binnall
Professor, California State University, Long Beach

CUTTING LIFE SHORT

Framing the Issue

I wanted to write this book for several reasons. Primarily, I hope to raise awareness about the pressing issue of life sentences in America and shine a light on how the use of life sentencing has grown unnecessarily and dramatically over the past fifty years. My opinions and conclusions are based on the firsthand perspective I gained while working at the Wyoming parole board. From 2007 to 2017, I sat through thousands of parole hearings where I listened to hundreds of inmates serving life sentences plead for mercy and petition for a recommendation that the governor reduce their sentence. The vast majority of those pleas were rejected, even when the parole board, the Department of Corrections, and in some cases the victims and other stakeholders in the criminal justice system all supported the offender's release.

Wyoming is not unique in this regard. Until recently, over 200,000 people were serving some form of life sentence in US prisons, which is more than the entire US prison population in 1970.[1] Individuals who have been sentenced to life in prison are called "lifers."[2] There are three primary types of life sentences: (1) life without the possibility of parole, (2) life with the

https://doi.org/10.5876/9781646428557.c000b

possibility of parole, and (3) virtual life, which includes sentences of fifty or more years.[3]

While overseeing hearings for lifers serving the latter two types of life sentences, over the years I came to believe that many of them deserved to be released and that to continue to imprison them for life was not only cruel but fiscally irresponsible. My experiences in those hearings compelled me to write this book. The individuals with life sentences who agreed to cooperate on this book were chosen based on the impact they had on me, both when I heard their cases and while helping to compile the written recommendations and accompanying documents that were forwarded to multiple governors as part of commutation recommendations. In my position at the parole board, I had access to hearings and extensive information that were hidden from public view, and some of those firsthand observations will be recounted in the following pages.

People I profile in this book who are serving a life sentence individually provide an example of someone who I believe should be released, will soon be released, or has recently been released from prison. In each narrative, I introduce legal and historical research, as well as relevant trends, data, and criminological theory. In my conclusion, I offer recommendations to stem the rising tide of life sentences in the United States. It is my hope that this book will appeal to national and perhaps global audiences.

While most of the people profiled are from Wyoming, the issues and concepts I address are universal: murder, retribution, mercy, and forgiveness—acts and emotions that are common across all cultures. Nonetheless, this book is written from the perspective of someone who was born and raised in Wyoming and worked in Wyoming's criminal justice system. Wyoming is a jurisdiction so small that the connections between stakeholders are often close. Because of the variety of positions I held—public defender, prosecutor, and parole board official—I had the opportunity to experience the system from a variety of different points along the continuum.

Part of this increase in the use of life sentences stems from a reluctance on the part of executive officials, from governors to the president, to grant clemency through the commutation process. In the book's final chapter, I make several recommendations for reducing life sentences and refining the criminal justice system. My primary recommendation is for the State of Wyoming and other government bodies to create a system of reviewing all sentences of twenty years or more, including life sentences, thereby removing an elected official—that is, the governor—from the decision-making process. The review could be conducted by the sentencing court, a parole board, or both. My additional proposals include restoring the right to vote and serve on a jury to all former felons and reducing barriers to employment following their incarceration. I further recommend educating the media and the public about the essential societal need to report responsibly on crime rather than giving in to sensationalism and fear-mongering. Equally important is the need to build productive coalitions and relationships with interested stakeholders, which ideally is the entire community.

It is important to make clear that while I support the release of people who are serving life sentences, I believe that release should be earned after they have served significant time in prison with exemplary behavior. I greatly enjoyed my time working at the Board of Parole, and I believe in the rehabilitative power of decently run prisons, which I believe Wyoming has.

I am grateful to the individuals who have shared their stories with me. It is my hope that their narratives will paint a picture of real human beings, capable of transformation and of doing great things after committing serious crimes during difficult points in their lives. The life histories of these individuals share common traits: They committed their crimes under extreme personal circumstances, often in the throes of addictions, with issues of low self-esteem triggered by youthful impulsivity. The simple fact is that after decades of sustained effort at rehabilitation, many of these people are ready for release, and in some cases they could have been safely returned to the community years ago. It is also my intent that this book will be part of a growing dialogue in the criminal justice system regarding the proper role of life sentences and retribution versus the need for a renewed focus on redemption and restoration.

1

Dealing with Life

James Boule and Darla Rouse were young lovers from Texas who were on the run, wending their way across the United States after Boule had escaped from jail in Texas. According to her Wyoming Supreme Court appeal, Boule and Rouse had fled Texas in late July 1996, after Rouse aided and abetted Boule's escape.[1] The couple packed firearms, cash, and provisions for a two-week jaunt through Louisiana, Arkansas, Missouri, Nebraska, South Dakota, and finally Wyoming, where they ran out of money.[2]

Once in Wyoming, they hatched a plot "to kidnap and kill the owners of [a] truck and trailer rig, thereafter disposing of the bodies in some remote area."[3] The court observed: "Only the exceptional courage of the victims thwarted the plan, leading to appellant's [Rouse] convictions on charges of conspiracy, kidnapping, aggravated robbery, and aggravated assault."[4] There are many facts to unpack and sift through when analyzing the litany of criminal charges Darla Rouse was convicted of, and before doing so, it is helpful to keep in mind that the facts recited in that opinion do not represent the complete story of how Rouse would end up spending the majority of her life thus far in prison.

https://doi.org/10.5876/9781646428557.c001

A significant portion of the evidence cited in that Wyoming Supreme Court opinion comes from James Boule, the charismatic young man who involved Rouse in his criminal lifestyle and later became the star witness against her at trial. Boule's testimony recounts that he and Rouse were waiting at a Wyoming rest area for a victim who suited their needs, ready to abandon their vehicle "because we were going to kill them and she [appellant] figured it would be better if we got an older couple. That way they've already lived and experienced a lot more life than someone younger."[5] Boule claimed he was having second thoughts but that Rouse urged him on, stressing that they were running out of time and money.[6] Boule approached Gerald and Rose Rockne. The older couple was in their trailer when Buele and Rouse entered, carrying a loaded .38 caliber revolver "supplied by appellant [Rouse]." Boule informed the Rocknes that the outlaw couple "needed [their] services for a couple days to get across state lines." The opinion then describes Boule readying the Rocknes' rig for departure as an agitated Rouse urged Boule to complete the execution of the older couple while Rouse held them at gunpoint.[7]

Boule returned after securing the truck and ordered the Rocknes into the trailer, where he handcuffed their hands behind their backs and to the chairs they were seated in, further tying the handcuffs together with nylon cord that he also used to tie Mr. Rockne's legs to his chair.[8] As the truck came to a rest in Buffalo, Wyoming, the Rocknes were convinced they would eventually be killed and they began to loosen the nylon cords between them, taking care to still appear tethered together in case their captors checked on their status.[9] Boule returned to the trailer to inform the Rocknes that while Rouse was buying groceries, he would be standing guard outside the trailer. Mrs. Rockne had managed to break free from her chair and slip her bonds except for the handcuffs, and she was able to keep this hidden from Boule. The Rocknes had privately discussed their plight and decided that their only chance for survival would be for Mrs. Rockne to jump from the trailer once it began to move again. With her hands still handcuffed behind her back, Mrs. Rockne jumped from the moving trailer, hitting the roadway with such force that she fractured her pelvis, the humerus in her left arm, and several ribs and suffered numerous bruises and abrasions. She was able to maintain consciousness and report the status of her husband's ongoing captivity to Good Samaritans who stopped to render assistance. Law enforcement was able to quickly locate Boule and Rouse, and an hour-long pursuit followed from Buffalo north to the Montana border. Officers successfully ran the truck and trailer off the highway.[10]

Rouse's trial began on December 16, 1996. Boule claimed that Rouse had devised the kidnapping plot. To further complicate matters, Rouse's court-appointed attorney was hospitalized with illness mid-trial, requiring that a new attorney take over the case.[11] At the trial's conclusion, Rouse was convicted of two counts of aggravated assault and battery, aggravated robbery, kidnapping, and conspiracy to commit kidnapping.[12] The sentencing judge had little sympathy for Rouse, handing down four separate prison terms varying in length from five to thirty years, for a total sentence of fifty-three years to life—a "virtual" life sentence.[13] If the sentencing judge lacked sympathy for Rouse, the Wyoming Supreme Court appeared to be equally, if not more, outraged. In the opinion, the court stated that "Sentient minds are left only to wonder whether any sentence or combination of sentences could truly fit the crimes of which appellant was rightly convicted."[14] Clearly, the court implied that Rouse should spend the rest of her life in prison, if not suffer a worse fate.

LIFE AFTER LIFE

Rouse was only twenty years old when she walked into the Wyoming Women's Center, located in Lusk, Wyoming, a small town on the state's sparsely populated eastern border, two hours from the nearest city of any size. Not only had Rouse never been to Wyoming, she recalls not knowing that it was a state until her arrest. Now she was trapped in prison in the middle of nowhere—Wyoming—for life. Boule's version of the crime worked against Rouse at trial and would haunt her for years.

However, the severity of her crime did not stop Rouse from immediately dedicating herself to her rehabilitation. Rouse's conduct during her incarceration has been exemplary; she is the epitome of the "model" inmate. Since her imprisonment began in 1996, Rouse has incurred only a single disciplinary violation, for using the kitchen without permission after she was caught frying eggs when she was supposed to be making French toast. Rouse has been a member of an inmate panel, answering questions from visitors on tours of the prison, her home for over twenty-five years. She has participated in a prison dog program, training rescue dogs for adoptability; obtained several fitness and exercise degrees; and taught exercise classes to other women in the institution. Rouse has also taken a few online college classes while incarcerated and was part of the first cohort of participants in Wyoming's newly created prison education program, outlined in chapter 10. As a result of her productive record, the parole board recommended several times that the governor commute her sentence.

In Wyoming, when the parole board considers an inmate for release or other action, such as making a recommendation to the governor for a commutation of sentence, it meets with the inmate in person for an interview. To prepare for the interview, the board members are supplied with an informational document called a "parole summary." The parole summary includes the individual's pre-sentence investigation (PSI) report that is prepared for the judge when sentencing decisions are made, after a defendant is found guilty following criminal prosecution. It gives the judge a wide range of information to consider when sentencing an individual, such as the facts of the current offense, the defendant's criminal record, family and employment background, mental health and medical information, and input from the probation and parole agent as well as the victim(s) of the crime, among other pieces of information. Prison staff members utilize the PSI to create the parole summary, basically updating the PSI with the individual's progress while in prison, highlighting programs taken as well as disciplinary and behavioral history. The report also includes the defendant's version of the crime for which they were convicted, often repeated from the PSI and updated in later parole summaries.

James Boule's testimony and the Wyoming Supreme Court's rendition of the facts of her trial would continue to surface as the parole board attempted to seek a commutation for Rouse. In July 2009, the parole board recommended that the governor convert all of Rouse's sentence to be served concurrently rather than consecutively, which would have made her eligible for parole sixteen years sooner than the court-imposed sentence would have allowed. Then-Governor Dave Freudenthal, a Democrat, denied that recommendation. In reviewing some of the documents submitted to the governor, I noticed a memo from the attorney general's office that took issue with Rouse's version of the crime as reported in her parole summary. The attorney recited Rouse's version as including statements that she was fearful and afraid of Boule. The memo noted that Rouse claimed to not want to hurt anyone, that she was just doing what she was told, and that she was praying she would be caught by police. The memo also cited letters of opposition from the prosecuting attorney and a victim, Mrs. Rockne. The memo concluded: "What is clear from her statements is that Rouse is not honest about her involvement in the horrendous crimes she committed. She does not take responsibility for what she has done to two innocent senior citizens, and shows no real remorse."[15]

"Real" remorse—what does that mean exactly? There are several problems with offering an opinion about whether a person is truly remorseful. It can be difficult to do so having only reviewed an inmate's parole summary, yet that is what happened to Rouse repeatedly: Individuals who had never met her passed judgment on the degree of her remorse.

Not everyone involved closed their mind to Rouse's potential to become a productive member of society, though. In 2007, the judge who sentenced her experienced a change of heart and began writing letters of support to the parole board on her behalf.[16] Rouse also gained the support of several families who came to know her after she had been incarcerated. Cheri and Charlie Reese, ranchers from nearby Shawnee, Wyoming, supported Rouse, as did Lyn and Russ Underdahl of Minnesota, who met Rouse during a prison tour and also developed a strong bond with her.[17] When Charlie Reese died in 2020, Rouse was referred to as his "beloved daughter" in his obituary.

Beginning in 2007, the parole board consistently recommended Rouse for commutations, forwarding a total of four requests to the governor's office. Republican Governor Matt Mead (2011–2019) refused to sign any of the recommendations for Rouse, but he did acknowledge in his denial letters that she appeared to be progressing nicely through the system.[18] The victims, the Rockne family, consistently opposed commutation recommendations for Rouse, which was apparently enough to dissuade two governors to deny her until two events occurred: the Rockne family withdrew their opposition to Rouse's release and Governor Mark Gordon was elected in 2018.[19] In December 2021, Governor Gordon, a Republican, granted Rouse a commutation that effectively made her parole-eligible on April 23, 2025.[20] The commutation also brought Rouse within two years of parole eligibility, enabling her to transfer to a halfway house in Casper, Wyoming, in November 2023.[21] As of early 2026, Rouse had progressed from the halfway house to the community and is enjoying life.

WOMEN'S PATHWAYS TO CRIME AND THE EVIL WOMAN HYPOTHESIS

The testimony of James Boule in 1996 had undoubtedly hampered Rouse's earlier chances at clemency. At that time, there was a paucity of research on the unique pathways that lead women to crime. However, several feminist legal and criminology scholars began making important contributions to the field beginning in the late 1980s. In 1989, renowned criminologist Meda Chesney-Lind addressed the inadequacy of delinquency theories in accounting for female behavior and identified the societal criminalization of women's survival strategies—such as running away from abusive situations or self-medicating with alcohol and drugs—as key factors leading to a female's involvement in the criminal justice system.[22]

This feminist perspective on crime recognizes the unique risks girls and women face as active contributors to their entry into, or escalation of, criminal behavior. Emily J. Salisbury and Patricia Van Voorhis connect women's pathways to crime to the ways girls and women are differentially exposed, or respond differentially, to the risk of criminal behavior compared to boys and men.[23] With regard to pathways to incarceration, certain predictors, called gender-neutral factors, are common to both genders—for example, education, criminal history, and criminal associates. However, gender-responsive factors, such as unhealthy relationships, victimization, and mental health, also often play a more significant role in developing a pathway to deviance and crime for women than for men.[24]

In 1992, criminologist Kathleen Daly designed a qualitative model that identified five prototypical pathways to crime for women, beginning with the street woman—who is in escape and survival mode—fleeing abuse and violence to live on the streets, often engaging in prostitution, petty theft, and substance abuse. The second pathway is the drug-connected woman working in the drug trade, often alongside and at the direction of an intimate partner or family member. The third pathway is the harmed and harming woman, who, having experienced extreme physical and sexual child abuse and neglect, develops problems at school and exhibits delinquent behavior, becoming more withdrawn over time. The fourth pathway is the battered woman, reflected by frequent and extreme victimization by an intimate partner, leading to criminal behavior otherwise viewed as out of character. The final pathway—which is often unique to women—is the *other* woman, who follows a pathway of greed and economic gain, committing crimes such as embezzlement, fraud, and theft.[25]

In an article published in 2014, Becki Ney, a national expert on justice-involved women, identified ten facts about women in jails that distinguish them from men. One fact is that "women's engagement in criminal behavior is often related to their connections with others." Another important difference noted when women are incarcerated is that "women entering jails and prisons often report histories of victimization and trauma, and continue to be vulnerable to victimization within correctional settings."[26]

Without question, Darla Rouse's involvement in victimizing the Rocknes was voluntary on her part. However, the fact remains that she had no criminal history before she met James Boule. She was barely an adult, age nineteen, and waiting tables. After they began a relationship, he, not Rouse, was the one who initially ended up in jail, creating the fugitive situation. He was the one who made the decision to escape; tragically, she decided to aid and abet his efforts.

Rouse's decision to cross the line into a world of crime, to knowingly commit a string of felonies, was an extreme act of defiance. As a woman committing those crimes, she violated multiple social norms, following the pattern identified by criminologist Joanne Belknap as the "evil woman" hypothesis. In 1996, Belknap proposed three hypotheses for testing for the presence of gender discrimination in crime. The equal treatment hypothesis holds that no sex discrimination exists in the processing of crime and that men and women are treated identically when arrested, regardless of the type of crime committed. The chivalry or paternalism hypothesis states that there is discrimination against male offenders, and females are treated with more lenience than men. The third hypothesis, and the version that arguably applies to Rouse, is the evil woman hypothesis, which claims that women are treated more harshly than men when being processed through the criminal justice system. The often hidden rationale for treating females more harshly is that they have violated not only criminal laws but gender roles as well.[27]

At the time she committed her crime, Rouse was young, had never been married, and had no children. Current research would suggest that these factors worked against her at sentencing and may have likely continued to play a role in the repeated rejections of commutation recommendations.

Citing other research, Belknap noted that the chivalry hypothesis is more likely when women commit less serious crimes; when the crimes are violent, such as Rouse's, women are treated more harshly than men who commit the same crimes.[28] According to the evil woman hypothesis, the severity of the crime corresponds with gender-role stereotypes. Women whose crimes are minor, such as shoplifting, will receive better treatment than male counterparts who commit violent robberies, assaults, murder, and other serious crimes. But women who commit "masculine" crimes have also defied their expected gender role; consequently, they receive more severe punishment.

Having children or being the guardian for dependent children may lend support to the chivalry hypothesis. Belknap explained: "For example, rightly or wrongly, persons in charge of dependent children and with little access to legitimate means may be given special consideration by crime-processing decision-makers. In most cultures, such persons are usually women. Thus, evidence of chivalrous treatment in crime processing might in fact be a manifestation of institutionalized gender roles in society at large. If women are fulfilling their 'natural' roles as mothers, and to some extent wives, they may be given more lenient sanctions."[29]

While Rouse was young and impressionable at the time she committed her crimes, she was still a willing participant. James Boule testified that he was having second thoughts about approaching the Rocknes until Rouse urged him on. That self-serving testimony did not result in a lesser sentence for Boule. A check of the Wyoming Department of Corrections Offender Locator reveals that Boule is currently serving forty years to life for kidnapping, with consecutive sentences.[30] Before her commutation, Rouse's kidnapping sentence was shorter than Boule's: She received a thirty-years-to-life term.

Trying to unpack exactly what happened that day is difficult. People's memories fade; different people can have different recollections of the same event only moments after witnessing or being involved in the situation.[31] If Rouse were getting out solely based on having served enough time in light of the extreme severity of her crime, then it could be argued that Boule should also get a reprieve, with some type of release date set for him. That is for others to consider. However, Rouse earned her release primarily through her determination to change herself after her conviction. Her growth, resilience, and progression as a human being speak to redemption.

AGE-CRIME CURVE AND BRAIN DEVELOPMENT

When Darla Rouse committed her crimes at age nineteen, she was legally an adult. But thanks to medical advancements in what we know about human brain development, neuroscience can now explain what may have motivated Rouse to follow Boule on his pathway of crime. In the years since Rouse obtained her General Educational Development (GED)

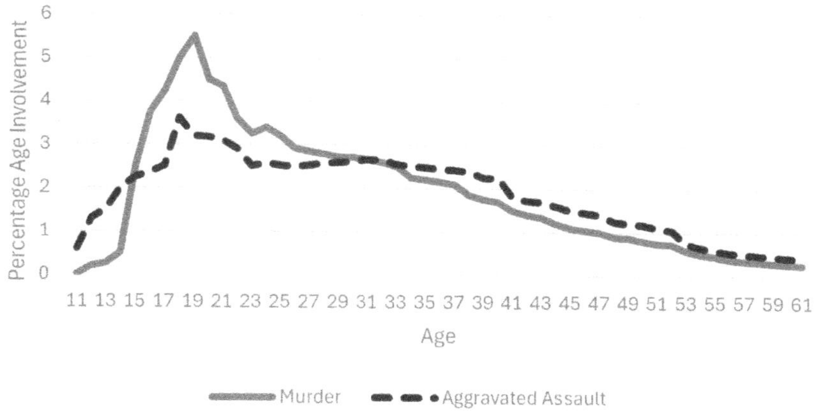

FIGURE 1.1. 2024 age-crime arrest curves. James Tuttle, "The Age-Crime Curve Is Dead, Long Live the Age-Crime Curve! An Examination of the FBI's 2024 Arrest Data." *Journal of Crime and Justice* (2025): 1–12. doi:10.1080/0735648X.2025.2571411.

degree in 1994, significant discoveries in the neurosciences have helped criminologists explain the connection between age and crime. The age-crime curve is derived from the statistical count of the number of reported crimes in a population over a given time period, mapped according to age (figure 1.1). Beginning with early adolescence, the curve tracks an increase in deviant and illegal behavior, with a peak of criminal activity in mid-adolescence, a sharp drop in early adulthood, followed by a steady decline throughout the remainder of the human life span. This age-crime curve has been noted throughout history and in all cultures worldwide; it has been referred to as "the most important regularity in criminology."[32] Criminologists Travis Hirschi and Michael R. Gottfredson have stated that "no fact about crime is more widely accepted by criminologists" and that the age-crime distribution is "one of the brute facts of criminology."[33]

While youth and background have long been considered possible factors leading to crime, no proof existed to support this theory until the recent and rapid expansion in the neurosciences. In 1983, Hirschi and Gottfredson commented: "The age distribution for crime cannot be accounted for by any variable or combination of variables currently available to criminology."[34] Suddenly, the age-crime curve that had defied explanation for decades had a possible scientific explanation: The adolescent brain is not fully developed until much later in life than had previously been believed;

as a result, the juvenile and early adult periods of our lives are when we are most likely to engage in crime. Reinforcing the certainty of the age-crime curve, data from 2024 have confirmed that the age of arrest has remained consistent with historical norms—revealing that desistance after the teenage years is continuing for most crimes, including murder and aggravated assault.[35] With this new knowledge, various public institutions have begun to incorporate brain development theories into their decision-making.

Beginning in 2005, the United States Supreme Court announced a series of opinions that relied upon both developmental research and brain theory in striking down excessively harsh sentences for juvenile offenders. That year, in *Roper v. Simmons*, the Court prohibited the death penalty for crimes committed by juveniles.[36] In *Graham v. Florida*, decided in 2010, the Court struck down as unconstitutional the sentence life without parole (LWOP) for juveniles convicted of any non-homicidal crime.[37] Most consequential, the Court decided in *Miller v. Alabama* in 2012 that a statute mandating LWOP for murder amounts to cruel and unusual punishment when applied to a juvenile offender.[38] Each of these opinions was based on a proportionality analysis in sentencing that accounts for a juvenile's development, holding that juveniles have "greater prospects for reform" than adults because much teen offending is the product of "transitory" developmental influences.[39] In the course of this legal evolution, the Court identified three important factors that mitigate the culpability of juvenile offenders. First, juveniles can be impulsive, reckless in their risk taking, and deficient in their ability to evaluate possible consequences—making their overall decision-making skills suspect.[40] Second, adolescents are susceptible to negative external pressures from peers and family, and as children, they are less able to escape their social context than are adults.[41] Third, given that a juvenile's character has yet to fully form, their crimes are less likely than an adult's to be indicative of irretrievable depravity.[42] The Court further acknowledged that the immaturity of the human brain corresponds to immaturity in human behavior.

These rulings were largely influenced by the research of neuroscientist Aaron White. White's main points were delivered in a 2003 address to the New York Academy of Sciences:

1. Much of the behavior that characterizes adolescence is rooted in biology intermingling with environmental influences to cause teens

to conflict with their parents, take more risks, and experience wide swings in emotion.

2. The lack of synchrony between a physically mature body and a still maturing nervous system may explain these behaviors.
3. Adolescent sensitivities to rewards appear to be different than those in adults, prompting them to seek higher levels of novelty and stimulation to achieve the same feelings of pleasure.
4. With the right dose of guidance and understanding, adolescence can be a relatively smooth transition.[43]

Prior to these groundbreaking findings, most, if not all, of the major changes in brain development were thought to occur prior to adolescence. White defines adolescence as "the period of transition from childhood to adulthood, a time during which an individual acquires the skills, and biological substrates, necessary to survive on his/her own. It involves changes at numerous levels, some of which are defined biologically and some of which are defined behaviorally. It is now clear that a variety of changes also take place during adolescence."[44]

Another difficult characteristic of adolescence is the onset of puberty, which ushers in a ten- to twenty-time increase in testosterone level for boys, a hormone that is linked to aggression and dominance-seeking behavior.[45] The brain chemicals that lead us to seek excitement increase during adolescence, while the chemicals that tend to inhibit our risk-taking behavior decrease.[46] There are obvious physical signs that the human body is changing during adolescence. These changes disappear eventually as the person ages, but the effects of puberty can last well into a person's twenties.

The thrill-seeking behavior continues into the twenties in part because the human brain has not fully developed. Psychologist Laurence Steinberg has specifically observed that "sensation-seeking—the tendency to pursue novel, exciting, and rewarding experiences—increases substantially around the time of puberty and remains high well into the early 20s, when it begins to decline."[47] When the brain finally does reach a fully developed state, a more mature personality emerges, one that it is hoped shows greater restraint, discretion, and conscientiousness.[48] Psychology professors Avshalom Caspi and Terrie E. Moffitt analyzed data revealing that this maturation leads to a desistance or retirement from crime for most individuals, since by age twenty-eight, roughly 85 percent of all former juvenile delinquents have stopped offending.[49]

Most individuals follow the pattern of what Moffitt calls the *adolescent limited* (AL) offender, growing out of crime as they take on the responsibilities of adulthood.[50] Moffitt describes an individual who continues to offend well into adulthood as a *life course persistent* (LCP) offender.[51] LCP offenders are often found to suffer from neuropsychological and temperamental deficiencies, compounded by genetic and environmental influences on brain development—which can produce low IQ, hyperactivity, inattentiveness, negative emotionality, and lack of impulse control. Fortunately, LCP offenders account for only 7 percent of juvenile delinquents, yet those same youthful offenders commit at least 50 percent of all delinquent acts and tend to commit more serious crimes, such as assault, rape, and robbery. In contrast, AL offenders tend to commit minor acts of deviance, such as crimes of petty theft and vandalism.[52]

Professors and criminologists Mary Stohr, Anthony Walsh, and Craig Hemmens have observed that AL offenders have developmental histories with consistent pro-social influences and are temporarily sidetracked by youthful offending; they are "normal" children dealing with growing pains whose deviance does not portend an ongoing history of personality deficiencies.[53] In addition, the changing world has had an impact on the maturity gap between puberty and entry into the job market: Better health and nutrition have lowered the average age of puberty, while the average time needed to gain the skills necessary to succeed in the modern economy has increased.[54] This has resulted in a five- to ten-year maturity gap between puberty and entry into the job market, leading to more teens being diverted from a pro-social life trajectory.[55]

As the case of Darla Rouse suggests, it can be difficult to know from the outside whether a person is a "normal" child merely dealing with the complexities of navigating life as a teenager or if their environment is marred by abuse—abuse that often takes place behind closed doors.

FINDING HER VOICE

Nearly twenty years after Rouse committed her crimes, she was given the opportunity to take a college course through a University of Wyoming program called Pathways from Prison. Prior to being incarcerated in Wyoming, Rouse had obtained her GED and taken a few junior college classes in Texas. While taking the Pathways from Prison course twenty years after her crimes, Rouse wrote "Hard Won Lessons," a short essay that was published in a women's and gender studies journal at the State University of New York at Cortland.[56] I had the chance to observe several of her parole hearings. The first hearing was in 2007, on my first day of hearings as the new deputy director of the Wyoming Board of Parole. Previously, during my time as a prosecutor, I had tried cases before a jury and given oral arguments to various appellate courts, but I had never attended a parole hearing. I had no idea that Rouse's case would become one of the most compelling and difficult cases for me to reconcile, both professionally and personally.

Parole hearings are fascinating proceedings and like nothing I had ever seen outside of reality television. At first glance, Darla Rouse reminded me of actress Geena Davis (*Thelma and Louise*). She is tall, athletic, and attractive, with long, curly brown hair. As I listened to her speak, I was struck by how articulate and poised she was. It was very hard to imagine that the person I met that day had committed the crimes I'd read about in a scathing Wyoming Supreme Court opinion.

After that hearing, the Wyoming Board of Parole recommended a commutation of Rouse's sentence—an event that culminated in her first commutation denial. Over the next decade, I would see her at hearings a few more times before I left the parole board in 2017. Ironically, it was the same year her essay was published.

When I read it, I found Rouse's essay to be well-written and powerful. We know now about the pathways women often take to crime, as well as the neuroscience and developmental research that has conclusively demonstrated the environmental and biological factors that can increase the risks of exposing a child to something other than a "normal" childhood. Without strong family and peer support—including the right amount of guidance and nurturing—the chances increase that a child's development will deviate from a pro-social path.

In her heartfelt and courageous essay, Rouse reveals enough of her background for the reader to gain insight into the emotional, physical, and sexual abuse to which she was subjected. Her words not only helped educate me, but they also illuminated the pain of her imprisonment in stark terms:

> At the beginning of my incarceration I had to make a decision between suicide and surrender. It was a very real and practical decision to make, it seemed. Anyone who has ever been in the depths of darkness will understand. I must admit that the main reason why I didn't commit suicide was my mother. I knew that it would take the life from her too . . . After that decision

came the determination that I would not be defeated by prison or what I had done . . . I refused to allow this to be the sum total of my life. These walls and fences keep me here, but the health of my life and its effectiveness is not limited or confined by them.[57]

Although Rouse alludes to her abusive and chaotic childhood, she makes no excuses for her crimes: "There is nothing I can do to make things right again," she states.[58] Her motivation to share her feelings, she explains, is that she can't keep her experience to herself, as she feels a need to share what she has learned and how she was able to grow. "My crimes were terrible for my victims, their family, my own family, and the community where it happened," she says. "It would remain a gaping wound, a black hole of regret and pain in our lives if we left the event as only what it was: terrible."[59]

Rouse also shared how she kept going in spite of her life sentence. She points to "nature's law of self-preservation" in describing her perseverance. Her thought-provoking conclusion is that life keeps on keeping on, that people keep waking and sleeping: "Life wants to survive, and it matters very little how we feel about it." Lastly, Rouse offers this advice: "Take whatever happened yesterday and let it make you better. Move forward, enjoy your days, love your people well, and do good things."[60]

A SECOND CHANCE AT LIFE

Rouse can remember the precise date and time she was notified that her sentences would be commuted. At 4:00 p.m. on December 21, 2021, she was fulfilling her familiar role as a mentor to young women in the Youthful Offender Transitional Program when one of the lieutenants pulled her out of class, telling Rouse the other "ladies would be fine on their own."[61] Recalling the event, Rouse remembers initially thinking she was being called to provide information about a routine investigation. "Not a fun feeling," she said. Instead, the lieutenant led Rouse to the warden's office, which meant something else—but what?

The warden was Rick Catron, who has since retired after a long and distinguished career in corrections. After Rouse entered his office, Warden Catron asked her to sit down. She recalls the warden telling her that he had something to read to her, and he grabbed a stack of papers, tapping their edges on his desk to straighten them.

"It seemed like a formal act," Rouse recalls, "like he was performing an important step in a special ceremony of some kind." In a letter to me, she described the moment: "As soon as the Warden started reading the papers, 'Whereas, Darla D. Rouse, WDOC #874 . . . 'I put my head in my hands and started crying. Warden Catron read the entire Grant of commutation aloud to me and I cried through the entire thing. There were even a couple moments I thought I might hyperventilate. Even Warden Catron got a little emotional. I heard his voice quiver as he read the grant. So, of course, that will endear him to me for the rest of my life, even though I already had an affinity for him."[62]

Rouse was originally sentenced to four separate terms of imprisonment, varying from five to thirty-five years each for a total of fifty-three years to life. The commutation shortened Rouse's sentence by thirteen years.[63] Following her commutation, Rouse reported that her life changed completely. Everyone in the prison, both staff and inmates, became aware of the rare turn of events. Rouse was frequently congratulated and asked about her plans after she was released. Prior to her release, Rouse said she had looked forward to choosing her own clothes, using a cell phone, and "answering a ringing phone when someone calls me instead of me having to call them."[64] At one point during the writing of this book, Rouse called me from prison while under the supervision of a caseworker. I was riding my bike and pulled over immediately to answer the phone.

This led to a conversation about other things she was looking forward to: "I want to get my driver's license and drive a car. I want to walk down the sidewalk in town and just take in the scenery. I want to go outside at night and see the stars, without having razor wire in view. I want to play with puppies, go swimming, grocery shopping, cook in a real kitchen on a real stove with real silverware and plates and bowls. I want to go out to eat. I want to ride a bike."[65]

Her expression of longing for those simple pleasures that had been withheld from her for so many years made me realize how much I'd completely taken for granted the simple freedom of riding a bike. I could not help but be inspired by Rouse's positive energy. She said her other goals included having a family, earning a degree, balancing her own budget, starting a career, and being an active member of a church community, maybe as part of the choir. Even though it "sounds weird," she added, she wants to pay bills and take care of a home, including the simple act of cleaning it. And

Darla Rouse wanted to give back: "I also want to have enough so that I can give some away. God has given me so much that I pray I manage it well enough to bless other people the way He's blessed me through all of this. And that's not limited to money. I want to pour out everything He's poured into me emotionally, spiritually, physically, and monetarily. There's been so much and I can't keep it to myself."[66]

Rouse's words are a potent reminder to all of us to appreciate what we have in our lives. Far too many of us take for granted the freedom of riding a bike or walking around town and taking in the scenery—until it's taken away. Rouse was like thousands of other inmates who are waiting in US prisons, clearly rehabilitated and ready to rejoin the community. But commutation "success" stories like hers will continue to be rare—so rare that her commutation was regarded as "ceremonial," given the current miracle-like nature of executive clemency that exists in the United States.

In my opinion, the dormant state of commutations in America is counterproductive and does not need to continue. In the chapters that follow, I will explain why governors and presidents alike should adopt a reasoned, evidence-based approach to granting commutations and begin granting sentence reductions more frequently. Unquestionably, the proliferation of life sentences calls for other, more constructive approaches to reconsidering the cases of inmates who are in a situation similar to the one Rouse found herself in for so many years, praying for a political miracle. She was among the lucky few lifers whose prayers were finally answered.

2

The Misunderstood Power of Executive Clemency

After spending more than ten years in prison, Darla Rouse received her first commutation recommendation from the parole board in 2007, only to be denied four times until receiving clemency from Governor Mark Gordon shortly before Christmas in 2021. As the beneficiary of that commutation, Rouse won the equivalent of the criminal justice lottery. To understand the rarity of her case, I trace how the decline in the exercise of commutations came about, recounting some of the history associated with this extraordinary power of clemency. There are various forms of commutation, but a simple definition is that a commutation is the reduction of a prisoner's sentence granted by an executive official, typically a state governor or the president of the United States.[1] Commutations were once granted regularly by American presidents and governors; however, with the onset of the "tough on crime movement" of the last fifty years, the number of commutations has dwindled drastically, particularly in Wyoming.

The power of clemency is nothing new; it has been in use as long as there have been tribal chiefs, monarchs, and chief executives. The Code of Hammurabi, which dates back to 2000 BC, included a clemency provision.[2]

https://doi.org/10.5876/9781646428557.c002

Greek and Roman rulers exercised the power of executive clemency.[3] Under common law in England, the king possessed the pardon power.[4] The common law also served as the doctrinal basis for the adoption of clemency in the United States: "As this power had been exercised, from time immemorial, by the executive of that nation whose language is our language, and to whose judicial institutions ours bear a close resemblance; we adopt their principles respecting the operation and effect of a pardon, and look into their books for the rules prescribing the manner in which it is to be used by the person who would avail himself of it."[5]

In the modern criminal justice system, state constitutions generally place the power of clemency, which includes commutations and pardons, with the governor.[6] On the federal level, the power to grant clemency is vested in the US president by the second article of the United States Constitution. The law provides that the president "shall have power to grant reprieves and pardons for offenses against the United States, except in cases of impeachment."[7] Similarly, in Wyoming statutes, the governor's power of commutation is found in the state constitution: "The governor shall have power to remit fines and forfeitures, to grant reprieves, commutations and pardons after conviction, for all offenses except treason and cases of impeachment; but the legislature may by law regulate the manner in which the remission of fines, pardons, commutations and reprieves may be applied for."[8]

However, there are several important distinctions between the federal approach to clemency and how the process works in Wyoming. For one, Wyoming's statute limits the governor's power of clemency to offenses for which a conviction has been obtained. Presidential pardons and commutations are also traditionally granted to individuals who have been found guilty of a specific crime, yet presidents can ignore the fact that the individual being pardoned has not yet been convicted of a crime but has only been charged. Former President Joe Biden took the unprecedented step of preemptively pardoning Dr. Anthony Fauci and the members of the United States House committee that investigated the January 6 attack on the United States Capitol, prior to any investigation being undertaken.[9] The Biden administration called the pardons a protective measure against "revenge" from the Trump administration.[10]

Second, the Wyoming State Legislature has the power to regulate the manner in which pardons and commutations can be applied for; as will be discussed later, Wyoming lawmakers have limited that ability by creating a life without parole (LWOP) sentence, which is not commutable by the governor.[11] At the federal level, presidential pardons cannot be overturned by the United States Congress or the judicial process, which makes the federal power of executive clemency a powerful tool both to correct miscarriages of justice and unfortunately, when abused, to also benefit political cronies.[12] The only limitation placed on the presidential power of clemency is that the president may not commute or pardon someone for a state offense; further, the president cannot prevent Congress from impeaching and removing a federal official.[13]

The word *clemency* is derived from the Latin word *clementia*, which was associated with a "willingness to show benevolence towards others, despite conscious suspicion, belief or knowledge that they do not deserve it."[14] The definition of clemency has varied somewhat over time and place. In Great Britain, clemency was defined by former Prime Minister Herbert Henry Asquith as the "most important of all the prerogatives of the sovereign."[15] In the United States, the very idea of executive clemency is seemingly contradictory to one of the key motivations behind the founders declaring independence in 1776: the rejection of a ruling king. Before the creation of the rule of law and the rise of Parliament, the English crown was the lone authority, and whoever sat on the throne held the power of life and death over everyone in the kingdom.[16]

The founding fathers did not completely reject the idea of an executive, but they took steps to limit the powers of the president. The president has the power to sign or veto acts of the United States Congress.[17] The president is the commander in chief of the military.[18] The president has the power to make treaties, with concurrence of the United States Senate.[19] The president has a duty to provide an address to Congress from "time to time."[20] The president also has administrative duties and implied powers to implement the powers specified in Article II of the United States Constitution.[21] Nonetheless, the president's clemency power "quite visibly stands out from the others because it *does* have a regal nature to it."[22] In July 2024, the Supreme Court also decided *Trump v. United States*, finding presidential immunity from prosecution for "official acts" of the president.[23]

PARDONS VERSUS COMMUTATIONS

While important distinctions exist between pardons and commutations, both are forms of executive clemency. In terms of differences, a pardon is the granting of clemency for a criminal offense and is typically granted after the offender has served their prison sentence. A commutation, in contrast, shortens the amount of time served for an offense and is usually granted while an offender is serving their sentence. A pardon, unlike a commutation, also restores the offender's civil liberties if they were convicted of a felony, allowing them to serve on juries, vote, and possess firearms.[24]

At the presidential level, there are multiple types of pardons and commutations, including conditional pardons, commutations of sentence, conditional commutations of sentence, remissions of fines and forfeitures, respites, and amnesties.[25] Similarly, the Wyoming governor can fashion a variety of commutations and pardons. With respect to commutations, Wyoming governors can commute an offender's sentence to time served, or they can reduce the amount of time to be served on a sentence. The governor can also modify consecutive sentences to concurrent sentences.

Several governors in recent Wyoming history have granted successive commutations to inmates over a period of years, particularly inmates serving life sentences. For example, after an extended period of good behavior, such as ten years, an inmate might receive a commutation reducing their life sentence to fifty years to life. After another five years of good behavior, the inmate might receive a second commutation, reducing their sentence to forty years to life. Another commutation might come five years later, reducing the sentence to the point where, after a period of twenty to thirty years in prison, the inmate becomes eligible for parole. The aforementioned hypothetical scenarios were fairly common in Wyoming for several decades, but the use of this executive prerogative has diminished in the United States in recent years, including in Wyoming.

Once a robust feature of the American criminal justice system, the number of requests for executive clemency granted by governors and the president dropped sharply beginning in the 1970s with the Nixon administration.[26] Several factors led to presidents and governors using the power of executive clemency less in recent decades. During the past sixty years, due process improvements in the criminal justice system have made the need for executive intervention in cases of miscarriage of justice far less common.[27] The advent of parole and sentencing guidelines also reduced the need for executive intervention in cases of inmates burdened with unduly harsh sentences.[28] However, other reasons for the diminished use of executive clemency have nothing to do with improvements to the criminal justice system. Despite the low recidivism rate of parolees convicted of murder, the highly visible nature of an executive clemency decision makes it a risky political move. There is little "political boost" for a governor or president who grants executive clemency.[29] In addition, a government official's exposure to political disaster can hinge on one mistake in granting a commutation—if just one released inmate commits a horrific crime, a political career can come to a crashing halt. This risk has only increased with the 24/7/365 news-cycle environment in which we now live.[30]

DECLINE AND CORRUPTION OF EXECUTIVE CLEMENCY

Both Democrats and Republicans began to back away from executive clemency out of fear of being portrayed as "soft on crime." In 1988, Democratic presidential candidate Michael Dukakis was heavily criticized for both his opposition to the death penalty and his oversight of a prison furlough program in Massachusetts that was viewed as too lenient.[31] One man who had been furloughed during Dukakis's administration, a Black man named Willie Horton, raped and killed a white woman and bound and stabbed her boyfriend.[32] Republican presidential candidate George H. W. Bush and his campaign pounced on the tragedy to portray Governor Dukakis as soft on crime.[33] In response, the media and public focused only on the Willie Horton example and failed to mention that the Massachusetts furlough program had a success rate greater than 99 percent.[34]

Similar fears of being perceived as soft on crime had a noticeable effect on Democratic President Bill Clinton. Not only did Clinton sign off on the first execution in Arkansas in twenty-six years while governor in 1990, he championed tougher sentencing laws as president, which added to the snowballing of mass incarceration in America and disproportionately affected minorities.[35] Clinton thus played a significant role in contributing to the nation's ballooning prison population.

There were allegations that Clinton used his clemency power unethically. As one of his outgoing acts as president, on January 20, 2001, he pardoned Marc Rich and Pincus Green, wealthy financiers and Clinton donors who had been indicted for tax evasion. There are other troubling facts concerning Clinton's use of clemency. Hugh Rodham, Hillary Clinton's brother and a Florida attorney, accepted hundreds of thousands of dollars on behalf of clients to promote clemency cases in the White House. Clinton was also the first president to grant clemency to a family member when he pardoned his half-brother, Roger Clinton, for a 1985 drug trafficking conviction. The former president's other controversial pardons were given to personal friends or family members of his supporters. Significantly, many of those recipients were not eligible for a pardon under Department of Justice (DOJ) rules and had not submitted an application.[36]

Also ethically troubling were Bill Clinton's pardons in the infamous Whitewater real estate scandal. In that instance, Clinton pardoned his former business partner, Susan McDougal, who had been convicted of fraudulently obtaining and misusing a $300,000 loan—a loan Clinton had allegedly pressured the investment company to make while governor of Arkansas. McDougal spent eighteen months in jail after being held in contempt for refusing to testify against the president. Former President Jimmy Carter called the pardon of Marc Rich "disgraceful," and then-Senator Joe Biden called Clinton's pardons "totally indefensible." Biden added: "I think either the president had an incredible lapse in memory or was brain dead."[37]

If Clinton had poisoned the well for future presidents, former President Joe Biden and current President Donald Trump amplified the corruption in executive clemency without apparent concern for appearances or protocols. During his first term, Trump's initial pardon was of the notorious human rights violator, former Sheriff Joe Arpaio of Maricopa County, Arizona. Ignoring the established DOJ petition process, Trump pardoned Arpaio before he was sentenced on charges of criminal contempt for failing to stop the practice of racial profiling.[38] In a preemptive response to allegations of wrongdoing during the investigation into Russian interference in the 2016 election, Trump tweeted, "As has been stated by numerous legal scholars, I have the absolute right to PARDON myself, but why would I do that when I have done nothing wrong?"[39]

While Trump did not grant himself a pardon for alleged Russian interference in the 2016 election, he did grant his former national security adviser, Michael Flynn, a full pardon for lying to the FBI. After they pleaded guilty to making false statements to investigators, Trump pardoned his former foreign policy adviser George Papadopoulos and attorney Alexander van der Zwaan. Trump also issued pardons to Roger Stone Jr.—who had been convicted of obstructing official proceedings, witness tampering, and five counts of making false statements—and to Paul Manafort, his former campaign chair, who had pled guilty to conspiracy to defraud the United States through undisclosed lobbying with a pro-Russian politician and a political party in Ukraine.[40]

President Trump's former attorney, Michael Cohen, testified before the United States Congress that Trump had floated the idea of a pardon to Cohen in exchange for lying to investigators about campaign finance crimes. The long-awaited report, released by special counsel Robert Mueller in 2019, included information that Trump allegedly promised pardons in exchange for silence from co-conspirators about Russian interference in the 2016 election.[41] Trump also pardoned Charles Kushner, the father of his son-in-law Jared; three former Republican members of Congress accused of white-collar crimes; and ex-service members and military contractors convicted of wartime crimes overseas, including four contractors who were involved in the murders of fourteen unarmed civilians.[42]

Despite promising not to pardon his son Hunter, Biden did exactly that before leaving office, in addition to granting a commutation to former "cash for kids" judge Michael Conahan.[43] Conahan's commutation was part of a mass commutation granted to 1,500 federal inmates who had been released to home confinement during the Covid pandemic.[44] Biden also commuted the life sentence of Leonard Peltier, a Native American activist who was convicted in the 1975 killing of two FBI agents.[45]

In the most controversial act of executive clemency in US history, President Trump issued a blanket pardon and commutations to almost all of the participants in the riot and attack at the United States Capitol on January 6, 2021, including at least two men from Wyoming.[46] Prior to Trump's pardons, Vice President JD Vance said that rioters who engaged in violence "obviously" should not be pardoned.[47] The largest police unions in America, the Fraternal Order of Police and the International Association of Chiefs of Police, issued a joint statement condemning the pardons issued by both the Biden and Trump administrations as sending "a dangerous message."[48]

While recent presidents have ignored the guidelines, the process created by the federal pardon attorney, a DOJ employee, has clear standards regarding pardons and commutations.[49] The federal standards for a pardon are based on "the petitioner's demonstrated good conduct for a substantial period after conviction and service of sentence."[50] Other "principal factors" for considering a federal pardon application are: (1) the applicant's post-conviction conduct, character, and reputation; (2) the seriousness and relative recentness of the offense(s); (3) the applicant's remorse, atonement, and acceptance of responsibility; (4) the applicant's need for a pardon; and (5) any official recommendations and reports.[51] The standards adopted by the pardon attorney with respect to commutations are similar to the pardon standards, and they note that a commutation is an "extraordinary" and "rarely granted" form of relief.[52] Some of the cited reasons for past presidential commutations are: an offender's punishment differed greatly from the sentences handed down to other offenders for the same offense, or the sentence was unduly severe; the offender was elderly or near death; or the offender had performed a meritorious service, such as assisting with prosecutions.[53] Unspecified "equitable factors" might also justify a commutation, but apart from providing historical instances where presidents had commuted sentences, the standards provide no tangible guidance as to when a president should grant a commutation.[54]

The pardon process established by Wyoming statute requires that an applicant must have been convicted of a felony and that an application be submitted to the governor's office. The application is rather basic. It calls for a description of the sentence for which the pardon is sought, any subsequent criminal history, and "any pertinent information the governor may request such as parole and community correctional program records." Notice must be given to the district or county attorney at least three weeks before the governor can consider the application. However, if a physician certifies that the applicant is in imminent danger of death and the Department of Corrections recommends a pardon, the application rules do not apply.[55]

The Wyoming Board of Parole is composed of seven members, and the board may make recommendations to the governor to grant commutations and review inmate matters.[56] A recommendation from the parole board is not the only method by which the governor can grant a commutation, though. While the vast majority of commutations in the state are referred to the governor by the parole board, at least one decision during my tenure bypassed the board.

In 2011, Governor Matt Mead commuted the sentence of Joe Welch, an escapee from the Wyoming Department of Corrections who had been arrested after thirty-one years on the lam. Welch's underlying crime was burglary, and he was eventually discovered in Alaska and returned to Wyoming to serve his sentence. His attorney was able to secure a commutation of Welch's sentence by contacting Governor Mead directly, bypassing the parole board.[57] The attorney was named in the press, but the article omitted the fact that Welch's lawyer was also the brother and former law partner of Governor Mead's attorney general at the time, Greg Phillips. This is just one example of many little-known facts that often do not surface. Welch's commutation was one of only three Governor Mead granted during his eight-year tenure as governor.

Though the politics involved in the Joe Welch decision raise questions of fairness, at least Welch did not appear to be a personal friend or political pawn of the governor. There was a legitimate fiscal rationale for his release.

By contrast, governors in a number of other states have unquestionably abused their executive clemency powers. In 1976, Marie Ragghianti, who was serving as chair of the Tennessee parole board, exposed a "cash for clemency" scheme being run by then-Governor Roy Blanton. The scheme involved inmates who had ties to Governor Blanton or his allies paying the governor in exchange for pardons. Ragghianti became suspicious of the corruption when the governor's legal counsel continually pressured her over the proposed pardon of an inmate convicted of a double homicide. Before she resigned, Ragghianti was the catalyst for an FBI investigation. Eventually, the governor's legal counsel and other participants were convicted for their involvement in the corrupt scheme. Blanton did not run for reelection and was later convicted for his participation in selling liquor licenses.[58] Ragghianti was vindicated further when her story of ethics and courage was made into an acclaimed film, *Marie*.[59]

RESURGENCE OF EXECUTIVE CLEMENCY

While he may not have lived up to his promise of using clemency to effect meaningful change, President Barack Obama did not engage in corruption or abuse his power of clemency. Near the end of his tenure, he touted his efforts at resurrecting the power of executive clemency.[60] In 2017 Obama wrote: "By shifting the narrative to the way clemency can be used to correct injustices in the system—and reminding people of the value of second chances—I worked to reinvigorate the clemency power and to set a precedent that will make it easier for future Presidents, governors, and other public officials to use it for good."[61]

Without question, Obama used his powers of executive clemency, particularly the power of commutation, to grant many second chances. The president granted 1,715 commutations—more than any president in history at the time. His approach to executive clemency also differed from that of his predecessors in that he granted far more commutations than pardons, freeing people from prison rather than pardoning people after their release. In contrast, under previous presidents, commutations for inmates were granted much less frequently, as they were considered riskier political moves than pardoning a person who had already been released.[62]

In 2014, the DOJ announced a new initiative to support commutations of inmates who met specific criteria, including that their sentences would have been shorter had they been convicted following recent legislative changes. The initiative led to presidential commutation petitions more than tripling, from 6,561 in fiscal year 2014—up from 2,370 the year before—to 11,028 petitions in 2016.[63]

However, Obama could have done much more. When he left the Oval Office, 13,000 commutation applicants awaited a response.[64] Moreover, he was sworn into office on January 20, 2009, but his clemency initiative did not begin until 2014.[65] The spike in commutation petitions created a tidal wave that caught the DOJ unprepared. By 2016, author Brittany Barnett observed, "Obama's Clemency Initiative, once and still a beacon of hope for so many, had turned from being a potential tool for mass liberation to a bureaucratic nightmare."[66] Earlier, in the spring of 2015, US Pardon Attorney Deborah Leff had resigned in frustration because of the lack of resources needed to process the increase in commutation petitions.[67] Leff claimed the DOJ was reversing her recommendations and that many deserving petitions had not been submitted to the president.[68]

Although Obama claimed to have reinvigorated executive clemency, the president's overall grant rate, encompassing both commutations and pardons, was a modest 5 percent. His grant rate was in line with those of George H. W. Bush (5%) and Bill Clinton (6%), higher than the rate of George W. Bush (2%), but far lower than the rates of Presidents Richard Nixon (16%), Gerald Ford (27%), and Jimmy Carter (21%).[69] Obama also had a record number of denials, including the failure to grant commutations to more than 2,500 people who met his criteria for commutations.[70] His initiative only granted commutations to individuals convicted of drug trafficking; those convicted of other nonviolent offenses were not included in the initiative.[71] Furthermore, Obama excluded those with violent crimes or extensive criminal histories from consideration.[72]

Despite the shortcomings of his commutation initiative, President Obama's efforts were a step in the right direction. His successor, President Donald Trump, however, continued to engage in the ethically suspect clemency practices that had been part of Bill Clinton's presidency. Before Trump was elected president, he specifically asked then-President Obama to not pardon Hillary Clinton.[73] Trump asked: "Will you pledge not to issue a pardon to Hillary Clinton and her co-conspirators for their many crimes against our country and against society itself? Will you make that pledge?"[74] Ironically, Trump later pardoned many of his own staff and allies for crimes committed against the United States.[75]

Larry Kupers, who served as acting pardon attorney and deputy pardon attorney during Trump's first two years in office, quit in 2019 out of frustration.[76] In the *Washington Post*, Kupers commented: "Donald Trump conducted his presidency for his profit, making virtually every policy decision on a transactional basis—not what the Constitution required, not what benefitted our country and our people, but only what increased his power, wealth, and status."[77] Liz Oyer was the US pardon attorney at the beginning of Trump's second term, and she reported being fired in March 2025 after refusing to restore actor Mel Gibson's right to carry a gun following a domestic battery conviction.[78]

In terms of actual numbers, Trump granted a total of 143 pardons and 94 commutations during his first four years in office, while Obama granted 212 pardons and 1,715 commutations over the eight years of his presidency.[79] The only one-term president in modern times who granted clemency at a lower rate than Trump during his first term was George H. W. Bush, who granted 74 pardons and commuted only 3 sentences.[80] While Trump was roundly criticized for pardoning his cronies and political allies during his first term, he also commuted the sentences of some prisoners who were serving life sentences for nonviolent drug offenses.[81]

A few legal scholars viewed Trump's initial corrupt use of executive clemency as an opportunity to revamp the clemency process.[82] In an essay quoted in *The Marshall Project*, former US Pardon Attorney Magaret Love wrote: "We should instead be asking more basic questions about what, if any, role the pardon power should play in the ordinary operation of the federal justice system."[83] Law professor Rachel E. Barkow was quoted in the same article as saying that President Biden needed to confront the issues surrounding executive clemency, especially considering his role in the mass incarceration crisis: "It's the most direct way to confront Biden's past. Some of the very people who need clemency in federal prison are there because of crime bills Biden supported."[84]

Biden may not have fully confronted his past role in mass incarceration, but he did manage to grant more acts of clemency than any president in history to that point.[85] Biden signed off on 4,245 requests: 80 pardons and 4,165 commutations.[86] Notably, Biden commuted the death sentence for 37 of 40 inmates on federal death row and reduced the sentences of more than 2,000 people convicted of nonviolent drug offenses.[87] Overall, Biden received 14,867 clemency requests and had a historically impressive grant rate of 29 percent.[88]

President Trump has also taken steps in his commutation policy approach that appear to be progressive and promising. In early 2025, Trump appointed former "lifer" Alice Marie Johnson as his "pardon czar."[89] In 1996, Johnson was convicted of multiple drug offenses and sentenced to LWOP plus an additional twenty-five years.[90] Reality star Kim Kardashian lobbied Trump for a commutation for Johnson during his first term, which he granted, and Trump has now given Johnson the task of recommending people for presidential commutations. Johnson has vowed to assist those who receive commutations in having not just a second chance but "their best chance at success."[91]

It is hoped that the Trump administration will set new records in granting second chances. Republican House Speaker Mike Johnson was quoted by the BBC as saying that doing so is the "ethos" and "worldview" of the Republican Party.[92] In defending Trump's pardons of the January 6 rioters, Johnson said, "We believe in redemption. We believe in second chances."[93] Since issuing his initial wave of clemency to the January 6 rioters, President Trump has signaled that those second chances will be offered only to those who support him.

At the end of May 2025, President Trump issued a flurry of pardons and commutations to dozens of political allies, campaign donors, law enforcement officials, and Republican politicians. In replacing Liz Oyer, President Trump appointed right-wing activist Ed Martin as the chief pardon attorney. Martin was previously unable to gain United States Senate confirmation as the US attorney for Washington, DC, over objections to his legal representation of the January 6 rioters.[94] After being sworn in as pardon attorney, Martin tweeted: "No MAGA left behind."[95]

The presidential norms associated with clemency that Trump primarily ignored during his first term stemmed from his pattern of rewarding people who "have spoken glowingly of him"—to the point of writing books praising him—and the fact that he started issuing pardons and commutations early in his term, whereas previous presidents, such as Clinton, waited until a few hours before leaving office.[96] However, President Trump's use of clemency at the beginning of his second term has once again shocked historians and legal experts.

Law Professor Rachel E. Barkow at New York University was quoted in *The New York Times* describing Trump's agenda with clemency: "The use of the pardon power is part of his effort to put the country on an authoritarian path. Instead of administering the pardon power evenhandedly with a regular process that is available equally to all, he is rewarding partisan allies. It is the carrot for supporters, and he uses the stick of weaponizing prosecutions and investigations against his partisan enemies."[97]

In the same article, former special counsel to the United States Sentencing Commission and law professor at the University of Missouri Frank Bowman III added: "Trump's twin ambitions are to be a dictator and to become ever more fabulously wealthy. Thus, in addition to using state power to crush his perceived enemies, he wants to be able to accept or extort political favors, both monetary and intangible, that keep him in office and centralize authority in his person."[98]

Leev Kovarsky, a University of Texas law professor, compares Trump's use of clemency to organized crime: "It's mafia stuff. They won't break your legs, but they'll publicly pardon the person who does."[99] Trump's pardons and commutations have also cost taxpayers. Former Pardon Attorney Oyer has created a "pardon tracker" that has tallied the cost of Trump's clemency at more than $1.3 billion in lost restitution and fines.[100]

President Trump also appears to have little regard for the impact his clemency decisions have on victims of sexual abuse. As the billionaire and convicted child sex offender Jeffrey Epstein's scandal continues to consume Washington, DC, Trump seems to be seriously considering pardoning Epstein's co-conspirator, Ghislaine Maxwell.[101] Maxwell had been convicted of recruiting female minors who were sexually abused by Epstein. When both *The New York Times* and the *Wall Street Journal* reported that Trump's name was in the Epstein files, Trump's former attorney and Deputy Attorney General Todd Blanche was dispatched to interview Maxwell. Through her attorney, Maxwell made it clear that she wanted a commutation or pardon in exchange for her testimony. When asked if he would pardon Maxwell, Trump replied, "I'm allowed to do it, but it's something I haven't thought about."[102]

When asked if he would pardon Sean "Diddy" Combs following the music mogul's conviction for federal sex crimes, Trump balked at the notion, citing Combs's negative comments about him: "But when you know someone and you were fine and then you run for office and he made some terrible statements . . . so I don't know . . . it makes it more difficult to do."[103] There was no mention of the victims, the cost of prosecution, or the need for accountability. In October 2025, Trump commuted the sentence of disgraced former New York Republican Representative George Santos, a fabulist liar who misused campaign funds on Botox, designer fashions, cosmetics, and OnlyFans purchases.[104] In a social media post, Trump hinted that the decision was based on politics, claiming that "at least Santos had the Courage, Conviction, and Intelligence to ALWAYS VOTE REPUBLICAN!"[105]

After the crypto sector contributed heavily to Trump's 2024 presidential campaign, Trump pardoned convicted Binance founder Changpeng Zhao in late October 2025.[106] Democratic Senator Elizabeth Warren commented: "First, Changpeng Zhao pleaded guilty to a criminal money laundering charge. Then he boosted one of Donald Trump's crypto ventures and lobbied for a pardon. Today, Donald Trump did his part and pardoned him."[107]

Fortunately, the federal system is only a small part of the nation's prison population. It may be that Trump's unchecked use of clemency will inspire governors to do the same, albeit with a greater sense of fairness. Steve Zeidman, a law professor at the City University of New York School of Law, summed up this hope: "President Trump is making shameless use of his constitutional clemency power, rewarding insurrectionists, cronies, campaign contributors and sundry others. But this is not the only problem. Mr. Trump's acts of commission are paralleled by American governors' acts of omission. Even though they control the bulk of the nation's prison population and typically have the power to grant clemency, many governors have consistently failed to exercise the power of forgiveness, to all of our detriment."[108]

COMMUTATIONS IN WYOMING

In some states, such as Wyoming, the governor's executive clemency powers include the ability to unilaterally commute people's sentences. I reviewed Wyoming commutation records dating back to 1954 and the tenure of Clifford J. "Doc" Rogers, the state's twenty-second governor.[109] I was unable to determine the commutation grant rate for that time period, but I was able to examine each individual commutation granted by reviewing records kept by the Wyoming State Archives. Beginning with the commutation of inmate Robert Kowinski on April 8, 1954, Governor Rogers granted 34 commutations. Rogers was followed by Governor Milward Simpson, who granted 116 commutations from 1955 to 1959. Governor John J. Hickey granted 90 commutations during his two-year term as governor (1959–1961), and Governor Jack R. Gage granted an impressive 223 commutations during his two-year stint (1961–1963). Between 1963 and 1967, Governor Clifford Hansen granted 205 commutations, and Governor Stanley K. Hathaway granted 198 commutations between 1967 and 1975. By comparison, Governor Edgar "Ed" Herschler was the "king" of commutations, granting a whopping 856 commutations between 1975 and 1987.[110]

The frequency of commutations in Wyoming began to decline with Governor Mike Sullivan—who granted 218 during the years 1987 to 1995—although the number of Sullivan's commutations was very much in line with governors prior to the prolific Ed Herschler. Herschler and Sullivan were Democrats; but soon, Republican Governor Jim Geringer would usher in a new era of gubernatorial commutation policy in Wyoming that would bring an abrupt halt to the practice and, consequently, add to the growing population of US inmates serving life sentences.

Governor Geringer served two terms, from 1995 until 2003; during that time he granted only 15 commutations. Similarly, the next governor, Democrat Dave Freudenthal, also granted 15 commutations during his two terms, 2003 to 2011. Republican Governor Matt Mead all but ended the practice of granting commutations in Wyoming, with the exception of Joe Welch's, described earlier. Mead was in office from 2011 until 2019 and granted commutations to inmates Orland Glenn and Brad Skinner, both of whom were serving life sentences.[111] Interestingly, Glenn was released and Skinner is still in prison, having had another commutation request denied by current Governor Mark Gordon (Skinner's case will be discussed later). To date,

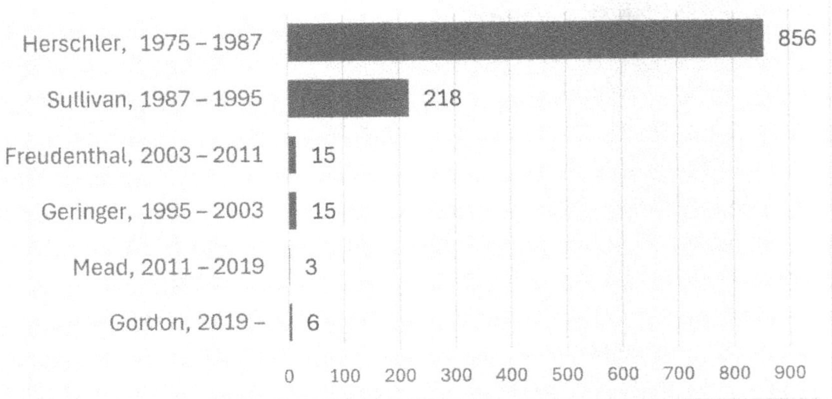

FIGURE 2.1. Decline in Wyoming commutations. Source: The author maintains a complete copy of commutations granted by governors beginning with Ed Herschler. The entire record is on file at either the Wyoming State Archives or the Secretary of State's Office.

Governor Gordon has granted only 6 commutations, one of which went to Darla Rouse and another to Mark Farnham, who will be introduced in chapter 6 (figure 2.1).

The chronic under-use of commutations is not unique to Wyoming. Commutation data are often not readily available or accessible on state websites, so in 2021 the Prison Policy Initiative conducted a clemency survey of eight northeastern states. Those eight states reported granting a mere 210 combined commutations from 2005 through mid-2021, an average of 13 grants a year.[112] When we factor in the combined average prison population across those states of about 130,000 incarcerated individuals, the governors granted a commutation to 1 of every 10,000 persons.

However, in several states, recently elected governors have turned the clock back to more forgiving times in their approach to commutations. In Missouri, former sheriff and current Governor Mike Parsons, elected in 2018, granted 613 pardons and 20 commutations by November 2023, the most since the period 1941–1945.[113] During her tenure ending in 2023, Oregon Governor Kate Brown commuted the sentences of about 1,000 people to reduce Covid-related risks and to fight Oregon wildfires. Governor Brown also granted 47,274 pardons of marijuana offenses and commuted the sentence of all 17 death row inmates to life without the possibility of parole.[114]

In 2024, Maryland Governor Wes Moore pardoned more than 175,000 cannabis-related convictions, the largest blanket pardon in US history.[115] Colorado Governor Jared Polis has made it a tradition to grant clemency around the holidays, pardoning 21 people and commuting the sentences of 7 others a few days before Christmas 2023, including commuting 1 murder sentence.[116] In 2024, Polis pardoned 22 people and granted 4 commutations, including 2 commutations in murder cases.[117] Since 2019, Polis has granted 29 commutations, reducing the sentences of all three men on death row after signing a bill abolishing capital punishment in Colorado.[118]

While there are exceptions, executive clemency—particularly commutations—has become politically risky for elected officials. For many politicians, the idea of reducing any prison sentence is unattractive if not out of the question. But for those in prison who are serving life sentences, what incentive is there for them to take accountability for their crime, to learn and grow from the tragedy? Still, some people in prison experience profound personal growth despite the fact that they know they may never be released. They maintain hope in the face of knowing that others have given up on them. In some cases, they receive a miracle, from either the courts or a forgiving governor—a governor like Mike Sullivan, who recognized what a demoralizing place prison can be, without any hope.

3

Profiles in Political Courage

Long before he became governor of the State of Wyoming and ambassador to Ireland, Mike Sullivan experienced the personal impact of a murder case—a case that ultimately led to a commutation granted by the governor at the time, Milward Simpson.

Governor Michael John Sullivan was born on September 22, 1939, and grew up in Douglas, Converse County, Wyoming.[1] During the summer of 1955, while Sullivan was enjoying his fifteenth birthday in Douglas, a murder was committed in Converse County that the future governor would never forget. The facts of the murder are not especially heinous or unusual, but what is noteworthy is that the young Sullivan loaned his suit to defendant Earnest Lindsay for his murder trial. Sullivan's father, Joseph Sullivan Jr., also known as J. B. Sullivan, was Lindsay's court-appointed defense attorney. Lindsay was convicted and sentenced to death in the gas chamber.[2]

On June 20, 1955, Earnest Lindsay, then twenty-two, had driven into Wyoming in a stolen Buick, along with a companion, Kenneth Phillips.[3]

https://doi.org/10.5876/9781646428557.c003

Both young men had escaped from jail in York, Pennsylvania.[4] Later that day, the two happened upon a blue Studebaker truck near Shawnee, Wyoming, in Converse County.[5] The truck was parked off the highway and had a camper that appeared to be open. The truck seemed to be abandoned. Lindsay and Phillips pulled over and discussed pilfering the truck for anything of value. Phillips served as a lookout while Lindsay started toward the truck.[6] He had a pistol stashed in his waistband.

Lindsay first tried the truck's door. Finding it locked, he proceeded to the rear, where the door to the camper was slightly open. Lindsay stooped down to peer through the open door. He later testified that his gun became loose in his waistband, which caused him to reach down and take the gun in his hand. As Lindsay looked back up into the truck, he was shocked to find himself confronted by a large man.[7]

The large man was named Herbert Diestler. According to Lindsay, Diestler hollered and then swung at him. Lindsay reacted by shooting and killing Diestler. In his testimony, Lindsay stated: "I don't know if he was fixing to hit me with something or shoot me or whether he was as scared as I was. I don't know, and I shot him."[8]

Lindsay fled the scene, was later apprehended in Indiana, and returned to Wyoming to stand trial. After only forty minutes of deliberation, a Converse County jury convicted him of first-degree murder and sentenced him to death on February 5, 1956.[9] The Wyoming Supreme Court upheld Lindsay's sentence on November 5, 1957, and he was scheduled to be executed on January 4, 1958.[10]

Since he did not have a dress suit for court appearances, Earnest Lindsay had worn a suit borrowed from his defense attorney's son, Mike. Following the affirmation of Lindsay's death sentence, J. B. Sullivan submitted a plea for clemency to Governor Milward Simpson, who on December 17, 1957, commuted Linsday's death sentence to a sentence of life without the possibility of parole.[11]

In many respects, the murder Lindsay committed fits the type of crime and subsequent punishment examined in this book: Lindsay was not a serial killer, and he certainly did not premeditate the killing. Both his and his accomplice's testimonies confirmed that they only wanted to rob Diestler's truck, not murder him.

Despite the fact that Governor Simpson explicitly reduced Earnest Lindsay's death sentence to a term of life without the possibility of parole, the

Wyoming Board of Parole later granted Lindsay a series of time cuts that eventually led to his release in his late thirties.[12]

Lindsay had a few acts of deviance left in his criminal career before he experienced the downward slope of the age-crime curve. Lindsay had been a model prisoner during his incarceration, to the point that he was transferred to the Wyoming Boys' School in Worland to serve as a trusty at the juvenile facility for delinquent boys. On May 21, 1962, Lindsay walked away from a work crew outside the Boys' School, committing the crime of escape. He was apprehended ten days later in Elko, Nevada, after breaking into a company garage.[13]

While Lindsay was sometimes a problematic inmate during his incarceration, that did not prevent attorney J. B. Sullivan and others from recognizing his potential for redemption. In a letter to the parole board dated September 5, 1963, Sullivan acknowledged Lindsay's escape but added that he had interviewed staff at the Boys' School and learned that Lindsay "was a very model trusty at the State Industrial School; that he had the confidence and respect of the boys at the school, and was, prior to his escape, doing a very worthwhile job with the boys at the school."[14]

During his trial and appeal, which culminated in 1957 with Lindsay being sentenced to death in the gas chamber, J. B. Sullivan had been his court-appointed defense counsel.[15] A few years later, Sullivan was elected Converse County attorney, meaning he was also the county prosecutor. As is still the custom today, the parole board requested Sullivan's input on later commutation recommendations for Lindsay, even though he had transitioned to prosecution. J. B. Sullivan wrote:

> In the course of my representing Lindsay I became very well acquainted with him, and have always had a personal interest in his progress. I realize any remarks I make may be somewhat prejudiced; however, I do feel that Lindsay at the time of the commission of the crime was a very young man. I believe at the time of sentence, he was 21 years of age, or perhaps 22. I can in no way condone or excuse his actions for which he was convicted. However, I do have a sincere feeling that with proper guidance this man could be rehabilitated and become a useful and worthwhile citizen.[16]

Lindsay was a young man when he committed his crime, which science now tells us may explain some of his impulsivity and criminal behavior.

The elder Sullivan also recognized the promise of Lindsay's rehabilitation and his positive work record before escaping.

The complication of Lindsay's escape conviction did not seem to hamper his progression through the Wyoming correctional system, as he obtained seven commutations from 1957 through 1975. The last commutation came on April 4, 1975, reducing Lindsay's sentence to time served and allowing his sentence to expire on May 1, 1975—nearly eighteen years after the murder of Herbert Diestler.[17]

Lindsay was subsequently released to parole on January 6, 1971, and appears to have completed parole without incident, given his discharge in 1975. Lindsay died in his mid-forties without ever re-offending. According to his obituary, Lindsay was living in Laramie and died of a heart attack on December 10, 1977.[18]

A LIFE OF SERVICE

The Lindsay case had clearly made a lasting impression on the young Mike Sullivan, giving him an understanding of the burdens a small-town attorney could face when prosecuting or defending a murder case. After watching his father deal with the pressures of the Lindsay case, Sullivan graduated from Douglas High School and "went off to school" at the University of Wyoming. Sullivan later recalled that he did not want to be a lawyer, "so I went to engineering school."[19] However, after two years studying petroleum engineering, he changed his mind about the legal profession. "Being a lawyer didn't sound nearly as bad as being an engineer," so after graduating with his engineering degree, Sullivan attended law school.[20]

After graduation, he moved to Casper, Wyoming, to practice civil law. As an attorney with the firm of Brown, Drew, Massey & Sullivan from 1968 through 1986, he engaged primarily in trial practice, specializing in medical malpractice defense and personal injury claims.[21]

When I first met former Governor Sullivan, he told me he'd had no experience in criminal law, with the exception of a few court appointments he had been required to accept as a young lawyer. Fresh out of law school, Sullivan recalled with a chuckle that he had "one appointment for a guy who was accused of violating the Mann Act. I had no idea what the hell I was doing."[22] When Sullivan interviewed his client in jail, the man said, "Sully, if you'll just get me out of jail, I can sell some siding and pay your bills."[23]

Again with a laugh, Sullivan recounted how he had read in the next day's paper that the man had pleaded guilty and "been shipped off someplace. He probably assessed the quality of his defense counsel and figured he was better off."[24]

In my discussions with the former governor, I was continually impressed by his self-deprecating wit and humble good nature. Governor Sullivan may not have thought much of himself as a criminal defense attorney, but his reputation as a skilled civil litigator became widely known throughout Wyoming. Prior to running for governor, he had served on a handful of boards but had never run for office. However, by the mid-1980s, Sullivan had grown weary of civil litigation, particularly medical malpractice. "It was getting kind of repetitive," he said. "I was taking expert medical witness depositions where I felt like I had taken the same deposition ten times before. I finally said to myself, 'I don't know if I want to take another deposition again in my life.' "[25]

Around that same time, fellow Democrat Dave Freudenthal, who later served as governor from 2003 to 2011, began pushing Sullivan to consider running.[26] Sullivan recalled: "Finally, I woke up one day and said, 'you know, if I don't embarrass myself, I can maybe contribute to the conversation, and it would be a pretty good sabbatical.' "[27]

That "pretty good sabbatical" produced a governorship for Mike Sullivan, from 1987 to 1995.[28] When asked to explain his ability to win the governor's race despite being a political unknown, Sullivan credited his experience litigating cases around the state and his family roots in Wyoming as factors that added to his name recognition.

While Governor Sullivan would go on to grant 218 commutations, he said he had not given the topic of commutations any thought prior to becoming the chief executive, although he avoided taking any firm position on the death penalty prior to assuming office. "Look, it's on the books, and I know there are instances, depending on the nature of the crime, that I would believe the death penalty is appropriate," he explained.[29]

Sullivan added that he'd been aware of one infamous death penalty case when he took office: that of Mark Hopkinson. Hopkinson's case had been made famous, in part, because of the man who prosecuted him, legendary Wyoming attorney Gerry Spence. In her book about the case, author Marion Huseas recounted not only the prosecution of Hopkinson but also that Spence was unsuccessful when he sought a commutation for Hopkinson from Governor Sullivan.[30] According to Huseas: "Sullivan knew, when he ran for office in 1986, that he might have to face this decision. While some people might favor the death penalty without reservations, he said it had not been that easy for him. 'I go into it as a human being, as a lawyer, as a citizen, as a governor, and as a practicing Catholic. All of those things form a part of the ultimate decision I reached. The ultimate decision is that I support the death penalty in this case.' "[31]

By his own admission, Governor Sullivan took no pleasure in allowing Hopkinson's execution to proceed, and he issued a statement shortly after Hopkinson's death: "Be assured, one can feel only sadness that an execution has occurred. As governor, there is an added sorrow . . . I have prayed for the victims of these heinous crimes and their families. I now pray for Mark Hopkinson and his family."[32]

SULLIVAN'S COMMUTATIONS

Mark Hopkinson was the last inmate to be executed in Wyoming—by lethal injection in 1992.[33] Despite pleas from influential individuals, including Gerry Spence, Governor Sullivan had refused to intervene in Hopkinson's execution. However, he did engage in the liberal practice of granting commutations to inmates serving life sentences. Whatever one may think about the former governor's position on the death penalty, he clearly believed that people who commit violent crimes might be capable of rehabilitation. As chapter 2 documented, Sullivan's predecessor, Governor Ed Herschler, granted hundreds of commutations during his unprecedented three terms as governor of Wyoming.[34] Sullivan did not recall any conversations with Herschler about his approach to commutations, but Sullivan "was aware that he [Herschler] was granting a lot of commutations, particularly toward the end, and some people were raising their eyes about that."[35]

Mike Sullivan may not have granted as many commutations as Herschler, but his approach was still far more forgiving than that of those who followed him. When asked to describe his decision-making process when considering commutations, Sullivan noted that many of the commutation recommendations he had received involved cases in which Governor Herschler had already granted the inmate sentence reductions.

Wyoming governors prior to the Herschler era rarely granted an inmate serving life a commutation resulting in immediate release. Instead, commutations were granted in a gradual fashion, and its power was used as a management tool to promote good behavior. In reaching his decision on a commutation recommendation, Sullivan explained:

> There are two things I remember clearly: I relied heavily on the parole board. I figured they were there for a reason, and I put good people on it, and I expected them collectively to make good decisions. The other, I had a specific belief, if you were in prison, on a life sentence or seventy to ninety years, you probably needed some kind of incentive, to maintain management, to at least maintain a degree of hope that will keep you on the straight and narrow. You sure as hell don't want a prison fully populated with people serving eighty- to ninety-year sentences because they don't have much incentive to behave or pay attention. I always thought there's a carrot at the end of that stick, [if] you've behaved yourself for the last ten years, even though you committed a horrible crime, we'll give you something to look forward to for the next ten years and then you'll get some further help.[36]

After Governor Sullivan left office, the Wyoming inmate population had few "carrots," as succeeding governors began to abandon the long-standing practice of granting frequent and graduated commutations to inmates serving life—or any sentence—and commutations all but disappeared.

Two of the governors who followed Sullivan were former federal prosecutors: Dave Freudenthal, who had been the United States attorney for Wyoming prior to being elected governor in 2002, and Matt Mead, who had also been United States attorney prior to being elected governor in 2010.[37] During our interview, former Governor Sullivan expressed disappointment that a "prosecutorial syndrome" had overtaken the governor's office. Sullivan made it very clear that he is friends with all of Wyoming's past governors, but he has confided in them his feelings about the virtual abandonment of commutations in recent decades. "I've told Mead and Freudenthal both: You guys are prosecutors, you never saw anybody you didn't think belonged in prison for the rest of their life, and I think it's a shame," said Sullivan.[38]

Freudenthal openly admitted that his time as prosecutor tainted his view of commutations. "I never worried about the politics of commutations," the former governor stated in a 2022 interview. "I just had a bias against them that had been shaped by seven years as a prosecutor." However, Freudenthal expressed some regret over his reluctance to grant more commutations: "I believe it's a tool that ought to be used more often. You'd be surprised [at] how many people have felony convictions from their youth. I probably should have been more understanding about that."[39]

When the governor is considering a commutation recommendation from the parole board, he receives a packet of information that includes input from the prosecutor, the judge, and the victim's family. While he greatly valued the input from those stakeholders, Sullivan noted that it's "unlikely that you will get positive responses" from many of the involved parties, "so it was rare that I let that impact my decision, because it was a response that I expected."[40]

"VIOLENT" OFFENDERS AND RECIDIVISM

The responses from families of murder victims and other victims of violent crime can be understandably unforgiving. But it is a popular myth that all victims of violent crime want long sentences in every case. According to the results of a survey released by the Prison Policy Initiative in 2022, most victims of violence support violence prevention rather than lengthy periods of incarceration. The survey found that 52 percent of victims believed a prison sentence will make people more likely to commit a crime, and 61 percent preferred shorter sentences coupled with more spending on prevention and rehabilitative programs. Moreover, 82 percent of victims preferred investing more in programs for at-risk youth and other crime prevention programs than in jails and prisons.[41] These findings suggest that retribution is far less important to crime victims than is living in a safe, pro-social community.

Another complicating fact about crime victims is that many perpetrators of crime have been victims themselves, making severe punishments perhaps less fair than one might believe. A 2019 publication, the *Square One Project*, part of Columbia University's Justice Lab, observed: "Often growing up in poor communities in which rates of street crime are high, and in chaotic homes which can be risky settings for children, justice-involved people can be swept into violence as victims and witnesses. From this perspective, the violent offender may have caused serious harm, but is likely to have suffered serious harm as well."[42]

Many individuals who are caught in the cycle of violence come from poor communities with high unemployment and low graduation rates and are raised in single-parent households.[43] A growing body of research provides evidence to counter the conventional narrative that violent offenders are too risky to be released back into society.

Part of that disputed narrative is rooted in a faulty approach to determining the risk to re-offend, which is often judged by evaluating the type of crime rather than the facts and circumstances behind each crime.[44] This approach perpetuates the myth that violent offenders are incapable of rehabilitation and should therefore be locked up for long periods of time, if not for life. To reexamine this faulty approach, one should begin with a discussion about what it means to re-offend, or to recidivate. What does recidivism mean?

Generally speaking, recidivism means a relapse in prior negative behavior to the point of re-offending, basically engaging in criminal behavior after having been released from a prior sentence.[45] Recidivism can be measured in a number of different ways. It can be self-reported or, more commonly, gathered from reports of arrest, conviction, and incarceration.[46] However, measuring recidivism through the use of arrest data is problematic because an arrest is not a conviction or a pronouncement of guilt. In many instances of arrest, the charges are later dismissed, reduced, or pleaded down. It is more accurate and useful to measure recidivism by tracking convictions for crimes that result in a new sentence of incarceration, as this level of re-offending is severe enough to merit a return to prison.[47]

Another aspect of the public misconception of violent offenders is based on the view that they are at a greater risk than nonviolent offenders to re-offend. In fact, the opposite is true. People convicted of violent offenses have the lowest recidivism rate under each measure: rearrest, re-conviction, and re-incarceration.[48]

Recidivism data from that 2022 study also revealed that 82 percent of incarcerated people were arrested at some point within ten years after release. The vast majority were arrested in the first three years and over half within the first year.[49] In the same study, 69 percent of violent offenders were rearrested within five years, but only 44 percent of those individuals were arrested for another violent offense.[50]

Current data support the proposition that recidivism rates for violent offenders are lower than the rates of those incarcerated for all other offenses; however, evidence indicates that those involved in serious violence tend to be life course persistent (LCP) offenders.[51] Longitudinal studies have shown that about 5 percent of all people commit about 50 percent of crimes and that 5 percent not only commit more serious crimes but also offend at a higher rate than the rest of the population.[52] Predicting which individuals will develop into LCPs cannot be done with certainty, as previous efforts to identify higher-risk offenders at an early stage in the life course have failed.[53]

In a review of the literature on life course re-offending, criminologist Alex Piquero and his colleagues explain that incidents of people committing violent crimes are "rare," with the exception of the small group of LCP offenders discussed earlier, and that those particular LCP offenders do not specialize in any particular crime type.[54] Piquero and his coauthors concluded that "attempts to correctly predict the violent recidivist are virtually impossible regardless of the make-up of individual risk and protective factors available to researchers and policy makers."[55]

Governors in Wyoming began to back away from granting commutations after Governor Mike Sullivan left office. During his two terms (1987–1995), Sullivan signed off on 218 commutations. A rudimentary study of the inmates released as a result of Sullivan's commutations indicates that their recidivism rate was fairly low. The study is limited by a few factors, though. First, the sample size, coming from Wyoming, is small. Second, several of the inmates who received commutations were never released from prison, making it impossible to measure their capacity to avoid re-offending. Third, the study only captures inmates who were returned to the custody of the Wyoming Department of Corrections (WDOC). It is certainly possible and, in fact, likely that individuals in the sample moved out of state after completing parole, just as several individuals in the sample are now on parole out of state. Again, this study tracks only what could be obtained through searches of the internet and the information the WDOC was able to provide.

Of those 218 commutations, 66 were granted to inmates with life sentences; however, many inmates serving life received multiple commutations from Governor Sullivan. For example, 1 inmate received 6 separate commutations from Sullivan, and 2 other inmates received 5 each. In total, 31 individual inmates serving life sentences received commutations from Sullivan. For 17 of those individuals, the WDOC was unable to provide any data other than the facts that they died in prison or they successfully completed their parole and have not returned to WDOC custody. Eight of those 31 individuals are currently on parole, either in Wyoming or out of state. Six of those individuals are still in prison; of those, 2 were released on parole but are currently in prison, having re-offended.

Significantly, not one inmate from the sample has committed another murder, at least from a review of the available data. Moreover, the two inmates who have been returned to WDOC comprise 6.5 percent of the sample size, which is in line with the percentage of LCP offenders who comprise 5 percent of offenders who commit 50 percent of all crimes—committing more serious crimes and offending at a higher rate than the rest of the population.[56]

One of those recidivists is an individual who had his parole revoked several times, has been prosecuted for new crimes on multiple occasions, and is currently serving an eight- to ten-year sentence for influencing, intimidating, or impeding a witness. For the sake of privacy, I am not identifying the inmate, but he fits the LCP offender model discussed earlier. He did not seem to specialize in any particular crime type but rather committed a variety of crimes involving the illegal drug trade.[57]

In the wake of the three-term governorship of Ed Herschler, the Wyoming State Legislature placed a two-term limit on the governor's office.[58] At the end of his second term as governor, Mike Sullivan ran for the United States Senate against then-US Congressman Craig Thomas, but Sullivan lost the election as part of the historic "red wave" of 1994, when Republicans took control of both houses of Congress following the election of President Bill Clinton, a Democrat, in 1992.[59] After he left office in 1995, Sullivan completed a fellowship at Harvard's Institute of Politics in the John F. Kennedy School of Government. President Clinton later appointed him ambassador to Ireland in 1998.

We can only dream that more of our elected officials would demonstrate the strong moral character exhibited by Mike Sullivan. He used his commutation power as a reward for good behavior for *all* inmates rather than using clemency to reward his family or friends or not using it at all.

4

Pleading for Life

The act of committing murder is without question one of the most grave and shocking crimes one human being can perpetrate upon another. In the Bible's Ten Commandments, the Sixth Commandment states unequivocally "Thou Shall Not Kill."[1] We are taught at a young age that murder is perhaps the most unforgiveable of all sins and that those who commit murder should be punished harshly, with sanctions that match the severity of the act. However, it is important to understand that not all murders are committed in the same fashion, and not all murderers are the same. The circumstances of each case can and do vary greatly.

For those who have never witnessed a parole hearing—which includes most of the public—what occurs there is remarkably similar to the parole hearings dramatized in the 1994 movie *The Shawshank Redemption*, based on a Stephen King novella. Morgan Freeman's character, Ellis "Red" Redding, attends a succession of parole hearings over a thirty-year period of incarceration in a Maine prison.[2] Each hearing is conducted at the prison, where Red enters a classroom and sits in a front of a panel of parole board

https://doi.org/10.5876/9781646428557.c004

members who question him about the crime he committed and his efforts at rehabilitation. During the hearings, Red recounts his crime of armed robbery/murder. Until the final hearing, he professes that he has been rehabilitated. Only near the end of the movie, when Red speaks bluntly about the fact that he cannot change his past and has no idea what rehabilitation truly means, does the parole board release him.[3]

The Wyoming parole board conducts hearings in nearly that same format. There are some slight differences in our current era, such as technology upgrades like laptops, which have replaced paper files, but the essence of a parole hearing remains the same to this day: A panel of board members presides over the room, sitting at a table and interviewing individual inmates for possible parole release.

Not only does the State of Wyoming conduct every parole hearing live, but every inmate is eligible for a parole hearing at some point regardless of their crime, unless the inmate received a life without parole (LWOP) sentence or was sentenced to death.[4] At the outset of a parole hearing, the board usually asks the inmate to describe their crime. Some inmates' descriptions are brief and minimize their culpability. Others describe their crimes in great detail, explaining their motivation or memory of the acts in vivid terms.

LIFE BY THE NUMBERS

The data certainly support the argument that we should rethink our approach to life sentences, not only for murder but for all crimes that are eligible for such a severe sentence. While the case studies presented here focus primarily on crimes of violence, the general practice in the United States of administering life sentences even for nonviolent crimes has been overused and abused. For example, the proportion of individuals serving sentences of life without parole in the United States is 180 times higher than the number in England.[5]

According to a 2017 report by the Sentencing Project, 161,957 people were serving life sentences in the United States—or 1 for every 9 people in prison.[6] An additional 44,311 individuals were serving "virtual life" sentences, producing a total population of both life and virtual life sentences at 206,268, nearly 1 in every 7 people in prison.[7] The number dipped slightly in 2024, to 194,803; however, nearly half of the states had more people serving life in 2024 than in 2020.[8] Moreover, the pool of people

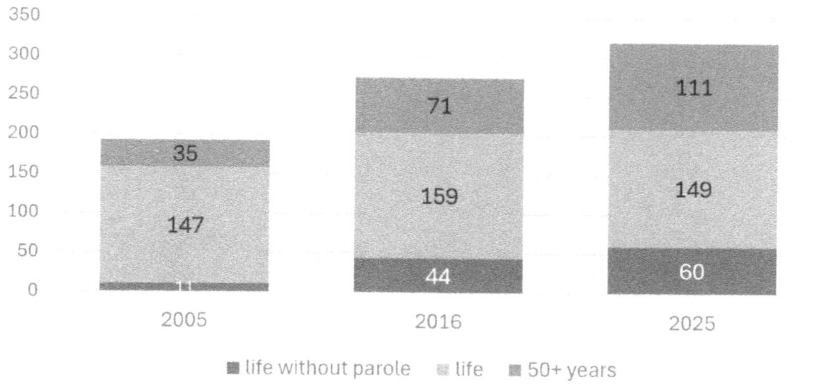

FIGURE 4.1. Growth of life/virtual life sentences in Wyoming over twenty years, 2005–2025. Counts represent sentences listed in Wyoming Correctional Information System, which are non-cumulative data. Source: Information provided by the Wyoming Department of Corrections, on file with author.

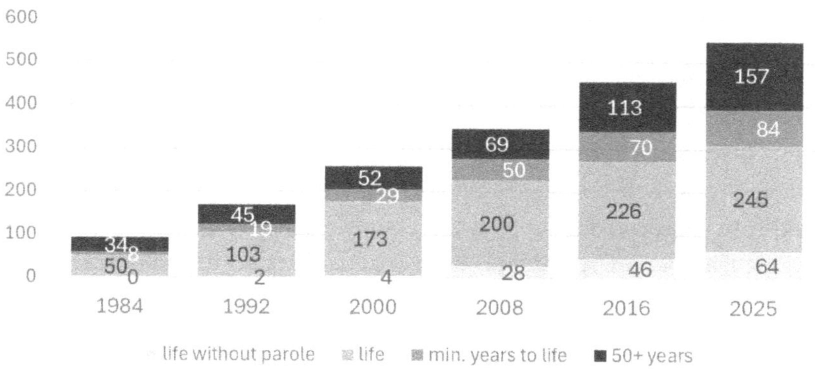

FIGURE 4.2. Cumulative growth of life/virtual life sentences in Wyoming from 1984 to 2025. Counts represent sentences listed in WCIS as of December 31 of the given year. Sentences are cumulative going back in time in WCIS. Source: Information provided by the Wyoming Department of Corrections, on file with author.

serving life sentences has more than quadrupled since 1984.[9] Nearly half of those serving life and virtual life sentences are African American (48.3%), equal to 1 in 5 Black prisoners overall.[10] In Wyoming, the number of life sentences has also more than quadrupled over the last four decades. In 1984, 93 individuals were serving virtual life sentences in Wyoming; as of

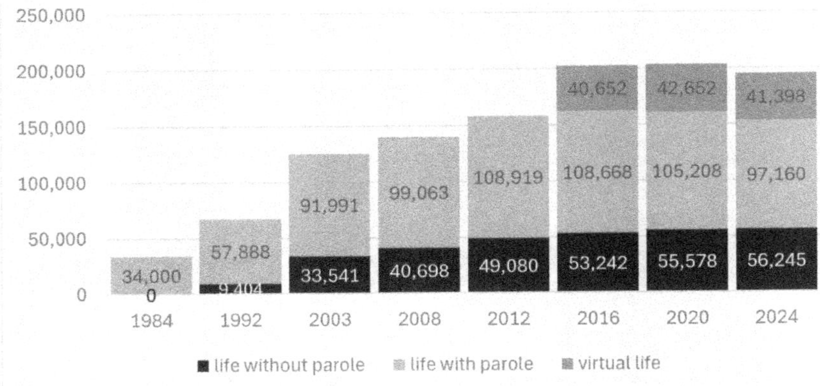

FIGURE 4.3. Growth of US life/virtual life sentences. Source: Ashley Nellis and Celeste Barry, "A Matter of Life: The Scope and Impact of Life and Long Term Imprisonment in the United States," *Sentencing Project*, January 8, 2025.

2025, 320 inmates were doing virtual life inside Wyoming prisons, and the total number of life sentences ordered by Wyoming courts had grown to 550 (figures 4.1, 4.2, 4.3).[11]

If you think those serving life or virtual life are all violent offenders, you are mistaken. More than 17,000 individuals serving life or virtual life sentences were convicted of nonviolent offenses. Currently, the United States incarcerates people for life at a rate of 50 per 100,000 US citizens, which is roughly the equivalent of the entire incarceration rates of the Scandinavian nations Denmark, Finland, and Sweden; the US is far ahead of the rest of the globe (figure 4.4).[12]

However, the recidivism rate for convicted murderers is the lowest of that for any offender. A 2002 study from the Bureau of Justice Statistics tracked 272,000 inmates released in fourteen states and found that only 1.2 percent of those freed after serving a murder sentence were rearrested on homicide charges within three years—the lowest rate among all reported crimes by released prisoners.[13]

The idea that a person who commits murder once is somehow beyond hope of rehabilitation is a popular notion that needs to be challenged and dispelled. Credible evidence indicates that most murders are committed in situations where the exact circumstances are unlikely to be repeated in that person's lifetime, which significantly reduces the chance of violent reoffending.[14]

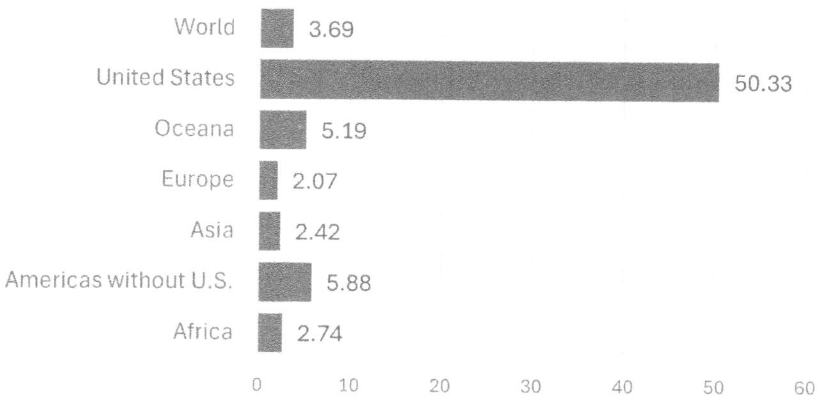

FIGURE 4.4. World and US prisoners sentenced to life (per 100,000 population). Sources: Dirk van Zyl Smit and Catherine Appleton, *Life Imprisonment: A Global Human Rights Analysis* (Cambridge, MA: Harvard University Press, 2019), table B.1, 340–347, data collected by the author; Helen Fair and Roy Walmsley, "World Prison Population List—Prison Studies," *World Prison Brief*, January 12, 2021.

In listening to individuals serving life sentences for murder during their appearances before the parole board, I recognized the validity of the research cited above. Most of the murders I recall involved a combination of several factors. Alcohol and drugs were involved in a majority of cases. Relationship issues and jealousy were common factors, and youthful impulsivity was also a component in many of the murder cases I encountered. And yes, without question, there were murder cases that involved depraved and calculated acts of cruelty and inhumanity and, in some cases, killers who seemed to thrive on their infamy and media notoriety.

After sitting through hundreds of parole hearings and hearing the stories of dozens of convicted murderers, I came to realize that most of those individuals had maintained hope, however dim, that they would one day be released. In some cases, the desperation in their voices was heartbreaking. This book does not seek to minimize the actions of these men and women but describes the humanity of many of them—a humanity they expressed in their hearings and in their conduct as inmates over many years. Some of the people I listened to had not premeditated their killings, and in several cases they had no significant prior criminal records. As former President

Barack Obama once remarked, the criminal justice system "takes young people who made mistakes no worse than my own and traps them in an endless cycle of marginalization and punishment."[15]

GROWTH OF RETRIBUTIVISM

A corresponding goal of this book is to reexamine the purposes of punishment in the United States and to advocate for a change in the prevailing perspective. The current approach to punishment favored by the American public is the retributive model.[16] The Model Penal Code, which is considered by some to be the most important influence in US criminal law, places retributivism as the official dominant principle for sentencing.[17] Not only is our system designed to be punitive, but undoubtedly, our criminal laws suffer from a lack of flexibility. Rachel E. Barkow, one of the leading voices of criminal justice reform, rightly finds fault with the US scheme of criminal justice, both at the federal level and among the states. Barkow has a uniquely informed perspective, as she served on the United States Sentencing Commission from 2013 to 2018 and coauthored the leading criminal law casebook used in US law schools.[18] She correctly points out that our criminal laws are too broad: "The popular discussion around a given crime tends to focus on the worst category of offenders, while the statute defining the elements of the crime often sweeps far more broadly, bringing in cases that no rational voter would have ever imagined belonged to that category."[19]

Not only is sentencing overly broad in the US, it is unduly harsh. Barkow points out that "people have different conceptions of what a just punishment for crime is, and retributive theory cannot settle what the exact amount of punishment should be."[20] A telling example of irrational sentencing, even under a retributive framework, is the fact that the average federal sentence for murder is twenty-three years, while people who sell drugs often receive much longer sentences. In one instance, a Louisiana woman who forged a $200 check received a twenty-year sentence. Also in Louisiana, more than 300 people serving life without parole have never been convicted of a violent crime.[21] Sentences in several recent federal cases indicated that possession of child pornography is considered more serious than the actual molestation of a child.[22]

The idea of just desserts has also supported the irrational, costly belief that those who commit felony crimes should be punished long after their sentence ends, in some cases for life. Voter disenfranchisement is but one example. In the 2016 election, an estimated 6.1 million US citizens were legally forbidden from voting, with 3.1 million of those disenfranchised having finished their sentence.[23] Jury service is another area of ongoing retribution. Twenty-six states and the federal government permanently ban convicted felons from serving on a jury. The remaining jurisdictions impose some type of less severe, record-based restrictions on jury service. Only Maine places no limitations on a convicted felon's right to serve on a jury.[24]

Perhaps the most under-recognized obstacle facing convicted felons relates to housing, a basic requirement for survival. Nearly a quarter of incarcerated persons were living in public housing before their imprisonment. Since the 1990s, the United States Congress has passed a series of laws that have made it more difficult for individuals leaving prison to find public housing. Roughly 10%–15% of people released from prison are unhoused, and in metropolitan areas the percentage is higher. Individuals who are required to register for life as a sex offender are permanently banned from public housing, without regard to their economic circumstances. While this may sound reasonable at first glance, should society impose this lifetime ban on, for example, individuals who texted a naked photo as a teenager or urinated in public while intoxicated?[25]

In 1996, Congress imposed a lifetime ban on food stamps for persons convicted of drug crimes and also prohibited anyone with a drug conviction from receiving student loans. These collateral penalties have disproportionately affected people of color, young Black men in particular. Professor Barkow has also focused attention on the disturbing ease with which Congress adopted these collateral consequences, using the ban on food stamps as an example.[26] The bill took only two minutes of debate before passage, despite Senator Edward Kennedy's (D-MA) warning that "under this amendment, if you are a murderer, a rapist, or a robber, you can get Federal funds; but if you are convicted even for possession of marijuana, you cannot."[27]

FEAR-MONGERING AND CRIME RATES

Not only do we sentence people much too harshly in America, we also have permitted politics to become detrimentally intertwined with the criminal justice system. The reasons for the mass incarceration era have been well documented.[28] The social unrest of the 1960s coupled with rising crime rates led a large majority of the public to report that they feared for their safety.[29] As a result, conservatives and liberals alike pushed for a tougher response to crime, and by the early 1970s the ideal of rehabilitation began to fall by the wayside.[30] To this day, the American public remains open to punitive crime policies, as most people are uninformed about criminal justice issues and tend to overestimate the actual threat of crime.[31] An estimated 95 percent of the public uses the news media as their primary source of information about crime in America.[32] The media, in turn, is fixated on crime: The lead story on the nightly news is either a crime story or an accident 77 percent of the time, and 32 percent of local news stories are about crime.[33]

Social media has changed the landscape of crime news consumption. In 2021, 48 percent of Americans reported getting their news from social media, with nearly a third getting news from Facebook, and other platforms such as YouTube, X (formerly Twitter), Instagram, Reddit, and TikTok following closely.[34] In 2023, researchers at Stanford University published a study that found Facebook users were overexposed to race-crime posts, overrepresenting Black suspects by 25 percent compared with local arrest rates.[35] The media has little interest in covering crimes other than those involving a victim of physical harm; news outlets typically focus on violent crime despite the fact that the majority of crimes are nonviolent.[36] Whether crime rates are up or down, stories about murder are almost always in the headlines.

The Center for Media and Public Affairs, based at George Mason University, conducted a study of television crime coverage during the years 1990–1995.[37] During that period, the number of murder stories (excluding the O. J. Simpson case) increased by 336 percent, from 80 cases in 1990 to 375 in 1995.[38] If this spike in media coverage had been the result of a murderous crime wave, the actions would have been understandable. However, the murder rate had actually declined by 13 percent during that five-year period.[39] The media's sensationalizing of murder and violent crime overshadows the scant attention to the real costs and benefits of criminal justice policies; the stories also tend to ignore or overlook important demographic statistics and the individual backgrounds of offenders and victims.[40]

If a political leader makes an issue of crime in their speeches, it also feeds the public perception that crime is spiraling out of control. President Donald Trump has been called a "master" at playing to the public's fear of crime. During his first campaign, Trump described the world as a "horrible mess" and falsely claimed that the murder rate in the US was "the highest it's been in 47 years."[41]

During his 2016 campaign, he stoked Americans' fears when he used language such as "crime and terrorism and lawlessness" and warned of "American carnage."[42] The president also focused continually on Chicago's murder rate during the campaign, emphasizing the allegedly rising crime rate and labeling crimes by immigrants and terrorist groups as the most serious threat to US public safety.[43] This toxic fear-mongering by politicians and a tabloid media has caused the public to believe that crime is rampant on the streets, when, in reality, crime rates had been falling since the 1990s.[44] According to a 2016 study by the Pew Research Center, "Despite double-digit percentage decreases in US violent and property crime since 2008, most voters say crime has gotten worse during that span."[45]

That misperception seemed to become a reality in 2020 when the US murder rate rose by 30 percent over 2019—the largest single-year increase in more than a century, and, as reported by the Pew Research Center, possibly the largest-ever single-year increase.[46] Although it would appear that the murder rate had skyrocketed, that assumption is false. The same report noted that despite the spike in 2020, *the murder rate in the US remains below the levels that were reached in the 1990s and "far below the rates recorded in much of the 1970s and 1980s."*[47] Even though murder rates during the pandemic were well below the rates reported a few decades earlier, the Pew Research Center found that more Americans saw violent crime as a "very big problem"—61 percent in July 2021, an increase from 41 percent in June 2020.[48]

According to Gallup, the belief that we are "too soft" on crime increased to 58 percent of Americans surveyed in 2024.[49] Trump continued his outrageous exaggerations leading up to the 2024 election, claiming "you can't walk across the street to get a loaf of bread. You get shot, you get mugged, you get raped, you get whatever it may be."[50] The recent fear-mongering has had an impact across the US, even in deep-blue cities like Washington, DC, and San Francisco, where policymakers have responded to these unfounded fears by adopting draconian measures to eliminate parole opportunities and increase the number of young people tried as adults and imposing extreme penalties for certain offenses.[51]

Despite these recent tough on crime proposals taking hold, public opinion polls indicate that Americans are not necessarily in favor of such approaches to the entire criminal justice system. A poll released in October 2024 revealed widespread bipartisan support for criminal justice reform, with support from 81 percent of likely voters and 72 percent saying we need to reduce the jail and prison populations.[52] Americans clearly have complicated and nuanced views of the criminal justice system, and simply getting tough on crime is not the long-term solution.

Homicide rates in the US continue to fall, posting a third straight year of record declines in the murder rate according to the Council on Criminal Justice.[53] These data are supported by Jeff Asher, who maintains the Real-Time Crime Index. In June 2025, Asher projected that the US will record the lowest murder rate ever and the lowest violent crime rate since 1968.[54] Criminologists are cautioning the public that the explanation for the drop in crimes rates is difficult to pinpoint. Adam Gelb, president and chief executive officer of the Council on Criminal Justice, commented: "Probably in the most simple form, it's simply that the shock waves of the pandemic that contributed to the spike have largely dissipated."[55] Gelb summarized the political reaction to the historic decline: "The theories and credit-taking claims are abundant. And a lot of the arguments have familiar contours. The right says it's tough enforcement and penalties. The left says it's better programs and community investment. The bottom line is it's likely a blend of both."[56]

* * *

Given these public perceptions, governors and presidents who actively engage in a policy of granting commutations see little political gain. Conversely, attacking proposed reform legislation and judicial nominations as "soft" on crime has remained a staple of some conservative politicians. Several current US senators routinely engage in fear-mongering. Even before the increase in the murder rate precipitated by the pandemic, Senator Tom Cotton of Arkansas claimed in 2016 that "if anything, we have an under-incarceration problem." Cotton continued: "The truth is you cannot decrease the severity and certainty of sentences without increasing crime. It's simply not possible."[57] The senator had no evidence to support his baseless claims. In his fervent opposition to criminal justice reform, Cotton blamed the Democrats for increases in crime and wrongly accused them of being responsible for criminal justice reform legislation that was sponsored by President Trump.[58]

"It's your party who voted in lock step for the First Step Act, that let thousands of violent felons on the streets who have now committed innumerable violent crimes," Cotton stated during a speech to the United States Senate.[59] Senator Dick Durbin of Illinois reminded Cotton that it was the Republicans who were in the majority on the First Step Act, a bill that passed the Senate by a decisive vote of 87 to 12. Cotton quickly pivoted, calling the First Step Act the "worst mistake of the Trump administration. Yes, it's true that a number of Republican Senators voted for it—they were wrong."[60]

The First Step Act created a new assessment process to identify low-risk offenders for possible early release.[61] When Trump signed the law in 2018, he had hopes that it would be the type of criminal justice reform that would have bipartisan support and, most important, increase his popularity with Black voters.[62] Then came the crime wave of 2020, which led many Republican legislators to attack anyone who did not adopt a retributive view of criminal justice as "soft" on crime.[63] These fear-mongering attacks were unmistakable in 2022, when several Republican senators repeatedly smeared judicial nominees who had backgrounds as public defenders.[64] In fact, presidents of both political parties have long been hesitant to appoint public defenders to federal judicial positions due to the political risks associated with the high-profile defendants those defenders often represent.

The Biden administration attempted to change that pattern by diversifying the federal bench with judicial nominations from the ranks of public defenders, many of them women.[65] During the confirmation hearing for former public defender Arianna Freeman, Biden's nominee for the United States Court of Appeals for the Third Circuit, Senator Ted Cruz of Texas commented, "There's a reason we see crime rates and murder rates and carjacking rates skyrocketing across this country, because the job of a judge is to follow the law, not to be a zealot pursuing a political agenda."[66]

The next confirmation hearing—for Nina Morrison, nominated for the United States Court of Appeals for the Eastern District of New York—drew similar criticism from Senator Cruz, who again aroused public fear: "Across this country, Americans are horrified at skyrocketing crime rates, at skyrocketing homicide rates, at skyrocketing burglary rates, at skyrocketing carjacking rates. All of those are the direct result of the policies you've spent your entire lifetime advancing."[67] Prior to Morrison's eventual judicial appointment, she had been an attorney with the Innocence Project, a reform-based legal organization that focuses on exonerating wrongfully convicted individuals through the use of DNA evidence.[68] Senator Cruz asked Morrison accusingly: "Why do you keep advising radical district attorneys who let violent criminals go and result in homicide rates skyrocketing? Do you care about the innocent people being killed because of the policies you're implementing?"[69]

Similar attacks were leveled against current United States Supreme Court Justice Ketanji Brown Jackson, who was nominated to the Supreme Court by President Biden after a distinguished legal career as a both a federal public defender and a judge. Justice Jackson faced a Republican line of questioning that focused on her sentencing record with regard to sex offenders during her tenure as a federal district court judge.[70]

Representative Marjorie Taylor Greene of Georgia prefaced the line of questioning nominee Jackson could expect by tweeting that the three Republican senators who supported Jackson's nomination were "pro-pedophile."[71] The notion that Jackson had been "soft" in her treatment of sex offenders began with Senator Josh Hawley of Missouri, who tweeted, "In every single child porn case for which we can find records, Judge Jackson deviated from the federal sentencing guidelines in favor of child porn offenders."[72] Senator Hawley failed to mention that he had voted to confirm at least three federal judges with sentencing deviations similar to those in the cases belonging to Judge Jackson.[73]

With respect to Jackson's confirmation hearings, Doug Berman, an expert on sentencing law and policy at Ohio State University School of Law, observed: "If and when we properly contextualize Judge Jackson's sentencing record in federal child porn cases, it looks pretty mainstream."[74] Concerning her service as a federal public defender, Judge Jackson told the Senate: "Federal public defenders don't get to pick their clients. They have to represent whoever comes in, and it's a service."[75] Even the conservative *National Review* dubbed the allegations that Jackson was soft on sex offenders "meritless to the point of demagoguery."[76] Moreover, Illinois Senator Dick Durbin noted that Republicans had decided to attack "assertive women of color" by suggesting they were "soft-on-crime." He added: "It is not somehow antithetical to the rule of law for an attorney to represent criminal defendants. The cause of justice is served when there is effective and competent counsel at both tables in the courtroom."[77]

Not only have cynical politicians engaged in fear-mongering over the recent increase in murder rates, but the available evidence also indicates that murder rates are up in jurisdictions controlled by Republican officials. The centrist think tank Third Way published a report that revealed murder rates were an average 40 percent higher in states won by Donald Trump in the 2020 election compared to the states he lost. According to the report, the state with the highest increase in murder was Wyoming, with a remarkable spike of 91.7 percent.[78] Wyoming was also the state that had the highest percentage of citizens who voted for Donald Trump in the 2020 election—69.9 percent—and that margin increased to 72.3 percent in 2024.[79] Third Way concluded its findings:

> The current narrative around crime and murder is convenient and wrong. Whether you're watching Fox News or CNN, or getting news online from a traditional newspaper, you would think that the increase in murder is a phenomenon found mostly in liberal cities. Many have tried attributing this to Democratic policies, specifically police reform. Republican lawmakers and ad makers have contributed to this narrative through clever messaging and strategies. The data clearly paints a different story. The increase in murders is not a liberal cities problem but a national problem. Murder rates are actually higher in Republican, Trump-voting states that haven't even flirted with ideas like defund the police. Eight of the ten most lawless, high-murder states are also Trump voting states but GOP bastions for the last quarter of a century. A more accurate conclusion from the data is that Republicans do a far better job blaming others for high murder rates than actually reducing murder rates.[80]

There is no simple answer to why murder rates increased in 2020, but several likely contributors have been identified: (1) the Covid-19 pandemic and its impact on communities and first responders, (2) the murder of George Floyd in 2020 and other police killings that sparked social unrest and multiple protests across the US, and (3) Americans having bought a record number of guns in recent years.[81]

Most Republican legislators are extremely reluctant to discuss placing any limitations on gun possession in America. Since the 2020 murder wave, they have become increasingly silent on the issue of criminal justice reform. President Trump's grand improvement to the criminal justice system, the First Step Act, has largely been forgotten and is sometimes attacked by Republicans. Frank Luntz, a popular Republican pollster and media figure, commented tersely: "The focus has changed because the situation has changed. We're not the same country."[82]

THE ARGUMENT FOR OVER-PUNISHMENT

Conservative scholars have argued convincingly that the tough on crime movement and subsequent increase in the prison population actually led to lower crime rates. Barry Latzer, in his book *The Myth of Overpunishment*, claimed that "the results of the great toughening were positive: crime began to drop in the mid-1990s and it kept dropping."[83] Latzer also identified murder sentences as a driving factor in the increase: "The long time that murderers spend behind bars is the key. Murder and manslaughter together account for only 2 percent of serious violent crime arrests, but 14 percent of state prisoners."[84]

Rafael A. Mangual, in his book *Criminal Injustice*, argued: "Notwithstanding the widely held belief that incarceration is driven by the drug war, just 14.1 percent of state prisoners were incarcerated primarily for a drug offense, and the vast majority of them were in primarily for trafficking, as opposed to possession—an offense category that constitutes less than 4 percent of [the] state prison population."[85] In the wake of the 2024 election, Mangual argued, "Yes, America is an international outlier on incarceration, but the vast majority of prisoners in the US are violent, chronic offenders who have squandered more than one 'second chance.'"[86] Charles Fain Lehman, a colleague of Latzer's and Mangual's at the conservative Manhattan Institute, claims that we should build more prisons, albeit "new and improved ones."[87]

John Pfaff, a law professor at Fordham, wrote that "drug crime is not what's driving the high prison population in the United States. It's crimes of violence."[88] Pfaff pointed to the fact that the public does not want to deal with the problem of violent crime in America and, for the most part, would rather ignore it:

> Now, of course, given the public's reluctance to think about violence, there's some risk to the politician who runs ahead of the pack to talk about it. But that, then, just creates a nasty vicious circle: The public doesn't want to change how we address violence, so no politician is willing to talk about how we need to change the way we address violence, so the public never learns that we need to rethink our approaches to violence, so attitudes stay fixed. And we remain where we are. And to be clear, changing how we approach violence is not just numerically justified, but actually good policy. The data consistently shows that tough prison sentences provide little additional

> deterrence over far less aggressive approaches, and often that spending more time in prison actually elevates the risk of future violence and offending, thanks to the traumatic nature of American prisons. Time spent in prison also undermines well-documented pathways out of violence, such as forming stable long-term relationships and gainful employment. And more and more research highlights programs that reduce violence and victimization in more effective—and humane—ways.[89]

Nonetheless, some conservative voices do remain invested in criminal justice reform. Brett Tolman, a former federal prosecutor and executive director of the conservative organization Right on Crime, stated: "I personally think there's just as many people that want to do criminal justice reform as the last several years, but I think their voices are quiet now, and those that are opposed to the First Step Act are still opposed and have gotten louder. It feels like we have to bide our time a bit and get past when the emotion of all of the political rhetoric is at the forefront."[90] Republican political strategist Zack Roday agreed: "Reform and calling out truths can coexist. It's not a binary decision. And there are achievable solutions available."[91] The search for those "achievable" solutions must endure beyond unpredictable shifts in the pendulum of public perception.

THE PROLIFERATION OF LIFE SENTENCES IN AMERICA

There is a pressing need for a rigorous examination of the utility of long prison sentences in America.[92] The number of life sentences has grown steadily in the US over the last forty years, expanding nearly five times since 1984, the year of earliest available data on life sentences at the national level. In eight states, one of every five inmates is serving life.[93] My experiences in the Wyoming criminal justice system combined with the abundance of research have convinced me that many inmates serving life—tens of thousands of people—should have their cases reevaluated for early release. We know that the impulse to engage in criminal behavior tapers off with age, and even life course persistent offenders begin to slow considerably when they hit their early forties.[94] Ashley Nellis, perhaps the preeminent scholar of life imprisonment in the US, has pointed out that "it is not 'tough' to imprison people long past their proclivity—or even physical ability—to commit crime; to the contrary, it is a poor use of resources that could be put toward prevention."[95] Nellis added: "Lifelong imprisonment with limited or no chance for review only serves a retributive purpose and is often counterproductive for purposes of crime control."[96]

Russell Harrison is an example from the Wyoming criminal justice system of an individual who is serving a life sentence and is arguably well past his physical ability to commit crime. While I was working at the parole board, Harrison wrote to the board many times, claiming to have had a deal with the board and governor to have been released earlier, years before he wrote the letters. As I will discuss, he had no deal, at least not an enforceable one. I had given some thought to contacting Harrison for this book, but from what I have learned by interviewing other individuals, health reasons would make a similar discussion with Harrison difficult. However, Harrison's worsening condition is what makes his story relevant to this area of reform. Harrison is serving life in prison, and even if he were to hit the criminal justice lottery like Darla Rouse did and somehow obtain a commutation from a Wyoming governor, he is likely past the point of being able to function in society.

On July 3, 1980, at age thirty-six, Russell Harrison murdered his ex-wife by beating her three times in the head with a lead pipe. Roughly four months later, Harrison was arrested in Texas and returned to Wyoming to face murder charges. An article in the *Casper Star-Tribune* began: "On advice of his attorney, who said the plea would mean a shorter sentence than a conviction on a lesser charge, a Casper man pleaded guilty Tuesday to first-degree murder in the beating death of his ex-wife last July." Harrison's defense attorney accepted the first-degree murder conviction because "it is probably more beneficial to Mr. Harrison. Those convicted of lesser homicide charges in Wyoming—such as second-degree murder or manslaughter—are actually . . . serving more time than under a life sentence." During his sentencing, Harrison's defense attorney proclaimed that "prisoners serving life sentences are being paroled after seven or eight years in prison."[97]

The only problem with Harrison's expectation of clemency is that governors change, and so do their respective approaches to granting sentence reductions. Harrison never had a deal with anyone, just an expectation built by the decades-long practice of commutations being freely granted by past governors. By the time Harrison might have received a commutation from a Wyoming governor, Mike Sullivan was about to leave office, and with him any realistic hope of a commutation for Wyoming prison inmates vanished.

5

A Pound of Flesh

Larry DeGraw had just been promoted to detective in the Casper (Wyoming) Police Department when he was assigned to investigate the murder of Melody Koester on June 5, 1988. Detective DeGraw knew the alleged gunman: a custodian named James Koester who removed his office trash at the courthouse every afternoon. As he walked into the interview room, the stunned detective informally asked Koester, "What happened?" Koester replied, "I shot Melody."[1]

DeGraw read Koester his Miranda rights and asked if he wanted to talk about the incident. DeGraw recalled that Koester began slowly, stating that he and Melody had been at a bar drinking and headed home when a verbal argument began, with Melody belittling Koester by comparing him to her previous relationships. The argument continued in their house, where according to Koester, Melody continued to insult him. Koester walked to the closet, loaded a clip into a .32 caliber automatic pistol, and shot Melody several times in the head.[2] Koester immediately called 911 and turned himself in.

https://doi.org/10.5876/9781646428557.c005

The affidavit DeGraw signed on June 6, 1988, indicates that shortly after midnight on June 5, 1988, dispatchers at the Casper Police Department received a call from Koester who reported he had just "blown away his old lady." When officers arrived at the Koester residence, Koester had his hands on his head and stated "I'm the man you want." Melody Koester was found dead inside her residence, with multiple gunshot wounds to the head.[3] The affidavit contains a short summary of Koester's confession, which is no different than DeGraw's recollection of the murder now, more than thirty-five years later.

The facts have never been in dispute when it comes to James Koester's case. Unfortunately for Koester, he pleaded guilty to first-degree murder, making the same gamble that cost Russell Harrison (see chapter 4). On the advice of his public defender, according to Koester he admitted guilt in committing first-degree murder under the promise of getting a commutation and being out in "10 to 15 years."[4] The *Casper Star-Tribune* quoted the district attorney as saying that Koester had "agreed to the deal before [he] entered the plea, although . . . it was not a 'plea bargain' because it affected only the penalty, and not a reduction of the charge." The district attorney elaborated: "In all reality I don't know that it would have qualified for a death penalty case anyway . . . 'The fact that Melody Koester was shot more than once, and that she was knocked down before she was shot might have made it possible to seek the death penalty,' he said. Nevertheless, [the district attorney] said, 'there were arguments made at the preliminary hearing that this was a manslaughter or second-degree murder case.' But the prosecution filed a first-degree murder case, and got its first-degree murder conviction, he said."[5]

That same district attorney was later convicted of a felony related to the handling of a family member's finances and was disbarred. On December 10, 2010, Governor Dave Freudenthal granted him a full pardon and restoration of civil rights.[6] Not only was the district attorney pardoned by a fellow prosecutor (Governor Freudenthal), but the two had been law school classmates.[7]

As mentioned, when the parole board recommended an inmate for a commutation, staff prepared a packet of information to send to the governor. The packet contained input from the prosecutor and judge, which was obtained by requesting their written recommendation regarding the proposed commutation. In many cases, both the judge and the prosecutor had long since left office. Koester's sentencing judge retired not long after his sentencing, but the new judge opposed the recommendation, writing: "The Defendant acknowledged that the homicide was premeditated. It appears that the investigator's opinion that the homicide is a crime of passion is not based in fact. I would also note that Mr. Koester accepted a plea agreement in which the State agreed not to pursue the death penalty, and the Defendant agreed to a life sentence. Since he accepted this agreement, it would not be appropriate to deprive the State of the benefit of its bargain by reducing the agreed upon sentence."[8]

The prosecutor's letter seemed to be an unwarranted attack on the parole board and the corrections department. By the time I received the letter, the district attorney who prosecuted Koester had been disbarred and forced to resign, and his replacement took the invitation to provide feedback as an opportunity to express his personal disdain for the concept of parole and early release from prison. What I recall most vividly about the letter is the prosecutor's threatening and bullying tone. The first page of the letter did not mention the facts of Koester's case; rather, the prosecutor engaged in a vitriolic diatribe aimed at both the parole board and the corrections staff, calling both state agencies a "secret sentencing society" that was actively "undermining the will of the citizens of Wyoming." (I am paraphrasing. Without the original copy of the letter, I can only recall bits and pieces.) I do remember a specific threat: that the district attorney would do whatever he could, either "publicly or privately," to oppose the commutation recommendation for Koester.

The discussion about the level of criminal homicide Koester's case exemplifies is also what has always interested me in the practice of law: the gray areas and arguing both sides of the question. Was his wife's murder premeditated? Under Wyoming law, yes. The Wyoming Supreme Court has held that "premeditation need not have existed for any given length of time before the act; it being sufficient that it existed at the time of the act; and the intent and the act may be as instantaneous as successive thoughts."[9] However, Wyoming case law also holds that "all evidence, direct and circumstantial, must be considered. It is for the jury to decide if the evidence presented establishes malice and premeditation."[10] Some factors the jury can consider are planning, motive, and a preconceived design for killing the victim.[11]

Koester was thirty at the time of his crime, and presumably, his brain was fully developed. However, to call his killing premeditated is debatable.

FIGURE 5.1. James Koester, present day. Image provided to author by James Koester.

Under Wyoming law, premeditation can be as instantaneous as successive thoughts, so in that respect the judge was correct in calling the murder premeditated. But there was no careful planning or deliberation by Koester in murdering his wife. He also took immediate accountability for his actions and has been a model inmate ever since. Arguably, his crime was closer to second-degree murder, which under Wyoming law carries a minimum of twenty years rather than the life sentence that is mandatory for a first-degree murder conviction.[12] While he did engage in the calculated act of loading a gun and ruthlessly killing his wife by shooting her several times, he did not plan the murder prior to their verbal argument, a situation in which both Koester and his wife were drinking. It is a tragedy that had devastating consequences, but I disagree with the view that the killing was premeditated (figure 5.1).

I was fortunate enough to become acquainted with the true champion of Koester's quest to gain his freedom: Larry DeGraw. DeGraw's perspective as a former law enforcement officer, private investigator, and county coroner was both unique and informed. I was well aware that Koester had the support of the detective who investigated his murder and planned to mention it in my book before ever speaking with DeGraw. Koester had suggested that I reach out to DeGraw, and he gave me DeGraw's phone number. In August 2022, I was able to have a lengthy phone chat with DeGraw, and I exchanged several emails with him, from which I quickly gained an appreciation for his sense of humanity and concern for James Koester's fate. He told me at one point, "I'd do anything to help James get out of prison."[13] I had meant to spend more time with DeGraw, but as I was compiling interviews and doing research for this book, his life was cut short by a heart attack.[14] I will discuss Larry DeGraw more in this chapter, as his legacy and impact on the people of Wyoming deserves more recognition.

I am still intrigued by the debate about what to charge in cases like Koester's: first- or second-degree murder? While I found aspects of charging decisions fascinating, I was never cut out to be a prosecutor. I am more inclined to look for the good in most people rather than treat them as criminals, even if they deserve the label. When I was working as a prosecutor, there were times when I felt I was living a lie. When I left my job as an appellate prosecutor at the Wyoming attorney general's office to work at the parole board, several of my friends and my immediate family were shocked—including the attorney general himself. At that time, in 2007, the attorney general had been a federal prosecutor in Wyoming before leaving that post to serve as attorney general for Governor Dave Freudenthal, who also had been the United States attorney for Wyoming.[15] When my boss learned that I was leaving to take the deputy director position at the parole board, he commented that he understood my leaving for employment elsewhere, but he could not understand why I would take at job at the parole board of all places.

While my prosecutorial duties were generally confined to appellate prosecution in the Wyoming Supreme Court, I also took on occasional special prosecutions around the state when the need arose. Most Wyoming counties were equipped with local prosecutors to handle their trial-level prosecutions, but issues sometimes arose in which local prosecutors were unable to participate in criminal matters arising in their jurisdiction. In some cases and in the smaller counties, an illness or a complicated pregnancy might sideline a prosecutor for months. In other cases, a local county official might have committed a crime; in that case, it became a conflict of interest for the duly elected county prosecutor or any of their subordinates to handle the case. I had been assigned to prosecute in both types of situations, but it was a case in which I was prosecuting a county official in place of the regular prosecutor where I found myself at odds with the attorney general.

In that particular case, a county official had embezzled nearly $20,000. However, the embezzlement had not been discovered until he turned himself in. To further mitigate his behavior, the individual had repaid the money before he reported his malfeasance. Had he not revealed his transgressions, I imagine that his conduct might not have eventually been discovered.

Nonetheless, I was sympathetic toward this man, appreciating the fact that he had repaid the money before anyone uncovered his misuse of county dollars. The man had hired an attorney I knew, and before filing any charges, we had reached a plea bargain in which the man would plead guilty to several misdemeanors involving misappropriation of public funds, pay a fine, but not be required to serve any jail time. I had also taken the precaution of having my direct supervisor approve the plea agreement, and I expected the case would be resolved in a fairly routine fashion.

The only problem with the plea agreement was that the attorney general did not approve. I still recall his objection: He wanted "his pound of flesh," as he put it. At that point in my life, I don't know if I had ever heard the phrase *pound of flesh*, but I later came to ponder that expression many times. For the attorney general, his "pound of flesh" was either a felony conviction or jail time for the county official; he made it clear that my initial plea offer was too soft. I had no choice but to produce the pound of flesh. While I was able to spare the guilty party the crippling consequences of a felony conviction, he still had to serve two months in the county jail, right next to the county courthouse where he had formerly worked. I knew at that point that my days of prosecuting were numbered. I had no stomach to go through my career constantly seeking a pound of flesh.

CONVICTION PSYCHOLOGY

The power to exact a pound of flesh—a power possessed by US prosecutors—is unparalleled in the criminal justice system, and this power can have disastrous consequences when abused. All too often this power is used to put more and more people in prison, adding to the mass incarceration crisis in America. Former public defender and law professor Angela Davis has described the enormity of the power prosecutors possess: "The power imbalance blew my mind, frankly: I couldn't figure out for the life of me how prosecutors had so much power with so little accountability." Davis observed that prosecutors "were allowed to do things, some unconstitutional, some perfectly legal but with horrific results that most human beings would think were unfair."[16]

Prosecutors, like everyone else, are susceptible to tunnel vision. It's a common human reaction when confronted with information that may be contradictory to one's established beliefs. Keith A. Findley, a law professor at the University of Wisconsin and founder of the Wisconsin Innocence Project, has written (with Michael S. Scott) about the effect of tunnel vision on prosecutors: "Tunnel vision is a natural human tendency that has particularly pernicious effects in the criminal justice system."[17] One example of tunnel vision is confirmation bias. In the field of psychology, confirmation bias is defined as the tendency to seek or interpret evidence in ways that support a person's preexisting beliefs, expectations, and theories.[18]

In her book *Charged*, Emily Bazelon quotes Findley to demonstrate how confirmation bias can affect the way prosecutors deal with evidence that undermines their theory of a criminal prosecution: "You have to believe in your case to prosecute it, and then cognitive dissonance sets in if someone confronts you with evidence that you were wrong. I saw it happen over and over again. Prosecutors say to themselves, 'I'm a good person. I wouldn't prosecute someone innocent. Therefore, this person must be guilty.' You sweep away the reasons for doubt."[19]

Other legal scholars have identified concerning issues in the current system of US prosecution. Constitutional law professor George T. Felkenes used the term *conviction psychology* to describe the mental state of many prosecutors who "think of the defendant as guilty, and reason that an innocent person would not be introduced into the system." According to Felkenes, the result of this conviction psychology is "a deterioration of the ideal purpose of the prosecutor—to seek justice."[20]

Although Felkenes published his findings in 1975, several other facets of his research resonated with me and my much later experiences as a young prosecutor. Felkenes surveyed more than 100 prosecutors from four counties in California and Alabama.[21] The responses revealed that prosecutors are generally young attorneys with little or no specialized training other than law school, and employment in a district attorney's office provided a substantial increase in pay: The average previous salary more than doubled when employed in the district attorney's office.[22]

I experienced a similar increase in my standard of living when I left my job as a public defender to accept employment in a prosecutor's office; my annual income also nearly doubled. While I may not have been cut out to be a prosecutor, the pay increase certainly made the job more palatable. There is also a certain amount of prestige that goes along with the job. My parents were very pleased when I became a prosecutor.

However, the most noticeable change to me was the lopsided difference between the resources a prosecutor has at their disposal and the scarcity of similar tools available to a public defender. I was a public defender in a relatively small Wyoming town from 1999 to 2001. At that time, the Wyoming Public Defender's Office had perhaps four full-time investigators to cover the entire state. Diane Lozano, until mid-2024 the director of the Wyoming Public Defender's Office, reported that in 2022 the office had five full-time investigators plus two contract investigators and two part-time investigators to serve the entire state.[23]

By comparison, when I started prosecuting, the investigatory power I had access to was at times overwhelming. The local police, state police, county sheriff, highway patrol, Game and Fish, federal agencies such as the Drug Enforcement Administration (DEA) and the Federal Bureau of Investigation (FBI) would contact our office to discuss and possibly seek prosecution of various crimes. Investigators from the State Engineer's Office would report to the prosecutor's office where I worked if someone tampered with the headgates on an irrigation ditch. It seemed we had an inexhaustible supply of law enforcement agents for the state, all at our disposal.

CHASING CONVICTIONS

From his research on conviction psychology, Felkenes also identified a tendency for prosecutors to reduce their measurement of achievement to conviction rates rather than the pursuit of justice.[24] Using conviction rates as a measure of success has produced shocking incentives in various jurisdictions around the US. One of the more infamous examples emerged from Illinois in the 1970s and 1980s, when prosecutors participated in a contest to determine who could successfully handle cases involving the heaviest criminal defendants in hopes of becoming the first to convict 4,000 "pounds of flesh."[25]

Law professors Ronald F. Wright and Kay L. Levine conducted interviews and surveyed more than 200 state prosecutors in the Southeast and Southwest in an attempt to learn more about the culture of emphasizing conviction rates over justice. Many of these prosecutors, particularly those with only a few years' experience, described themselves as virtual superheroes, battling the forces of evil rather than seeking justice. Some of the more experienced prosecutors in the study recalled their mind-set as young prosecutors as that of a "hardass," adding that rookie prosecutors too often go "for the jugular" or act like a "bully." One prosecutor went so far as to admit "I want to give the death penalty when someone steals a bag of potato chips!" Fortunately, Wright and Levine's study did conclude that after time, a prosecutor's outlook begins to change. Seeking justice does require "a variety of criminal justice responses, not just full conviction and punishment."[26]

Despite the fact that some prosecutors seem to grow out of the tunnel-vision mode of prioritizing convictions over justice, many defense attorneys and scholars continue to point to the lack of restraints or disciplinary mechanisms in place to serve as a check on the unfettered discretion prosecutors enjoy. During her years as a public defender, Angela Davis "noticed that prosecutors held almost all of the cards, and they seemed to deal them as they saw fit. Although some saw themselves as ministers of justice and measured their decisions carefully, very few were humbled by the power they had."[27] Davis further noted that the most troubling feature of a prosecutor's decision-making is that "these important, sometimes life-and-death decisions . . . are totally discretionary and virtually unreviewable. Prosecutors make the most important of these discretionary decisions behind closed doors and answer only to other prosecutors."[28]

Another complicating factor in the pursuit of justice is the lack of a clear description of what that should entail. The *Model Rules of Professional Conduct* provide that a prosecutor has a special duty to seek justice, but that vague admonishment fails to cover a wide range of situations where a prosecutor's discretion can undermine the fairness of a criminal judicial proceeding, such as plea bargaining.[29] For example, the Maricopa County attorney's office in Arizona had a policy of making plea agreement offers with the written warning that if the accused person requested a preliminary hearing, rejected a plea offer, or requested a jury trial, any subsequent plea offers "will be substantially harsher."[30] While this practice is not uncommon, it is unfortunate to see that written retaliation is used in advance of any chance for the defense to so much as investigate the case.

PROSECUTORIAL MISCONDUCT AND WRONGFUL CONVICTIONS

In recent years, a new level of attention has been focused on addressing some of the weaknesses in the criminal justice system that stem from prosecutorial misconduct. However, even with recommendations proposed to reform the system, the instances of prosecutorial misconduct will only be reduced if ethical legal professionals are committed to preserving our system of justice for all. Prosecutors currently have little incentive to seek to remedy injustice by bringing their concerns to the surface.

In the 2006 case *Garcetti v. Ceballos*, the United States Supreme Court ruled against a prosecutor who was retaliated against for exposing what he saw as a violation of a defendant's due process.[31] Richard Ceballos was a prosecutor in the Los Angeles County District Attorney's Office who submitted a memorandum to his supervisor explaining his concerns that a search warrant obtained by the police had serious flaws. The memo recommended dismissal of the case; however, the office continued with the prosecution. Against his supervisor's wishes, Ceballos provided a copy of the memo to defense counsel and was later called as a defense witness. Ceballos was subsequently passed over for promotion and sanctioned in other ways, causing him to file a Section 1983 claim arguing that his First Amendment rights had been violated.[32]

The Supreme Court ruled against Ceballos and held that the First Amendment did not apply to public servants during their public duties. The Supreme Court relaxed this rule in the 2014 case of *Lane v. Franks*, where the Court held that the First Amendment does protect public employees who provide truthful sworn testimony, under subpoena, in a hearing that is outside ordinary job duties, even if the testimony addresses information learned at work.[33] Justice Sonia Sotomayor concluded: "It would be antithetical to our jurisprudence to conclude that the very kind of speech necessary to prosecute corruption by public officials—speech by public employees regarding information learned through their employment—may never form the basis for a First Amendment retaliation claim. Such a rule would place public employees who witness corruption in an impossible position, torn between the obligation to testify truthfully and the desire to avoid retaliation and keep their jobs."[34]

Prosecutorial misconduct can be uncovered in ways other than disclosures from conscientious, self-reporting prosecutors. In discussing how to address prosecutorial misconduct, Thomas Sullivan and Maurice Possley argue that it is the job of other attorneys and courtroom officials who witness prosecutorial misconduct to report it.[35]

When prosecutorial misconduct has contributed to or caused a wrongful conviction, the prosecutors involved are rarely disciplined.[36] Prosecutors have immunity from civil lawsuits, which limits their personal liability for engaging in corrupt behavior.[37] Appellate courts also employ strict standards for review and rarely reverse a conviction based on prosecutorial misconduct, typically finding that the misconduct amounted to harmless error. The Supreme Court announced the harmless error standard in the 1967 case *Chapman v. California*, deciding that some constitutional errors are not significant or harmful and therefore do not require an automatic reversal of the conviction.[38]

A study of prosecutorial misconduct was conducted in 2003 by the Center for Public Integrity, a nonpartisan organization that engages in public policy research. A team of researchers and writers reviewed 11,452 cases over a three-year period that involved charges of prosecutorial misconduct heard by appellate courts. In the majority of cases, the alleged misconduct was found to be harmless error or was unaddressed by the appellate courts. However, the study revealed that judges found prosecutorial misconduct in over 2,000 cases in which charges were dismissed, convictions reversed, or sentences reduced. In hundreds of other cases, the judges indicated that the prosecutors' conduct was inappropriate, but the courts affirmed the convictions under the harmless error doctrine. The courts disciplined prosecutors in only 44 of these cases.[39]

Sullivan and Possley point out that when appellate courts determine that harmless error has occurred and a reversal of conviction is not warranted, they "issue their opinions without considering whether the conduct is sufficiently serious to require reference to disciplinary authorities." When appellate courts decline to make this referral, Sullivan and Possley argue that the justices fail to fulfill their judicial functions. Sullivan and Possley also recommend restricting the harmless error rule. They suggest that if errors occur during a trial because of misconduct on the part of prosecutors and law enforcement, new trials should be ordered unless the court is convinced beyond a reasonable doubt that the error was due to unintentional conduct and did not affect the defendant's right to a fair trial. Their recommendation also calls for the court to refer such prosecutorial misconduct to disciplinary authorities, with the offending prosecutor's name included.[40]

In many instances of prosecutorial misconduct, appellate courts describe the offensive behavior without naming the prosecutor involved. I had the opportunity to defend an instance of prosecutorial "dereliction of duty" by the same prosecutor who wrote the inflammatory and threatening letter to the parole board I referenced earlier in this chapter. That prosecutor had taken the time to insult the Wyoming Supreme Court in his arguments to his local trial court in a case involving a dispute over a forfeited bail, essentially calling the state high court clueless. In the subsequent legal opinion, the Wyoming Supreme Court devoted an entire paragraph to chastise him:

> Finally, we note that the State chose to interpret our remand as a mandate for the State and the district court to merely "go through the motions and say the words." *We view such an attitude as a dereliction of duty that is repugnant both to the courts and to the citizens of this State, and Natrona County in particular.* In addition, it was the State's contention that our former opinion was, "more than anything, this is yet another opinion of the Wyoming Supreme Court that seems to indicate they have no concept of how a busy docket runs. None. This is a classic example." *The prosecutor's fit of pique served no role in these proceedings other than to disparage this very important process and to demonstrate his unbridled arrogance. This sort of mindless posturing serves no useful purpose* [emphasis added].[41]

A rebuke from the Wyoming Supreme Court would be devastating to most attorneys, although from what I could gather, it seemed to have little effect on this particular district attorney—in part because his name did not appear anywhere in the opinion.

My name, however, *did* appear in the published appellate opinion on behalf of the Attorney General's Office. Once the opinion was issued, several attorney friends called to ask who the unnamed prosecutor was. The district attorney's identity was not a surprise to my friends. But outside of the attorneys who actively read Wyoming Supreme Court opinions, no one else in the non-legal world, including the media, had any idea of the insult that had taken place.

RECOMMENDATION FOR PROSECUTORIAL REFORM AND ABOLISHING ABSOLUTE IMMUNITY

In addition to narrowing the harmless error rule, Sullivan and Possley argue that appellate courts should include the names of offending prosecutors in their opinions, along with a description of the offending conduct.[42] The United States Supreme Court recommended this as an acceptable sanction when a court of appeals set aside a conviction for prosecutorial misconduct in *United States v. Hastings*, by "publicly chast[ising] the prosecutor by identifying him in its opinion."[43] Justice D. Brooks Smith of the Third Circuit also advocates for this approach: "I believe that the overwhelming majority of prosecutors would recoil at the notion of her or his name being publicly linked to what is, quite plainly, legal wrong-doing. Judicial opprobrium against a lawyer on ethical grounds is not the stuff of which successful careers are normally built—at least not in the prosecutorial realm."[44] Sullivan and Possley also recommend that appellate courts use their contempt powers to craft corrective remedies from an array of available sanctions, based on the severity of the misconduct involved.[45]

Another protection prosecutors enjoy that fails to discourage misconduct is absolute immunity from civil damages in lawsuits based on conduct undertaken as a function of prosecutorial duties, as recognized by the Supreme Court in the 1976 case *Imbler v. Pachtman*.[46] For example, in 2011, in a lawsuit against notorious New Orleans prosecutor Harry Connick Sr., the Supreme Court overturned a $14 million verdict for the victim based on prosecutorial immunity. In that case, Connick withheld a crucial blood sample test that showed the wrongfully accused victim had a different blood type than the perpetrator.[47] Justice Clarence Thomas suggested that the proper way to discipline prosecutorial misconduct is through "professional discipline, including sanctions, suspension, and disbarment."[48] However, as alluded to earlier, prosecutors are rarely referred to the state bar for disciplinary action. Both the harmless error rule and the absolute immunity doctrine are based on the application of federal law, not constitutional principles. Therefore, they need not be followed in civil actions brought under state law.[49]

Margaret Z. Johns, a law professor at the University of California at Davis, has made a recommendation for qualified immunity for prosecutors.[50] Under the current legal scheme, if prosecutors are sued under 42 U.S.C.

§1983, they enjoy either absolute or qualified immunity depending on the action they were engaged in at the time of the alleged misconduct.[51] When serving as advocates, prosecutors enjoy absolute immunity even when they have acted maliciously and intentionally.[52] When engaged in administrative duties or investigation work, prosecutors receive qualified immunity, which shields them from liability unless they violated a clearly established law a reasonable prosecutor would have been aware of.[53] Johns explains that under the current framework, distinguishing whether prosecutorial conduct merits absolute immunity or qualified immunity is a complex process that has generated multiple conflicting decisions. She argues that the solution is simple: Apply qualified immunity in all cases, regardless of whether the prosecutor was engaged in advocacy or investigative work, and then determine whether the prosecutor violated a clearly established law of which a reasonable prosecutor should have been aware.[54]

Johns is not alone in her support of abolishing absolute immunity for prosecutors. Frederic Block, a federal district judge for the Eastern District of New York, wrote in 2018 that "the cloak of absolute immunity should be judicially or legislatively lifted. Police officers do not have it and they are held accountable in courts of law for their egregious behavior. We wisely do not give our law enforcement officers, or even the President, carte blanche to do as they please; bad prosecutors should be similarly held accountable."[55] Law professors Kate Levine and Joanna Schwartz also call for prosecutorial accountability by abolishing absolute immunity, noting that for those harmed by prosecutorial misconduct, "there is almost no way . . . to seek redress."[56]

Chief Justice John Roberts has pushed back against the idea of removing the cloak of absolute immunity from prosecutors, claiming it would have a "chilling effect" on them.[57] It would be interesting to ask Roberts if he believes law enforcement officers experience the same chilling effect from operating with only qualified immunity.

As a former prosecutor, I support all of the aforementioned recommendations, including the abolition of absolute immunity for prosecutors. Model Rule 3.8 of the Professional Rules of Conduct contains mandates for prosecutors to disclose exculpatory evidence discovered both during the trial phase and post-conviction, but prosecutors are rarely disciplined for violations of Rule 3.8, in Wyoming or elsewhere.[58] When I took my first job as a prosecutor, I was not aware that I suddenly had absolute immunity after leaving my public defender job. What I did know was that I had just doubled my pay, and the resources to do my job had expanded exponentially. Immunity was the last thing on my mind, and I find the claim that the absence of absolute immunity would have a chilling effect on prosecutors laughable. In a concurring opinion in the 2022 case *Wearry v. Foster*, Judge James C. Ho, a Trump appointee, questioned the existence of prosecutorial immunity because it is not supported by the text of 42 U.S.C. §1983, writing that "worthy civil rights claims are never brought to trial . . . because an unholy trinity of legal doctrines—qualified immunity, absolute prosecutorial immunity, and *Monell v. Department of Soc. Svcs* [municipal liability principles]—frequently conspire to turn winnable cases into losing ones."[59] Although this is unlikely to happen anytime soon, Judge Ho pointed out that Congress can abolish absolute immunity for prosecutors should it choose to do so.[60]

I also fail to understand why prosecutors should be afforded protection from legal liability beyond that which other members of law enforcement receive. Certainly, prosecutors face tough decisions that require a delicate application of discretion, such as whether to file or dismiss charges. Those decisions are no more serious or life altering, though, than a police officer's decision to arrest or not arrest or whether to use deadly force. Beyond that, the system is adversarial for prosecutors. The same cannot be said for the judge and jury members, who must maintain impartiality and are also granted absolute immunity. Having been a prosecutor, I know that the pressure to rubber stamp law enforcement's activities is real. For all of these reasons, absolute immunity for prosecutors is untenable in light of the abuse a few bad prosecutors have perpetrated on public confidence in the criminal justice system.

A SECOND LOOK FROM PROSECUTORS

Without doubt, many instances of prosecutorial misconduct associated with wrongful convictions have made headlines in US news media. However, I also believe prosecutors are similar to those in any other vocation. For the most part, they want to learn and grow in their chosen profession, and I also believe the vast majority of prosecutors are more interested in seeking justice than in increasing their conviction rates. While there may be some "bad apples," the fact remains that prosecutors are not going anywhere, and their power within the criminal justice system can be harnessed and directed toward helping change the deficiencies in the system.

Working as a prosecutor is a highly stressful job, and when engaging in plea bargaining or actively prosecuting a case, pressure can come from a variety of sources. Law enforcement officials often expect to see their "pound of flesh," and in many cases, prosecutors also must consider input from emotionally charged victims. Some defense attorneys advocate for a deal on behalf of their client, and ultimately, the judge must approve the deal. And the electorate—the public—is always watching. There are many moving parts at work, and all of this machinery is operating under a strict speedy trial deadline. Our system often asks too much of prosecutors and judges, on the front end of a sentence, to be able to look into the future and determine which defendants will be capable of rehabilitation and which are truly unredeemable. It is difficult to second-guess prosecutors' and judges' decisions at the time of sentencing, but why not provide them with a second look at the sentence years down the road? That is the idea behind a new wave of legislation in the criminal justice system called "second look laws."[61]

One rationale behind second look proposals is the recognition that the human capacity for change is real and cannot be accurately measured at sentencing. US criminal justice needs a mechanism for these discretionary decision-makers to take a second look at individual cases that are meritorious and deserve reconsideration, and many jurisdictions are open to the idea. According to a report released by the Sentencing Project in May 2024, second look legislation for both juvenile and adult offenders had been passed in twelve states, the Council of the District of Columbia, and the federal government, along with litigation challenging extreme sentences in at least fifteen states—including Wyoming.[62]

Skyrocketing incarceration rates are one reason for taking a second look at long prison sentences. In the 1960s, US crime rates ballooned, but between 1991 and 2019 crime rates fell by around half—a trend felt around the world. The US was unique in exponentially increasing its prison population in response to this crime wave: The number of inmates in prison went from under 200,000 in 1972 to nearly 800,000 in 1991. The number continued to grow after 1991—when crime rates were falling—climbing to 1.6 million people in prison in 2009, with another 767,000 people held in jails.[63]

While rising crime rates did not cause the increase in US imprisonment rates, many factors did contribute to the spike. This growth was fostered by the "war on drugs" and a policy of seeking longer prison sentences for all crimes.[64] A detailed analysis of US sentencing patterns by legal scholar John Pfaff demonstrated that the sharp increase that began in the 1980s was driven primarily by prosecutors seeking prison terms for convicted persons and, to a lesser degree, by longer sentences and changes that reduced the availability of parole release and increased parole revocations.[65] The prison population declined after reaching its crest in 2009, dropping by 11 percent prior to the pandemic.[66] The number of prisoners in jails and prisons had declined every year since 2008, and the rate in 2018 was the lowest since 1996.[67] Those reductions, however, were modest. Most of the downsizing was of low-hanging fruit—meaning early release for mainly nonviolent drug offenders.[68] Half of the US prison population is serving time for a violent offense, and only a slight reduction—5 percent in imprisonment rates for violent offenders—occurred between 2009 and 2018, despite the significant drop in crime rates.[69] Most recently, the prison population has begun to grow again, increasing in both 2022 and 2023, with prison populations increasing in thirty-nine states.[70]

PUBLIC SUPPORT FOR A SECOND LOOK

In December 2018, President Trump signed the First Step Act (FSA), which overwhelmingly passed through Congress, clearing the Senate with an 87 to 12 vote.[71] The act created a mechanism for prisoners who had been sentenced for crack cocaine offenses to apply for re-sentencing, making changes created under the 2010 Fair Sentencing Act retroactive.[72] Unfortunately, the FSA has been mired in problems with implementation. Years after its passage, thousands of nonviolent offenders who are eligible for release under the First Step Act remain imprisoned due to "confusion and bureaucratic delays."[73]

Courtney Curtis, a former state legislator from Missouri, was sent to federal prison for wire fraud and should have qualified for a time credit toward his sentence under the FSA. However, Curtis's time credits were not granted, delaying what he believes would have been his correct release date if the act had been properly applied to him. "As one of the many inmates that benefit from the FSA," he wrote, "I've made strides to take classes, work and stay productive, but the BOP [Bureau of Prisons] and its systematic way of operating inefficiently have stymied my ability to take the most amount of classes in an orderly fashion as prescribed in the FSA or to release me as soon as I should have been . . . I can only wonder if this is by design, and what the total extent of impacted inmates is."[74]

Prior to retaking the White House, Donald Trump also seemed to have given up hope on his showcase piece of criminal justice reform legislation and renounced the spirit behind the First Step Act. At a rally in August 2022, Trump called on Congress to institute the death penalty for drug dealers, despite obvious constitutional and humanitarian problems with the proposal, not to mention that Trump had "pardoned several people convicted of selling drugs before he left office" at the end of his first term.[75] At the same rally, Trump engaged in his normal fear-mongering, stating: "Under Democrat control the streets of our great cities are drenched in the blood of innocent victims."[76]

The initial failure of the First Step Act to deliver as promised should not overshadow the strong bipartisan support it generated in Congress. Second look legislation aimed at potentially releasing long-term offenders with a promising record of demonstrated effort at rehabilitation can help alleviate mass incarceration. The American Law Institute (ALI), a nonpartisan group of legal scholars who seek to advance and modernize US laws, has observed that in the face of evolving social norms, "it is unsound to freeze criminal punishments of extraordinary duration into the knowledge base of the past."[77]

The ALI is also responsible for authoring the Model Penal Code, which currently recommends that legislatures authorize judicial review of sentences after fifteen years of imprisonment for adults and ten years for juveniles.[78] Edward E. Rhine, Kevin R. Reitz, and the late Joan Petersilia—all experts in the field of parole—wrote a seminal document on the future of parole and concluded "we would have no argument with a shorter period such as ten years" for a re-sentencing review.[79]

While ample and convincing evidence indicates that the age-crime curve is a real phenomenon within the criminal justice system, many "tough on crime" advocates question second look proposals based on the outlier cases in which individuals who have committed murder or other serious violent crimes recidivate in a violent manner. Another common argument leveled against second chance proposals is that they would increase the crime rate and reopen old wounds. A popular sentiment, in some cases rooted in religion, holds that a life sentence is exactly what a person deserves for committing murder, the "pound of flesh" or an "eye for an eye." However, the circumstances of every violent crime and murder are unique. My experiences in parole hearings convinced me that the majority of people who kill another human are not heartless and vicious, and I would stop short of calling them murderers. They are human beings who have made mistakes with devastating consequences, and most of them want and work for a second chance.

Despite the fear-mongering against second look and chance proposals, public support for these laws does exist. In February 2020, Data for Progress, a progressive think tank, surveyed 2,400 likely voters across the nation to gauge their opinions on second chance laws. The poll found that overall, 69 percent of voters supported second look legislation and the support was bipartisan, cutting across geographic and ideological lines. Eighty-one percent of Democrats and 64 percent of Republicans supported second chance laws, and 67 percent of all voters supported the idea of "elected prosecutors reexamining past sentences to provide a second chance to people who have been in prison for ten years or longer and who can be safely returned to the community."[80]

REMEMBERING LARRY DEGRAW

While drafting this book, I shared this chapter with one of my classes, which is how I learned about the death of Larry DeGraw. I asked the students to read and reflect on the draft by discussing absolute immunity for prosecutors and whether they felt prosecutors deserved more legal protection than law enforcement officers. I pointed out that I was still interviewing DeGraw and asked them for questions they would ask if they had the chance. Within a few hours of posting the assignment, one of my students who works in the court system notified me that DeGraw had just died following a heart attack. The moment was sadly surreal, and I instantly felt guilt and regret for not following up sooner. Before his death, DeGraw had been serving as the coroner in Fremont County, Wyoming.[81] My student emailed: "It was a huge shock here in Fremont County. We had a great conversation about civil service and reservation jurisdiction about three days prior to his passing. He was an amazing man, and always had an open mind about things. I also know that he would have loved being part of this with the class. He always pushed me to do the best I could do and helped me through some really rough patches."[82]

I have a feeling that Larry DeGraw helped many people through rough patches, including James Koester. It might seem surprising that the detective who investigated his crime would also become Koester's most vocal supporter for a commutation, despite the rabid objections from the prosecutor and lack of support from the judge. However, DeGraw was clearly a man who lived for more than a pound of flesh. He recognized the good in people, and he refused to condemn for life the man who emptied his trash. DeGraw and I agreed that Koester deserved many years in prison but that he also deserved a second chance at some point. There are many more inmates in the United States like James Koester, who are serving life but arguably deserve a second look and a second chance.

6

Roads to Forgiveness

There are different ways of classifying homicides. By definition, a homicide is the act of one human being killing another. However, not all homicides are murder. Some homicides are justifiable or excusable, such as killing in self-defense or a killing committed by a person suffering from a serious mental illness. Homicides that do qualify as murder are graded, typically into first- and second-degree murder. First-degree murder requires some level of premeditation, and second-degree murder requires hatred and malice, but premeditation is not necessary. Then there are negligent killings, commonly classified as manslaughter, involuntary or voluntary.

Informal typologies or classifications of killers also exist in the criminal justice world. For instance, a parent who is responsible for a child's death is called a "baby killer."[1] A person who kills a member of law enforcement is often called a "cop killer."[2] Many consider the act of killing a police officer in the line of duty one of the most unforgivable types of murder. That is what makes the story of Mark Farnham and Steve Watt unique in the US criminal justice system.[3]

https://doi.org/10.5876/9781646428557.c006

FORGIVING A COP KILLER

While Mark Farnham did not actually kill a cop, he came as close as you can to doing so without succeeding. In 1982, Farnham robbed a bank in Craig, Colorado, and shot a Wyoming highway patrolman five times, leaving the officer for dead. Farnham's story has been told many times, in different media accounts. However, one cannot tell the story without also telling about his victim, Stephen "Steve" Watt, whom Farnham shot and nearly killed. Watt would not only later forgive Farnham, but the two men became good friends.

Before he went to prison, Farnham had a normal childhood and background. After graduating from high school, Farnham joined the United States Army and worked as a military policeman assigned to guard nuclear missiles. Following his discharge from the army, Farnham enrolled at the University of Minnesota, where he was introduced to cocaine.[4] It was the early 1980s, and cocaine was a popular drug that soon gained control of Farnham. He developed a $250-a-day habit, which led him to the Wyoming oilfields looking for work to pay off his ever-increasing debt. When the oilfields did not provide a solution to his money problems, Farnham decided to rob a bank.[5] He bought a $50 pistol at a pawn shop and headed south to Colorado to find a bank. On March 18, 1982, Farnham walked into a bank in the remote Colorado town of Craig with a pistol and $2 in his pockets and left with $10,000 cash in a duffel bag. He placed the bag of cash on his Plymouth Champ and headed north back to Wyoming.

That same day, Steve Watt found himself at work in the morning despite being scheduled for the evening shift because he had switched shifts with another trooper. It had snowed the previous evening, and the roads were icy. Watt figured he would spend the day writing accident reports, which led him to shun wearing his bulletproof vest. He was sitting in a restaurant in Rock Springs, Wyoming, when the call came that a suspected bank robber driving a red sports car was heading north into Wyoming on Highway 43. Despite not wearing his bulletproof vest, Watt headed south on Highway 43, looking for the red sports car. Watt passed Farnham in his Plymouth Champ, which was painted brown and did not match the description of the suspect's vehicle. Watt decided he would pull the vehicle over anyway to ask the driver if they had seen the red sports car.

The next few seconds would radically alter the trajectory of both men's lives. Watt recalls that Farnham slammed on his brakes and was out of his car, firing shots before Watt had a chance to radio the stop in to his dispatcher. The first two bullets came through the windshield, with one bullet hitting Watt in the left eye and the other ricocheting off the windshield. Watt threw himself over the front seat to avoid the line of fire and continued with his radio call, reporting that he had been shot. When he finished the radio transmission, Farnham fired four more shots into Watt's lower back from point-blank range before returning to his own car. Despite having been shot five times, Watt managed to crawl out of his patrol car and empty his .357 Magnum, firing six shots at Farnham and managing to hit him in the shoulder.

Alone on the highway and bleeding profusely, Watt said a prayer. Prior to his encounter with Farnham, Watt had not been a religious man, but in that moment he was fighting for his life. He prayed, "God, I don't know if I'm going to live, but if I die, take care of my wife, Marian. Please help me." A truck driver who happened upon the wounded Watt called an ambulance. On the way to the hospital, Watt could hear the emergency technicians calling out his vital signs and thought to himself: A guy whose vital signs are broadcast always seems to lose his life. Watt remembers being in the emergency room. He was awake when they inserted a catheter and when they broke his nose to insert a stomach pump. Watt spent eight hours in surgery; his left eye and a third of his liver had been removed, and they took bullets out his intestines that would require hernia surgeries every year for the rest of his life. As a cautionary measure, the doctors left a bullet in Watt's spine, fearful of causing more damage if they tried to remove it. The first bullet pierced Watt's left eye and stopped just short of reaching his brain. The second bullet had dug through Watt's stomach, intestines, and liver. The third bullet, the one that was left in Watt's body, nearly severed his spine. The fourth and fifth bullets ripped through his abdomen.

Farnham, meanwhile, had been captured in the desert, three miles from where he left Watt for dead. His wounded shoulder needed medical attention, and Farnham was brought to the same hospital where Watt had been transported. The two men were placed less than ten feet apart. Farnham could hear the doctor speaking and operating as Watt screamed in pain.

He was originally charged with attempted first-degree murder but accepted a plea agreement to a reduced charge of attempted second-degree murder. The robbery and shooting were his first criminal offenses. On the advice of his attorney, Farnham turned down a twenty- to twenty-five-year sentence in favor of a life sentence, relying on the same advice that would backfire and confine fellow lifers Russell Harrison and James Koester. Farnham's attorney had advised him that the parole board and the governor regularly granted commutations on life sentences, to the point that the average time served was nine years. If he took the twenty- to twenty-five-year sentence, Farnham would have to wait at least twelve years to become parole-eligible. Farnham did receive two commutations of his sentence: one by Governor Mike Sullivan in 1992, reducing his sentence from life to seventy to eighty-five years, and another a decade later, when Governor Jim Geringer further commuted Farnham's sentence to sixty-five to seventy-five years.[6] However, that second commutation was the last one Farnham received for thirty years, as the nationwide dissipation of commutations had finally reached Wyoming.[7]

Early in his prison sentence, Farnham also ran into trouble as an inmate that further complicated his quest to eventually gain release from prison. Farnham attempted to escape by bending his cell bars two inches outward. He also hit another inmate with a stool and brandished a hammer at still another inmate during prison altercations.[8] Unfortunately for Farnham, a Wyoming law renders an inmate ineligible for parole if they have attempted an escape or assaulted another inmate with a deadly weapon.[9] His failed escape attempt and assaultive behavior foreclosed his opportunity for parole, leaving a commutation to time served the only option for Farnham to be released without having to complete his entire sentence in prison.

At the beginning of his incarceration, Farnham made some bad decisions as he navigated life on the inside, but he began directing his energy and efforts to positive outlets. In 1993, after serving eleven years in prison, Farnham was promoted through the Wyoming Department of Corrections (WDOC) classification system, moving from maximum-security housing to a minimum-security facility in Riverton, the Wyoming Honor Farm.[10] While at the Honor Farm, Farnham was a model inmate and was able to take part in a variety of programs that demonstrated the value he could offer to society. To his knowledge, Farnham was the first inmate in Wyoming history to earn a bachelor's degree while incarcerated. At the farm, Farnham worked jobs such as reading books into cassette tapes for the blind. He volunteered at local churches—installing rain gutters, hanging sheet rock, painting, and mowing grass—all while being supervised only by church officials. Farnham volunteered at the local rodeo, working ten-hour shifts in the roping chutes without uniformed supervision. At other times, Farnham left the prison with other inmates to stack bales of alfalfa for local ranchers, with only the rancher supervising.[11] If Farnham had wanted to escape during his time at the farm, it would have been easy for him to do so. In 1997, a failed but deadly escape attempt during which a correctional officer was murdered by inmates rocked the WDOC; as a result, the classification system was changed.[12] Inmates with lengthy sentences, such as Farnham, were regressed back to maximum security, even though most had done nothing wrong.

Steve Watt was disgusted by the sentence Farnham had received, and he seethed at the thought of Farnham possibly gaining parole after serving only a decade in prison.[13] After waking up in the hospital and being informed his left eye was gone, Watt began to hate Farnham. The hatred became all-consuming. He described it as being like a "cancer."[14] Each morning he would look at himself in the mirror and see an empty eye socket, a constant reminder of his brush with death. Watt suffered from nightmares, depression, and anxiety, yet he felt compelled to return to work. However, he was afraid of the public and fearful of making traffic stops, and his hatred continued to smolder within him. Watt began to drink heavily, hiding his drinking from his wife. One night while drunk, he put his service revolver in his mouth and contemplated ending it all, ending the pain, but he thought of his wife, Marian, and put the gun down. His struggle did not end there. Soon after considering suicide, Watt nearly shot an unarmed motorist who jumped out of his car during a routine traffic stop, just as Mark Farnham had done. This driver was not holding a gun, just a wallet. After recognizing that the man was not a threat, Watt yelled at him to get back into his car and slow down. That was Steve Watt's last night as a Wyoming highway patrolman. He was done.[15]

Watt's wife, Marian, was also a police officer and had been a confirmed atheist prior to her husband's tragic run-in with Mark Farnham. Marian began to wonder how her husband had survived the attack. Although he was shot in the eye, no bone fragments penetrated his brain. One of the bullets passed through his liver and missed a major artery by a quarter of an inch. The bullet that lodged in his spine stopped just 1/16th of an inch from his spinal cord. Watt should have been dead or paralyzed, and Marian's need for answers led her to the police chaplain. The chaplain introduced Marian to Christianity, and she was later baptized. As Marian's faith grew,

Watt's anger and bitterness toward Farnham continued to fester. Marian could see the pain and misery her husband was enduring and offered to take Steve to the chaplain's home. Watt agreed to the visit, and at one point the chaplain asked Steve, "Have you forgiven the man who shot you?" Watt initially answered that yes, he had forgiven Mark Farnham. Sensing Watt's struggle with truly forgiving Farnham, the chaplain suggested he write him a letter.[16]

In 1986, Watt wrote a letter of forgiveness to Farnham.[17] After doing so, Watt felt his life suddenly improve, as if a massive burden had been lifted from his shoulders. He picked up the Bible and began reading scripture and attending church. Soon after he sent his letter to Farnham, Watt received an eighteen-page letter in response.[18] Later that same year, Watt attended church at the prison, where he was able to meet Farnham face to face. They embraced and told each other how relieved they were that neither man had killed the other that day when they both emptied their pistols while shooting at each other. "I found out that day that he wasn't the monster who shot me," Watt said. "He was just a man."[19] Since that time, Farnham and Watt have become friends, and Watt has spent considerable time and effort trying to secure his forgiven friend's release. In 2002, Watt launched an unsuccessful bid for governor. As one of his campaign promises, Watt vowed to pardon his friend Mark Farnham. Watt's run for office was unsuccessful; he finished fourth out of five candidates, with 6 percent of the vote.[20]

In 2003, after being locked up for twenty-one years, Farnham got into an altercation with an inmate that landed him in solitary confinement.[21] While locked in the "hole," Farnham faced a crossroads in his life. While he had done some positive work as an inmate, he knew that things were not progressing the way he wanted and that he needed help to change his life. Farnham got down on his knees and prayed, and at that moment, he began to let Christ into his life. From that day forward, Farnham says things were different. Farnham has continued to try to be a positive influence on his community behind prison walls, co-founding Tell It Like It Is, an inmate outreach group that shares their mistakes with Wyoming youth in an attempt to influence their decisions. He also works with other inmates and prison ministries to help with the healing process. "Forgiveness is a choice, it's a conscious choice. And it doesn't have to be someone that shot you five times," Farnham said.[22] In an interview he commented: "If Steve had made the choice to stay unforgiving toward me, he would have remained locked in a cage worse than the one I'm in. People don't need to be locked in prisons of anger."[23]

Although Watt's bid for governor was unsuccessful, he did serve two terms as a state representative in the Wyoming State Legislature.[24] For years, Watt spoke to an occasional church group or school, always eager to tell his story and spread the word of forgiveness.[25] Over the years, a number of major newspaper and television programs have chronicled the story of Watt and Farnham and the unique circumstances surrounding their friendship. Forgiveness, however, is a complicated virtue. In September 2022, I reached out to Watt to discuss this book and get an update on his activities over the last few years. During our initial phone call, Watt had to cut the conversation short to visit the hospital to have fluids drained from his stomach, a reminder of the deadly encounter with Farnham. Watt experiences PTSD every time he visits a hospital, another nightmarish reminder of the day he and Farnham were taken to the same hospital, with Watt clinging to life.[26]

During our conversations, Watt had a comment when I mentioned the word *closure*. "Closure . . ." he began, "what the hell is that? I'll never have closure. I'll always be crippled. I'll always miss my eye. I'll always have pain, and I don't want closure." Watt recalled asking God several times why he was chosen for this fate. "Why me?" he asked, and the response was, "Why not you? Who better than you?" Watt said he didn't like that answer, but "how many other people could live through this? Me—the one too stupid and hard-headed to die," he exclaimed with a hearty laugh.[27]

We discussed his career in politics. Watt professes a strong dislike for politics these days. He recalls what his father told him when Watt first entered politics, "My God, son, when are you going to do something honorable? You've been a cop and now a politician?"[28] Watt was joking about his father's comment, and his good-natured humor is something he has not lost. We also discussed the commutation process in Wyoming, and Watt recalled Governor Ed Herschler, who was in office during the early part of Watt's law enforcement career. Although Watt viewed Herschler as a "bleeding heart liberal," his outlook has changed, and he now appreciates the approach to commutations Governor Herschler pursued. "It used to be that Warden [Duane] Shillinger would call up Governor Herschler and tell him that the prison was overcrowded," he explained. "Herschler would tell Shillinger to give him a list of names, and once he got the list, Herschler would commute them all."[29] It is a shame that things have become so complicated since the days of those simple but productive commutation practices, and it was refreshing to hear Watt speak fondly of that time in the not-so-distant past.

"As a politician, you will never get elected saying that you give people second chances, at least not in Wyoming," Watt continued. "It's more like 'let's grind 'em down, lock 'em up, and throw away the key.' I don't believe in that approach, and when I was in the legislature, I made criminal justice reform arguments over and over, and I was the bleeding heart," he lamented. Watt described how he lost most of his friends in law enforcement and how many of his family members do not support his forgiveness of Farnham. He said: "I've basically given up. I no longer go to parole hearings. I've said everything I can possibly say. The governor doesn't care, the parole board doesn't care." Watt bristled at being called a victim, though: "The parole board and governor want to make sure I stay a victim, and I'm not a victim. Don't treat me like a victim. If you want to be treated as anything other than a victim, they will fight you." He recalled meeting with former Governor Dave Freudenthal about Farnham's commutation and describing how Freudenthal told him rudely "you may have forgiven Farnham but I'm not going to." Watt added, "At least the other governors were polite, although they didn't care either."[30]

To this day, Watt battles with his anger toward Farnham: "This is forever for me, and sometimes I think Mark needs to know about it, how I feel, to keep him humble." However, Watt is always able move past the anger for one reason: "It always comes back to being a Christian, and it's based on one thing: forgiveness. It boils down to the fact that Christ forgave us. So, while anger may come and go, I always come back to forgiveness. We all have someone we need to forgive, and they don't even need to know you've forgiven them. I forgave Mark for me. I'm a selfish son-of-a-bitch and I did it for me. And then I started living a life"[31] (figure 6.1).

After years of waiting for his miracle, Mark Farnham had perhaps the merriest Christmas of his life, as on December 20, 2022, Governor Mark Gordon granted him a commutation that made him parole-eligible only a few months later.[32] Since that time, Farnham has transitioned to Gillette, Wyoming, and is thriving in the community. He and Steve Watt have been reunited on several occasions and have attended church services together.

FIGURE 6.1. Mark Corbett and Steve Watt (left) in a diner. Author photo.

The process of writing this book has taken more than three years, and Farnham has been an invaluable resource for me. He has sent me commutation research he has collected, journal articles, newspaper clippings, and other letters and memos that have provided key pieces of information I would not have found otherwise. In addition to collecting research related to life sentences and related topics, Farnham has been authoring a series of religious essays "about Moses, David, and Paul, all who were murderers and wrote much of the Bible." Farnham hopes the essays will demonstrate that the practice of mass incarceration in the United States is contrary to "what both the Old Testament and New Testament teach." After he was released from prison, Farnham changed his last name to Corbett, to honor his biological father who was a police officer. Farnham's father began speaking to his son only at the urging of Steve Watt.[33]

IN SEARCH OF FORGIVENESS

The "baby" killer typology is a subset of homicide that has been identified throughout human history. The late Carl P. Malmquist, who was a nationally recognized forensic psychiatrist at the University of Minnesota, noted: "Infanticidal acts have occurred for as long as *Homo sapiens* has been a species, and probably among its predecessors. Thus, infanticide has been noted among gorillas and other species of ape."[34] There are reports of infanticides in Babylonian and Chaldean civilizations from 4000 to 2000 BC, and the practice of abandoning a child someplace outside was common in Sparta.[35]

The murder of a child has several definitions. Maternal filicide is a generalized definition that encompasses any murder of a child by the mother; infanticide is the murder of a child in the first year of life, and the term *neonaticide* refers to the murder of an infant within twenty-four hours of birth.[36] In March 1995 in Casper, Wyoming, Amy Doerr killed her eight-month-old son, Justice, thereby committing not only infanticide but first-degree murder under Wyoming law, for which she received a life sentence.[37]

Justice died from a multitude of injuries inflicted on him throughout his brief life. At age twenty-seven, Doerr pleaded guilty to first-degree murder for killing her son in an effort to avoid the death penalty, although the reporter who covered the sentencing hearing called the chance of execution "unlikely."[38] The same attorney who prosecuted James Koester, who was later disbarred and then pardoned, prosecuted Amy Doerr.[39] "This case outraged me," the prosecutor commented after sentencing. The prosecutor explained that although executions of women in the United States are "rare," it would have ultimately been up to a jury to decide if the murder warranted the death penalty. "This is one of the most brutal, awful cases I've seen," he said. "I think it's horrible. What this child had to put up with his whole life, that's just outrageous."[40]

Justice Doerr died on March 24, 1995, and Amy Doerr explained that she had beaten him because she had been upset with her ex-husband in the days immediately preceding her son's death. Doerr believed she struck her son once "in the diaper area" and another time "on the side of the head." Later, when she was bathing Justice, who had been vomiting, he stopped breathing and Doerr unsuccessfully attempted to revive him with CPR, which may have contributed to the rupture of the lining of Justice's stomach. Autopsy reports would reveal that Justice Doerr had suffered a brain injury and several fractures to his arms and ribcage, some of which were recent and healing; he also had numerous bruises about his face and body. The police detective testified that his investigation pointed to Amy Doerr as the only suspect. During his interrogation of Doerr, the detective testified that she admitted to shaking her son severely when he was two or three months old and that on one occasion, his head was struck against a door frame and in other instance his head was slammed into a table.[41]

At the sentencing hearing, Amy Doerr's drug addiction was discussed at length. When he was born, Justice Doerr tested positive for methamphetamine, cocaine, and marijuana. In pronouncing the sentence, the judge made a point of highlighting his frustration with the frequency of drug-related crime in his jurisdiction: "In my brief time on the bench I have been dumbfounded by the methamphetamine use, the cocaine use, in this community." In exchange for her plea of guilty to first-degree murder, along with three counts of aggravated assault and one count of felony child abuse, the prosecution agreed not to seek the death penalty and dismissed four additional counts of aggravated assault and one count of felony child abuse. Prior to sentencing, Doerr's attorneys claimed that she did not recall the specifics of the aggravated assault charges because she was using drugs at the time. The article from her sentencing hearing reported, "Doerr shook her head No but still pleaded guilty to the premeditated murder of Justice." The article also noted that Doerr was the mother of two "little girls."[42]

Recounting the facts of Amy Doerr's case is not easy, and one can understand the outrage and frustration expressed by both the prosecutor and the judge. However, maternal filicide is a crime that predates human history, and Doerr's case is hardly unique. Phillip Resnick reviewed extant literature dealing with maternal filicide and found "filicidal mothers to have frequent psychosis, prior mental illness, and suicidal thoughts." Resnick and Susan Hatters Friedman identified five major motives of perpetrators of maternal filicide, the first of which is altruistic filicide, where a mother kills her child out of love in the belief that death would be in the child's best interest. An example would be a psychotic mother who kills her child thinking she is sparing the child from a cruel world, a fate worse than death. The second motive applies to acutely psychotic filicide, in which a "psychotic or delirious mother kills her child without any comprehensible motive," such as a mother who kills her child after some form of hallucination. The third motive would apply to the case of Amy Doerr: fatal maltreatment filicide. With this motive, death is not the desired or anticipated outcome; rather, it results "from cumulative child abuse, neglect, or Munchausen syndrome by proxy." The final two motives are unwanted child filicide, where a mother kills her child because she views it as a hindrance, and the rarest of motives, spouse revenge filicide, where "a mother kills her child specifically to emotionally harm that child's father."[43]

Without question, Amy Doerr deserved to be punished harshly for killing her son. However, her crime is no more gruesome than many of the case studies I came across when researching this issue. What may be unique about Doerr's case, particularly on a global level, is the severity of punishment she received. The response to infanticide by the criminal justice system can vary greatly. In one study of maternal filicide, the authors found that some women were charged with first-degree murder, while others were not charged at all. Some of the women were convicted of crimes other than first-degree murder, such as "child abuse, negligent homicide, second-degree murder, felony child endangerment, involuntary manslaughter, negligent manslaughter, and abuse of a corpse."[44] In another study based on identified media accounts, more than two-thirds of the women and girls who committed maternal filicide were charged with murder.[45]

Not only is the response to infanticide arbitrary and inconsistent in the United States, it also differs in the treatment of perpetrators of the crime in dozens of other countries around the globe.[46] In his study of neonaticide and infanticide, Malmquist noted that other countries "typically distinguish infanticides from other forms of homicide, and [they] carry a lesser punishment."[47] At the time of his study, Malmquist noted an absence of any US federal or state statutes that distinguish infanticides or neonaticides from other homicides.[48]

Former Governor Sullivan was involved in a similar case when he was a new attorney, as he was appointed to an occasional criminal case by the court. One case involved infanticide. Sullivan recalls that he was at home eating dinner one night when he got a call from a man who said, "I need a lawyer; my wife is in jail for the death of a baby." Ever humble, Sullivan admits being initially overwhelmed by the gravity of his task in defending the young woman: "I didn't know what to do. I thought, 'Oh my gosh, we need to find you a real attorney.'" Sullivan credited the case with opening his eyes to the realities of criminal defense work: "That's when I really appreciated for the first time what a burden and what a responsibility representing someone charged with a serious crime is."[49] Sullivan ended up obtaining a plea agreement with prosecutors in which the woman received probation. The facts were once again much different in Sullivan's case than in Doerr's case, but I continue to question the necessity of her life sentence.

The fact that the United States takes a much more retributive approach to infanticide than does the rest of world is a pattern that is mirrored in US incarceration rates. Some would argue that these disparities are an acceptable part of our unique position in the world, a concept that has been called "American exceptionalism."[50] The late United States Supreme Court Justice Antonin Scalia embodied this spirit of American exceptionalism when he argued that we should not be influenced by legal approaches that exist in other countries.[51] Should we persist in this worldview of exceptionalism when our approaches to criminal justice create a sense of injustice, when those approaches are applied arbitrarily and unevenly?

Amy Doerr's last commutation petition was denied. As with other people I've profiled, I was moved by my initial encounter with Doerr at her parole hearing. She is intelligent, thoughtful, and obviously very remorseful regarding her crime. Doerr is also very active in her rehabilitation. Most important, like Rouse and Farnham, Doerr has support waiting for her on the outside and could likely have been safely released years ago.

THE UNFORGIVEN

When I first began writing this book, I had a clear perception of the type of incarcerated individual I did *not* want to profile. Such a person would need to have committed a serious crime, most likely violent, and the individual would have made no effort at rehabilitation and demonstrated a lack of remorse for their crime. A couple of inmates came to mind when I envisioned the typology I wanted to avoid, and one person in particular surfaced in my memory: Aaron McKinney.

Aaron McKinney is the man who murdered Matthew Shepard in October 1998 in what became one of the most widely reported news stories in Wyoming history, a crime some called "one of the most notorious anti-gay hate crimes in American history."[52] McKinney's murder trial ended in November 1999, and little was known about the complicated motives and circumstances surrounding the crime until months after he had been sentenced. The judge had imposed a gag order, and the file was not unsealed until three months after the legal proceedings concluded.[53] Some important, unknown facts about the crime were eventually reported by the national media when McKinney and his co-defendant, Russell Henderson, gave interviews to ABC News co-anchor Elizabeth Vargas in a one-hour special report in 2004.[54]

Prior to beating Matthew Shepard to death, McKinney had been awake for days on a meth binge. On October 6, 1998, McKinney and his co-worker Russell Henderson were drinking together at a bar in Laramie, Wyoming, where they encountered Matthew Shepard. The three men, all twenty-one at the time, eventually left the bar together in McKinney's father's truck. They drove a short distance to the outskirts of Laramie, where McKinney robbed and brutally administered what turned out to be a fatal beating of Matthew Shepard with a large .357 Magnum pistol. Henderson was present during the entire incident; in fact, he was driving the truck owned by Aaron's father because McKinney's license had been suspended. When the men reached a secluded area, McKinney stole thirty dollars from Shepard and commenced to repeatedly beat him with the pistol. McKinney told Henderson to retrieve some rope from the truck and tie Shepard's hands behind his back to a fencepost. Henderson later reported that he tried to stop McKinney as he was beating Shepard, but McKinney responded by pistol-whipping him in the face, leaving a wound for which he received nine stitches in the emergency room later that night. The scar, verified by police, is still visible today. According to Henderson, he retreated to the truck out of fear. Shepard was still alive when McKinney ceased his murderous attack. McKinney then stole Shepard's wallet and shoes and told Henderson to drive away.[55]

There are more facts and extenuating circumstances to this horrendous crime, but the details in the previous paragraph are undisputed. Much has been written about the complicated motives behind the murder, but the factors that may have driven McKinney's murderous actions are not my focus in telling this story. My perspective stems from the parole hearings for both men that I had the chance to attend. Based on those experiences, I do not believe that Aaron McKinney deserves a second chance given his lack of serious efforts at rehabilitation. Russell Henderson, in contrast, is a very different story.

Henderson was polite, motivated, and realistic about his chances at parole when we met with him for his initial parole hearing. McKinney, conversely, was less than respectful and had no interest in discussing anything remotely related to rehabilitation or remorse. McKinney wanted to talk about two things: money and donuts. McKinney's money inquiry had nothing to do with the parole board; rather, the Wyoming State Legislature had passed a law in 2010 creating a mandatory savings account for every inmate unless the prisoner is awaiting execution as part of a death sentence or serving life without parole (LWOP).[56] As explained earlier, LWOP is a separate sentence from an ordinary life sentence, or what has informally been called a "straight life sentence." A straight life sentence can be commuted by the governor, whereas LWOP specifically states that it "is not subject to commutation by the governor."[57] Both Aaron McKinney and Russell Henderson received two "straight" life sentences, to be served consecutively. During his hearing, McKinney essentially told the board that he was never getting out of prison since he had the equivalent of life without parole, so why couldn't he have the money?

In such situations, my job at parole hearings was to explain relevant legal issues to inmates. I told McKinney that his sentences were "straight" life sentences, meaning they *could* be commuted by the governor, which meant there was a possibility that he could get out someday if the governor agreed to commute his sentence. McKinney seemed content, if not satisfied, with my answer. He then looked at the parole board members and said, "I heard there are donuts here."

One of the parole board members stared back at McKinney and, pointing to himself, sternly replied, "Donuts are for people on this side of the table." And that was basically the substance of Aaron McKinney's parole hearing. Not once did he exhibit any contrition or even mention his crime—just money and donuts. (The Wyoming Supreme Court later issued an opinion upholding the mandatory savings account as it applied to inmates serving "straight" life, noting that "parole from such a sentence is only available in those relatively rare cases where the sentence is commuted to a term of years."[58] The court has acknowledged that commutations are rare in Wyoming and virtually impossible if the inmate makes no effort at atonement.)

Russell Henderson's story is far different from McKinney's and worth briefly mentioning. While I was able to attend McKinney's parole hearing in person, Henderson's hearing was conducted through video conferencing; thus I do not remember it as vividly as I do McKinney's hearing. That may also be because Henderson was polite, humble, and obviously remorseful while McKinney was arrogant and, frankly, rude, even if he tried to appear respectful. The donut comment insulted the entire parole process, not to mention the memory of Matthew Shepard.

I do recall that Henderson was very careful to make it clear that he did not expect anything from the board in terms of a commutation recommendation, at least not at that point. He was aware that it was much too early in his incarceration to make such a monumental request. He said he simply wanted to introduce himself to the board, report on his progress as an inmate, and try to build rapport for future hearings when he might one day ask for a commutation recommendation. Even McKinney has acknowledged being responsible for Shepard's murder, telling ABC News: "It's really hard for me to talk to Russ. To see him in this situation, knowing that I'm the one that put him here."[59]

Henderson certainly bears some legal culpability for Shepard's death, in several respects. His failure to notify the police after leaving McKinney is the most obvious criminal omission on Henderson's part, and he acknowledges his responsibility and guilt. Henderson told ABC News: "I'm sorry to the Shepard family. They've had the hardest of all this. I'm sorry to the nation as a whole because this affected a lot of people and I wish every day I could change or fix it."[60]

I posed the question of whether Russell Henderson should ever be released to a few people who are close to Matthew Shepard's memory. Malcolm Lazin, executive director of the Philadelphia LGBTQ group Equality Forum and a former federal prosecutor who has met Henderson in prison, believes Henderson has paid his dues for being "in the wrong place at the wrong time." Lazin added: "I think he [Henderson] has atoned. I think he has a contribution to make to society." The late Jason Marsden, a Wyoming native and former director of the Matthew Shepard Foundation, pointed out that only the governor can reduce Henderson's sentence, a prospect he labeled "super unlikely."[61] Sara Burlingame, the director of Wyoming Equality, a LGBTQ advocacy group in Cheyenne, said she believes in redemption but doubts that Henderson has really atoned for the crime.[62]

The quotes in the previous paragraph are from a 2018 article, roughly seven years ago, and people change over the years, in terms of personal growth and their perceptions of other people. Matthew Shepard's mother, Judy Shepard, told Katie Couric on national television that she believes Russell Henderson "is as much a victim as Matt was."[63] In an interview on October 12, 2023, commemorating the twenty-fifth anniversary of Matthew Shepard's death, his parents spoke about the tragedy. When asked about Henderson's professed remorse, Matthew's father, Dennis Shepard, replied that he "didn't believe it for a second."[64] Judy Shepard quickly pointed out that she differed from her husband with regard to Henderson: "Up until he became involved with McKinney and drugs, he was a good kid."[65]

Dennis Shepard went further in 2024, speaking for the family when he said "there's no forgiveness in either one of us." He continued, referencing Aaron McKinney: "I personally believe I'd like to have torched him. But my smart wife, she convinced me otherwise. And in this instance, it was the right thing to do: to put both of them in prison, with two consecutive life sentences, so they will never see daylight again outside of those cement walls."[66]

In September 2024, the full membership of the Wyoming Board of Parole denied Russell Henderson's commutation petition, despite having received an initial recommendation from a panel of three board members.[67] He must wait five years before he can file for a commutation again.

In his 2013 nonfiction book *The Book of Matt: Hidden Truths About the Murder of Matthew Shepard*, journalist and gay rights activist Stephen Jimenez concluded that Shepard and McKinney knew each other prior to the murder, were sexually involved, and were both active in the methamphetamine scene.[68] The prosecutor in the case, Cal Rerucha, agreed: "A lot of people didn't appreciate [that book] because they don't think it helps in what folks are trying to do in getting equal protection to all people regardless of sexual orientation." Rerucha concluded that the book did "get to a lot of the facts."[69]

There's no excuse for what happened to Matthew Shepard, but calling his murder a pure hate crime ignores contradictory information that was known to both law enforcement and prosecutors in the case—information that has been thoroughly researched, documented, and vetted since 1998. Life is rarely that black and white. What is also verifiable is that Russell Henderson's involvement in the murder was not as simple as initially reported by the national media, and the true facts of his actual participation bear repeating, particularly in light of an inaccurate popular narrative that is often taken for granted.

Aaron McKinney, in contrast, may never atone for the murder of Matthew Shepard. He was not remorseful in his parole hearing, but beyond that I have no way of knowing whether he's truly remorseful. I do know that prison can be a dangerous and dehumanizing place, and showing weakness of any kind can invite predators. Some inmates know they are never getting out of prison, and they try to make their life there as comfortable as possible. Asking the board for money and donuts was undoubtedly McKinney's way of trying to have some control over his grim situation, and I'm sure it made a good story to tell other inmates back in the pod. Underneath the facade, might there be some remorse? My hunch is that we will never know, at least not with Aaron McKinney. His personal attitude toward prison is perhaps hinted at in the Wyoming Supreme Court's language in *Nicodemus v. Lampert*, when referring to the petition of another Wyoming lifer: "He [Nicodemus] does not expect to ever be paroled or released, and he anticipates that he will die in prison."[70]

For Russell Henderson, the hope for a commutation continues. Judy Shepard herself assessed Henderson as a victim in the crime, and his potential for success was obvious to those who knew him growing up. While he was governor, Mike Sullivan awarded Henderson his Eagle Scout badge, captured in a photograph that appeared in local newspapers and was reprinted in Jimenez's *The Book of Matt*.[71]

Another Wyoming politician, former US Senator Alan K. Simpson, penned an opinion for the *Washington Post* in 2009, in which he spoke about his own time on federal probation as a juvenile. In writing about second chances, Simpson observed: "When a young person is sent 'up the river,' we need to remember that all rivers can change course."[72]

7

Mercy as a Virtue

Randi Losalu, a former victim's advocate for the Wyoming Board of Parole, often encountered the "sense of injustice" the criminal justice system creates. In her role with the parole board for over ten years, Losalu worked closely with victims of violent crime, people who had suffered tremendous grief and loss—including every Wyoming case profiled in this book. Many of the victims Losalu worked with were opposed to parole, and in many cases the board would parole that person after having considered the victim's input. Losalu had the unenviable task of informing the victim or victim's family member that the board had elected to release someone. She also had the opportunity to inform victims when the board denied parole, a much easier task. Either way, somebody was unhappy. Because of that, Losalu's job as a parole board victim's advocate involved regularly working with a "sense of injustice."

Losalu was always interested in victim's advocacy in some form. Growing up in Evanston, Wyoming, she volunteered for the teen talk suicide hotline as a high school student and always felt a desire to meet the needs of those

https://doi.org/10.5876/9781646428557.c007

around her. Losalu attended the University of Wyoming and graduated with bachelor's degrees in criminal justice and psychology in 2003, during which time she was first introduced to the concept of restorative justice.[1]

Following graduation, Losalu joined the Peace Corps and was assigned to the Kingdom of Tonga, where she assisted with the development of a victim advocacy program based on traditional Tongan principles of restorative justice. From that experience, Losalu was impressed by the healing power of restorative justice: "For me, it's easy to see both sides individually and it takes more work to mesh them together, which is really what restorative justice does. It can help the other person see the situation from another perspective and works toward a more meaningful resolution or end, whatever that may be in each case, with each case being different."[2]

Within a few years of returning to the United States from Tonga, Losalu was hired as the victim's advocate for the Wyoming parole board, where her passion for restorative justice led her to create a victim-offender dialogue (VOD) program—the first restorative justice program in the State of Wyoming. A VOD program is a "guided face-to-face dialogue between the victim and the offender regarding a particular case for which participants have been prepared in advance."[3] Losalu received training from Jon Wilson, an expert VOD educator and facilitator who has worked with numerous criminal justice agencies throughout the United States.[4] After completing that training, Losalu launched the Wyoming parole board VOD program in 2013 and quickly garnered recognition around the state, winning several awards, including an Innovation Award from the Wyoming Division of Victim Services in 2014.[5] Another job duty was writing letters to judges and prosecutors, seeking input whenever the board prepared a commutation recommendation for the governor. She had to bear the initial shock of reading the letters from prosecutors and judges, some of which could be insulting, derogatory, and mindless posturing.

TEMPERING JUSTICE

I often recall the attorney general telling me he wanted his pound of flesh whenever he rejected my proposed plea agreement, or at least I remember the phrase, which I had never understood or studied. It was an influential point in my career. At the time, I had no idea how closely his statement was tied to the virtue of mercy. In *The Merchant of Venice*, Shakespeare artfully demonstrates the connection between justice and mercy.[6] The play involves a merchant in Venice, Antonio, who defaults on a large loan provided by a lender, Shylock. Shylock agrees to loan the money with one condition: If Antonio were unable to repay the loan by a specified date, Shylock could take a pound of Antonio's flesh as payment. In the scene, Shylock has demanded the court's enforcement of his legal right, which in this case is his claim to a pound of flesh from Antonio. The quoted speech about mercy was delivered by Portia, in disguise as Balthazar, who pleads for Antonio, but Shylock is unmoved and demands specific performance. The court sides with Shylock. As Antonio prepares to meet Shylock's knife, Portia intervenes and points out that the contract called for a pound of flesh, not the spilling of blood, thus sparing Antonio through a legal technicality.[7]

Shakespeare was able to dramatically convey the centuries-old idea that mercy is a virtue that seasons justice—a notion that has been criticized by several modern scholars. Jeffrie G. Murphy and Jean Hampton have expressed the view that the US criminal justice system should seek justice rather than grant mercy. While that position may not necessarily mean that mercy cannot temper justice, Murphy and Hampton further claimed that there is "simply no room for mercy as an autonomous virtue" and that actors within the system should "keep their sentimentality to themselves for use in their private lives with their families and pet."[8] Dan Markel, also skeptical of mercy as a virtue, wrote that "mercy is a source of especial shame for a nation secure in its institutions and confident in its desire to share the blessings of equal liberty under law."[9] University of Pennsylvania Law School Professor Stephen J. Morse observed that the literature on justice and mercy "is sparse and scholars rarely agree." Morse also noted that philosophers have not provided a "definitional and conceptual clarification" of mercy, which leaves the proposed virtue of limited assistance to those seeking to temper justice.[10]

While some may question the usefulness of mercy in the criminal justice system, many scholars and philosophers have identified the necessity for principles such as mercy to impact sentencing and clemency decisions made by judges and chief executives. Friedrich Nietzsche explored the interplay among revenge, punishment, justice, and mercy in *On the Genealogy of Morals*.[11] Nietzsche believed the virtue of justice could exist only in an organized society governed by laws; primitive societies, in contrast, are motivated by revenge, where private parties seek to redress grievances personally.[12] With the advent of law and government, a new system is born that requires all citizens to follow the rules of society, including respecting each other's rights; this creates a situation in which everyone is in a state of debt to one another.[13] At this point, the government assumes control of the legitimate use of physical coercion to enforce the reciprocal debt between citizens and also takes control of the means of punishing offenders, which balances the scales of justice whenever a citizen breaches the social contract that has been created.[14] As society endures and stabilizes, the need for punishment becomes less important to the orderly function of society, and the ruler can accordingly offer mercy to those who break the law. Because they need not extract punishment in each case, the most developed societies can also be the most merciful.[15]

With regard to the idea that mercy has no place in the criminal justice system, Professors Carol S. Steiker and Paul Larkin have found fault with Jeffrie Murphy's contention that we should limit mercy to household pets.[16] Larkin observed that Murphy's conception of justice is very similar to what people would call "mercy."[17] Steiker noted that Murphy's criticism of mercy acknowledges a role the virtue can play in justice, in that "it embraces as justice many of the most powerful examples of lenient treatment that might also be claimed to be the product of mercy."[18] Murphy doubts the sincerity of an individual's remorse at sentencing but finds such expressions more plausible at a much later point, such as when an executive official might consider clemency. He agrees that metanoia, although rare, is possible.[19] If a person does undergo a fundamental change, Murphy would agree that just as it is unfair to punish someone for crimes they did not commit, it is unjust to continue to punish an individual who has undergone a transformation of moral character.[20]

Alwynne Smart argued that mercy is an autonomous virtue, claiming that mercy is justified when one crime is less evil than another, when a person is provoked, and when extenuating circumstances exist—such as mental illness, impaired judgment, coercion, and ignorance.[21] Other situations Smart identified as warranting mercy are cases when an individual has already been punished severely, when the punishment would cause grave harm to third parties, and when the crime was committed remotely in time.[22] Smart also provided examples in which mercy would not be justified: if it causes an innocent person to suffer, if it is harmful to the individual's welfare, when it appears that the individual is not remorseful, or when it is clear that the person is not remorseful despite displaying an attitude that is "temporarily repentant."[23]

Philosopher Claudia Card espoused the belief that justice is a virtue that emanates from institutions, which concern themselves with the proper balance of rights among citizens, whereas mercy is the forsaking of the right to apply or continue punishment of another—a virtue that resides with individuals who have the power to grant clemency.[24] Card felt that a wrongdoer should receive mercy in two situations: where the individual would be made to suffer more than they deserve in light of their basic character, and where the person would be harmed more severely than those who would benefit from punishing the offender.[25] Accordingly, Card believed the role of mercy in the criminal justice system is embodied in the executive's ability to extend clemency to a specific wrongdoer without disrupting the institutional need to administer criminal sanctions that are applied equally to all those who break the laws created by the institution.[26] Borrowing language from Shakespeare, Card reasoned that her analysis would permit a government to "temper institutional justice" with "a chief executive's mercy."[27]

Philosopher Nigel Walker also examined the executive motivation for granting mercy, citing compassion as a valid reason to be lenient. However, Walker also discussed other rationales for mercy that he deemed inappropriate, such as personal gain, favoritism, and whimsy. Some justifications for clemency, such as prison overcrowding, are not commendable or improper but merely a practical exercise of the power of clemency. Other justifications for mercy might include unprompted, helpful actions by an inmate many years after conviction and imprisonment, such as intervening to quell a riot, saving a correctional officer's life, or providing information to authorities that thwarts an escape attempt or planned acts of violence against prison staff.[28]

MERCY IN ACTION

There have been well-documented acts of mercy by chief executives in US history. In 1970, Arkansas Governor Winthrop Rockefeller commuted the sentence of all fifteen death row inmates to life in prison. In a public statement announcing the commutations, Governor Rockefeller wrote that the individual records of the condemned men bore "no relevance to his consideration" and that his decision was "purely personal and philosophical."[29]

Governor Rockefeller elaborated on his rationale: "My position on capital punishment has been clear since long before I became governor. I am unalterably opposed to it and will remain so as long as I live. What earthly mortal has the omnipotence to say who among us shall live and who shall die? I do not. Moreover, in that the law grants me authority to set aside the death penalty, I cannot and will not turn my back on lifelong Christian teachings and beliefs, merely to let history run out its course on a fallible and failing theory of punitive justice."[30] Governor Rockefeller's death row commutations generated a response. His office received 397 letters regarding the commutations, 324 of which supported Rockefeller's decision.[31] Of the fifteen men who were spared execution, nine were later released on parole and only one inmate ever returned to prison, validating what the research tells us: Individuals who are convicted of murder and later paroled have extremely low rates of recidivism.[32]

In 2000, Governor George Ryan of Illinois declared a moratorium on executions when 5 death row inmates were exonerated as the result of DNA evidence. As one of his final actions before leaving office, Governor Ryan commuted the sentences of all 160 death row inmates to life without parole.[33] Other governors have been less benevolent. Governor Rick Scott of Florida used his power as governor to intervene in a case in which a local prosecutor refused to seek the death penalty against a cop killer in 2017. Elected prosecuting attorney Aramis Alaya made it clear that not only would she not pursue the death penalty against a cop killer but that she would not seek the death penalty in any cases, citing continuing constitutional challenges to Florida's death penalty and the expense involved. After Alaya refused to recuse herself from the cases, Governor Scott issued an executive order removing her from twenty-three death penalty cases and assigned them to prosecutors in neighboring counties.[34] Alaya contested the orders, but the Florida Supreme Court sided with Scott. In 2020, the governor took another case from Alaya, and she later announced that she would not run for reelection because Florida law conflicted with her belief system.[35]

Governor Mike Sullivan did not intervene to halt the execution of Mark Hopkinson in 1992 despite strong pressure from a variety of groups to spare his life. One writer noted: "A coalition of civil rights, human rights, and church groups asked Governor Sullivan for clemency on the grounds that Hopkinson would be the first person in the United States executed since the 1977 re-imposition of the death penalty, where the actual trigger men weren't known. 'Unless something unforeseen takes place, I anticipate it will be carried out. I'm not looking for anything. I'm just saying you never say never,' the governor said. Sullivan explained that he had great respect for life and had reservations about the death penalty, so any decision he made would be made carefully."[36] Robert Reese, one of the few Wyoming legislators who opposed Hopkinson's execution, "conceded that it was bad politics to be against it."[37] For Governor Sullivan, the death penalty was a complex issue, like many of the issues an executive official confronts.

Working in an environment that creates a "sense of injustice" also carries many complex issues and complicated decisions, and Randi Losalu thrived in that setting. When Losalu accepted the job at the parole board, her official title was victim service coordinator. The position "was exactly what I was looking for and held so much potential for many of my interests and passions. I was able to grow that position not only toward basic victim's advocacy, but I was able to take it much further by incorporating restorative justice principles and programs in the Apology Letter Bank and victim-offender dialogue (VOD) program. While these programs are not for every victim and their participation, it is extremely powerful to have [them] available to those who do want to participate."[38]

In addition to the VOD program, Losalu created the Apology Letter Bank, a program in which offenders can write letters of apology to their victims; the letters are screened for appropriate content. The victim has the option to access a letter of apology from the offender, and participation is completely voluntary. Losalu says the VOD program in particular was "special" to her: "It's amazing to see the process and progress of the individuals who choose to participate in VOD."[39]

In some VOD cases, Losalu provided the victim with information they could not otherwise get. For instance, Losalu facilitated dialogues that gave victims the opportunity to ask questions only the offender had answers to. The dialogues allowed some victims to gain a sense of control over their relationship with not just the grief but the entirety of the crime. In some cases, the interaction helped reduce the intensity of the victim's fear.

For Losalu, her decision to leave the parole board was another complex issue. The Wyoming parole board is a small agency in a very small state, and eventually, someone with Losalu's talent and ambition is bound to move on. While she was at the parole board, Losalu obtained a master's degree in social work from the University of North Dakota, and she is currently a licensed and certified social worker. Losalu has become both the operations manager and one of many therapists for a busy counseling business that has multiple offices in Wyoming and Colorado, and she continues to focus on trauma by helping victims in their journey of processing, healing, and moving forward with their lives.[40] The VOD program, however, is what she misses most about working at the parole board. Many of the dialogues and individual cases created lifetime memories for Losalu. One case in particular, a first-degree murder involving a juvenile offender named Tommy Rivera, was a classic example of the complexity and power of restorative justice.

8

The Power of Restorative Justice

When he pleaded guilty to first-degree murder at age seventeen, Thomas "Tommy" Rivera exhibited many of the markers of juvenile immaturity acknowledged by the United States Supreme Court: He was impulsive and reckless in taking risks; further, he lacked a fully developed brain and was deficient in the ability to evaluate the possible consequences of his actions.[1] The facts of Rivera's case originate around a story of high school jealousy involving two teenage boys in competition over a girl, perhaps one of the oldest sources of conflict in human history and rarely the stuff of irredeemable monsters.

A prime example of Rivera's adolescent impulsivity and lack of sophistication is that he stole the gun he used to kill his victim from an unmarked police car in February 1995, when he was sixteen. Roughly a year later, on January 18, 1996, Rivera used that gun to shoot and kill his victim, Jeremy Kragness. The gun was later traced to the chief of the Cheyenne Police Department.[2]

https://doi.org/10.5876/9781646428557.c008

Stealing items from cars was part of Tommy Rivera's lifestyle as a teenager. He was insecure and eager to prove himself, and when he and the rival student were set to confront one another, he wanted people to respect him. According to the affidavit of probable cause completed by the prosecutor, "This all stemmed from the fact that Jeremy Kragness wanted to date a girl that Thomas Rivera also wished to date."[3] Rivera did little to conceal his motive from classmates, as several students observed him and Kragness leaving school together in a vehicle driven by Rivera. The affidavit continued: "The students were aware that there were on-going problems between the two and that a fight had been discussed. When they left together the word was they were leaving to fight in Hol[l]iday Park."[4] The pair never reached Holliday Park. Instead, Rivera drove to a remote location in Cheyenne.

A friend of Rivera's called him, and he admitted that "he had shot Jeremy Kragness in the leg and that now he was 'going to go through with it.'" Rivera hung up, and his friend repeatedly tried to call him back; the friend then proceeded to tell the rest of the immediate friend group what Rivera had admitted to. Later in the day, Rivera met with the friend and admitted that "he shot Jeremy Kragness in the leg and then let him smoke a cigarette. When Jeremy Kragness tried to run, he shot him in the back." Rivera refused to tell his friend where the body was "out of fear he would tell the police." The following morning, Kragness was discovered by "a transient [who] found the body while walking through a culvert" near an area of Cheyenne that is frequented by the unhoused.[5]

Given the overwhelming amount of evidence pointing to him, Rivera was quickly arrested. According to the reporting at the time, the murder weapon was never recovered, but the holster was found during a search of Rivera's room. The holster was for a 9 mm handgun that belonged to Cheyenne's chief of police. He reported that prior to becoming chief, roughly a year before the killing, his patrol car had been broken into and the weapon had been stolen.[6] When I discussed the matter of the handgun with Rivera, he denied that he would have broken into a vehicle that was obviously a police car: "That's one of the first times I realized that people in positions of power would lie. I would have never broken into a marked police car. I was [a] sixteen-year-old kid. I took the gun from a regular car that was unlocked."[7]

Whether the gun came from an unmarked, unlocked vehicle belonging to a police officer makes no difference today. The facts are that at age sixteen, Tommy Rivera stole a gun and a year later, at age seventeen, he used

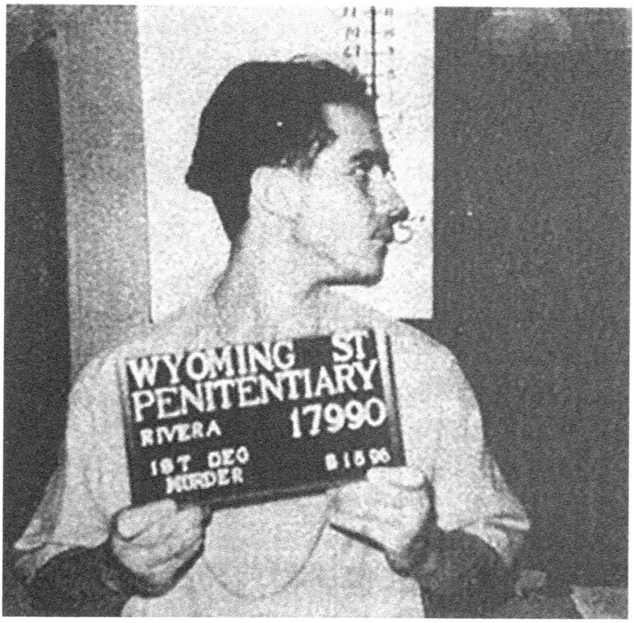

FIGURE 8.1. Tommy Rivera, age seventeen. Image provided to author by Tommy Rivera.

that gun to murder his high school rival, a crime whose motives he made no effort to hide from his classmates (figure 8.1). The brazen recklessness of the crime is matched by the utter lack of sophistication. There is no doubt that Rivera committed first-degree murder: The killing of Jeremy Kragness was obviously planned, and jealousy was an equally apparent motive. However, what is also painfully obvious is the lack of any mature self-evaluation of the consequences of Rivera's actions.

Without question, Rivera deserved to be punished, and, understandably, the family of Jeremy Kragness was devastated, just as Tommy Rivera's family was shocked to learn of his actions and then lose him after he received a life sentence for first-degree murder. In this case, retribution was necessary, and at the time, a life sentence was the only option for seventeen-year-old Tommy Rivera. However, as noted in chapter 1, the United States Supreme Court has recognized the rehabilitative potential for juvenile offenders, and, it is hoped, America is slowly moving away from past retributive approaches in some areas of the criminal justice system, such as declaring life sentences for juveniles to be unconstitutional.

RESTORING LIFE

However, overcoming the institutional inertia and support behind the retributive model of punishment in the United States will be difficult to achieve. In Wyoming, the punitive approach to dealing with offenders follows those who have committed felonies for the rest of their lives. Wyoming is one of the harshest US states when it comes to disenfranchising convicted felons, which is the practice of removing the right to vote following conviction for a felony offense.[8] Including Wyoming, only twelve states deny the right to vote to felons who have completed prison, probation, or parole.[9]

In 2012, former speaker of the Wyoming State House of Representatives and current University of Wyoming trustee Kermit Brown told the *Casper Star-Tribune* that the permanent loss of voting rights was "the price you pay for being dysfunctional in society."[10] Brown's statements reveal his pragmatic sense of government policy, and he also voiced fiscal concerns about life imprisonment: "When you deprive a person of liberty for the rest of his life, you assume the burden of care." Brown added, "When you look at the burden versus the benefit to be accomplished, you say, 'It's time to process that person out of the system.' "[11] Brown's quote with regard to life sentences embodies the Wyoming spirit of independence from tax burdens and government overreach, but it is not shared by the majority of conservative politicians. Brown's sentiments with regard to voting rights, however, *are* shared by many conservative politicians. During a 2002 debate, Kentucky senator Mitch McConnell remarked that "states have a significant interest in reserving the right to vote for those who have abided by the social contract that forms the foundation of representative democracy . . . those who break our laws should not dilute the votes of law-abiding citizens."[12]

Disenfranchisement laws are nothing new in America, as they were imported along with other common law customs by the colonists. Our founding fathers, who were wealthy white male property owners, also thought it was wise to grant themselves the right to vote but withheld the same liberty from women, African Americans, the poor, and the illiterate.[13] In light of that, it makes sense to question their judgment in excluding convicted criminals from voting, particularly if society wants to embrace and encourage rehabilitation as a societal goal for offenders rather than prioritize retribution.

People who have committed crimes can and do change, particularly youthful offenders. Are we to punish them forever by denying them the right to vote? Denying ex-felons the right to vote or to serve on a jury only reminds them of their past mistakes and lessens their feelings of inclusion. Zebulon Brockway, a nineteenth-century advocate for criminal justice reform and superintendent of the Elmira Reformatory in New York, believed that a return to citizenship was the ultimate goal of imprisonment and that his mission was to prepare inmates for "restoration to citizenship" and "personal fitness for future liberty."[14] Restoring the right to vote has many parallels to the restorative justice movement in America.

Some programs in the United States, like the victim-offender dialogue (VOD) program started by Randi Losalu (chapter 7), provide an alternative to the backward-looking approach to punishment that is embodied in the principle of retribution. Restorative justice approaches like the VOD program are methods of dealing with crime that have been in existence for centuries. Rather than focusing on retribution and punishing the offender, restorative justice programs focus on the harm done to the victim and the community. The approach seeks to rebuild the lives of the victim, the community, and the offender. While the restorative justice process places importance on the victim's needs, it also seeks to hold the offender accountable by making them understand the harmful effects of their actions. Restorative justice programs have existed in many societies but were mostly unheard of or rarely used in the US until recently. They have gained prominence in the US criminal justice system in recent decades after being resurrected by criminal justice reform advocates in the 1970s. Prior to colonization, restorative justice was actively practiced by Native Americans on this continent.[15] Restorative justice also has roots in the ancient Arab, Greek, and Roman societies that promoted a restorative approach to all crimes, including homicide.[16]

Condensing restorative justice into a single definition is not simple or even necessary. Restorative justice has been described as a philosophy that is flexible and capable of being tailored to suit the needs of the particular case and people involved.[17] The term is an overarching phrase used to refer to a spectrum of practices currently being developed in the criminal justice system. Restorative justice describes approaches to dispute resolution that are found in a variety of contexts, such as neighborhoods, schools, workplaces, and the legal system. The phrase is used to describe programs but also as an approach to living life. Recent Nobel Peace Prize recipients such as Buddhists Aung San Suu Kyi of Burma and the Dalai Lama are teaching these ancient lessons to the West: The more evil the crime, the greater the opportunity for grace to transform an act of retribution into one tempered with compassion.[18] The Dalai Lama said: "Learning to forgive is much more useful than merely picking up a stone and throwing it at the object of one's anger, the more so when the provocation is extreme. For it is under the greatest adversity that there exists the greatest potential for doing good, both for oneself and for others."[19] The lesson offered here is that crime is more than an opportunity to punish and prevent future criminal behavior but a chance to treat the offense as a way to prevent greater evils and transform both victims and perpetrators through pathways of kindness and giving.

Restorative justice has often been defined not as what it is but as what it is an alternative to: the extremely punitive criminal justice system. It instead focuses strongly on victim empowerment.[20] American restorative justice scholar Howard Zehr has been called the "grandfather" of the restorative justice movement. Zehr's interest in restorative justice was spawned by his work with victim-offender reconciliation programs; his articles, teachings, speeches, and books have greatly impacted the field.[21] His book *Changing Lenses* uses the metaphor of changing a camera lens to propose the idea that we can change our retributive view of crime and justice.[22] In later writings, Zehr summarized the different forms of restorative justice that have developed around the world.[23]

Family group conferences (FGC) are a form of restorative justice that began in New Zealand in 1989, inspired largely by the traditions of the Indigenous Maori people. FGCs are facilitated encounters between the victim and offender, but they also include family members, police, and other individuals. The juvenile justice system in New Zealand operates on an FGC model, with the courts serving as a backup rather than the primary option for dealing with youthful offenders. FGCs have also been created in various communities in Australia, South Africa, the UK, and North America.[24]

Another established restorative justice method is the peacemaking circle, which is composed of an even larger group of participants than the FGCs. Of the various restorative justice programs, peacemaking circles seek to include the community and are typically facilitated by a "circle keeper." The circle keeper uses a talking piece and a circular process to guide the interactions, and the circles often specifically identify and call upon the core values the participants are thought to possess. Peacemaking circles had their origins with one of Canada's Indigenous First Nations (Canada has three "First Nations"), and the concept has been extended beyond the criminal justice system to schools, businesses, and religious organizations with similar goals of having a facilitated, open dialogue about problematic issues within the organization.[25]

The other common approach to restorative justice is the victim-offender mediation approach. The use of the word *mediation* in the criminal justice concept does not sit well with some victims. The word is more fitting in a civil proceeding, where evidence of guilt is not an issue, so victims find the term *mediation* to be overly neutral.[26] Perhaps for that reason, some programs use the term *dialogue*, including the VOD program in place while I worked at the Wyoming parole board.

Unfortunately, the VOD program in Wyoming is no longer active, having ended after Losalu left the board. It would not require much to get the program operational again. Under whatever name, these programs seek to redefine the way we think about guilt and justice, shifting the focus away from punishment and redirecting it toward the harm suffered by and needs of the victim while still including the community and the wrongdoer in an effort to rehabilitate the offender through problem solving.

When the program was operating in Wyoming, one requirement for a VOD was that it had to be initiated by the victim. Not surprisingly, many crime victims have no desire to meet or confront the person who harmed them. For that reason alone, it makes sense to require that the dialogue be initiated by the victim. By placing the decision of whether to initiate a dialogue in the victim's hands, the VOD program restores some power to the victim over the offender, as the victim can decide whether they want to confront the offender at all. If the victim requests a dialogue and the offender agrees, a lengthy preparation process is carried out during which trained facilitators meet separately with both the victim and the offender, usually in two or three preparatory sessions. In most instances, VOD cases take place years after the crime, typically while the offender is still in prison.

Once the participants are adequately prepared, the dialogue begins. The meeting between the victim and offender usually takes place at the correctional facility housing the offender. The victim and offender meet in a private room at the prison with someone facilitating the encounter. The face-to-face meeting represents a chance for the victim to express their feelings of loss, suffering, rage, and loneliness—emotions that have been buried beneath the surface, hidden from the public, and often not fully recognized by the victims themselves. Victims can ask the offender questions, explain their pain and how the crime affected them, and describe what they need to gain closure and move forward with life. In turn, the offenders respond to the victims' questions; in doing so, they are forced to confront their actions that harmed the victim, and in many cases they end up examining their own history that led up to the crime—revealing a past that was likely marked by a tragic pattern of abuse, deprivation, and desperation. It is hoped that the dialogue will inspire an agreement between the parties to move forward with positive steps that will help both of them heal and move on in peace rather than remain embroiled in a continuing cycle of retribution.

Not all VOD cases conclude with what many people would call a happy ending. Every case is different, and there are few expectations other than an honest and open dialogue among all participants in the conversation. Forgiveness, while an attractive goal, is not necessary. As Zehr put it, "We don't impose a goal of forgiveness." He continued, "There are so many misunderstandings about what forgiveness is: that if you forgive, that means you are not holding people accountable or forgetting about the harm that was done to you." Zehr explained, however, that for victims who do forgive the offender, the act can be liberating, relieving the victim of a burden that has often plagued their life for years.[27]

Reducing recidivism is also not a goal of restorative justice practices, although empirical evidence supports the ability of restorative justice to help offenders lead law-abiding lives.[28] Perhaps the most radical departure from the traditional retributive model that restorative justice offers is the notion that offenders are capable of redemption, that we can change and transform our habits, that our moral character can be improved upon.[29]

Irish criminologist Shadd Maruna noted that redemption brings us together as a society in ways retributive models of punishment cannot. Maruna found parallels in Emile Durkheim's argument that punishment is not for the offender but for all of us; whether the offender is rehabilitated is a secondary concern relative to the benefit punishment confers upon all of society.[30] Maruna has argued that the power of redemption has the same effect on society. Borrowing from John Braithwaite's revision of Durkheim's view of punishment, Maruna explained that redemption and reintegration also benefit all of us. A society that can strategically forgive its wrongdoers by setting realistic goals for rehabilitation is a good society for restorative justice purposes.[31]

Restorative justice approaches may strike many Americans as foreign concepts, but such programs are beginning to gain a foothold in the US. In 2002, twenty-nine states had legislation that supported mediation or VOD programs.[32] In a 2014 study conducted by Shannon M. Silva and Carolyn G. Lambert and published in 2015, thirty-two states had restorative justice legislation on the books, with twenty of those states adopting statutes that specifically encourage restorative justice practices by providing structural support for funding and legislation. An additional twelve states have statutes that support restorative justice by deeming it desirable or an acceptable alternative to the traditional punishment-oriented approach to criminal justice.[33] However, Silva and Lambert's report also revealed that most of these laws have had little impact, as very few states provide meaningful support to implement restorative justice programs. Only Colorado, Minnesota, Missouri, Montana, New Hampshire, Texas, and Vermont have structured support for restorative justice in their criminal code; of those seven states, not one mandates restorative justice as part of the criminal justice process.[34]

Not only has restorative justice failed to gain a significant foothold in the US criminal justice system, it also has critics. Some have argued that under a utilitarian perspective, punishment may be warranted even if the victim forgives the offender, providing that the punishment produces a greater good to society through deterrence.[35] Some victim groups are suspicious of restorative justice programs, given that meeting the needs of the offender is also a component of the program. Many victim groups advocate for harsh punishments; they discuss "rights" rather than "needs" and base their moral legitimacy on retribution rather than restoration.[36]

John Braithwaite, a leading restorative justice scholar, noted that restorative justice benefits only a small part of the total number of victims, roughly 10 percent, considering that many crimes—like burglary and white-collar crime—have low clearance rates, which means that many victims are never truly served by the system. Because more than 90 percent of victimizations will not be affected by restorative justice practices, the approach has little impact on the overall crime rate. The restorative justice process can also increase victim fears of re-victimization. While evidence indicates that re-victimization can happen as a result of the approach, Braithwaite explained that the studies demonstrated that a reduction in fear was twice as common as fears of re-victimization. There are also concerns that restorative justice programs can be "shaming machines" that worsen the stigmatization of offenders. Braithwaite suggests that one way to prevent moral lecturing and shaming is to make sure that a large number of caring supporters are present for both the victim and the offender. Participants who support the offender can counter moral lecturing with statements that encourage a sense of responsibility in the person while extolling their virtues, thereby strengthening the bond between the offender and their supporters.[37]

VICTIM-OFFENDER DIALOGUE IN WYOMING

While the impact and reach of restorative justice definitely has limitations, its power in bringing closure and peace to victims while helping to reform offenders cannot be denied. Soon after *Miller v. Alabama* was decided in 2012, Tommy Rivera had the chance to participate in a VOD with Randi Losalu and his victim's aunt, Sherry Myrick. Myrick had learned about the VOD program after receiving a letter as a certified victim in Rivera's case. The decision to forgive Rivera was not easy for Myrick. "I hated him, and I told him [so] to his face," she said.[38] The hatred stayed with her for years, and she still has some anger—much like Steve Watt, the highway patrolman profiled in chapter 6. How could she not? Myrick's family members have shunned her or expressed disapproval of her decision to forgive Rivera. Myrick credits *The Shack*, a novel about grief and faith written by William P. Young, as inspiring her to contact Losalu and start the VOD process.[39] "Even after I contacted Randi, it took me years to finally get the courage to meet with her," she told me.[40] After undergoing multiple prep sessions, Myrick was finally able to meet with Rivera, and she left the meeting hugging him and feeling as though a burden had been lifted from her. Myrick described the feeling as a relief from "spiritual constipation."[41]

When he reflected on his life at the time of his crime, Rivera explained that he suffered from low esteem. When his conflict with Kragness began, he "became anxious because it seemed like everyone at school was watching and waiting to see what would happen."[42] In an interview with me, he explained:

> At the time, I truly felt like there were only two possible outcomes in this situation: be humiliated and ostracized at school or do whatever it takes to have the other kids still like me. That's when shooting Jeremy became the only option

> I felt I had left. Sitting here talking to you, that process and line of reasoning continues to haunt me. Hearing myself say that now sounds so abstract and far removed from reality. As an adult, I look back and see how senseless my decision was to kill Jeremy. If I just would have apologized to him for flirting with his girlfriend, I know without a doubt he would have forgiven me and the situation would have been resolved and we'd have moved on.[43]

When Rivera first reached prison at age seventeen, he was hardly in the mood or of the mind-set to be rehabilitated or to think about restorative justice. In fact, he racked up disciplinary violations and was generally a problem inmate:

> Upon arriving in prison, it was an immediate culture shock. I was surrounded by full-grown men who lived in this prison community and who live according to a different set of rules in a different kind of culture. I learned immediately that if you were to survive and not become a victim, you had to earn the respect of your fellow cons. I watched how other respected prisoners carried themselves, and I began to act accordingly. I ended up getting into trouble for all kinds of random acts of rebellion. I found that other prisoners respected that, and that seemed to be how one should conduct himself if he was to live as a successful convict.[44]

When he entered prison as a juvenile, life indeed looked bleak for Rivera. He was a kid, faced with the fact that he was going to spend the rest of his life in prison. After about eighteen months, Rivera tried to commit suicide by climbing one of the interior fences at the Wyoming State Penitentiary in broad daylight, in full view of the correctional officers. Luckily for Rivera, the officers did not shoot him. His partner in climbing the fence, Martin Gabriel, was hit with a shotgun blast that, fortunately, did not kill him either.

Like people living in free society or anywhere else, Rivera matured in his early and mid-twenties, as predicted by research into human brain development. The age-crime curve also had an impact on Rivera, and he found himself tired of acting out in prison. Rivera said he rebelled against prison authority for about six years, "but during that time, life was empty. Thoughts of Jeremy would come to mind. It was a painful existence, but there was no alternative, or so it seemed."[45] In 2003, Rivera met a caseworker named David Dingman who introduced him to restorative justice concepts and set Rivera up with projects he and other inmates could work on to benefit the community. Prior to meeting Dingman, Rivera had refused to engage in any rehabilitative programming, seeing no use given his life sentence. Rivera credits Dingman with reaching him on a level no one else had, at least not in prison. "He genuinely cared about us and wanted the best for us," Rivera recalled.[46]

In 2003, Rivera and a group of inmates created three-dimensional topographic maps of Wyoming that focused on the state's history, donating the maps to a local middle school.[47] Rivera also led an effort at the state prison to raise money for victims of Hurricane Katrina through a pizza fundraiser in 2005.[48] Rivera's last disciplinary violation was in 2002, after which he remained disciplinary violation–free for the remainder of his incarceration.

In 2012, the United States Supreme Court declared all juvenile life sentences to be unconstitutional, and the light at the end of the tunnel suddenly became an open window of opportunity.[49] By then, Rivera was familiar with restorative justice and understood that most restorative justice–based programs require that the victim initiate contact. He was amazed when Randi Losalu wrote him a letter indicating that Sherry Myrick wanted to participate in a dialogue with him. Rivera had not had much contact with Jeremy Kragness's family, but he had received negative feedback from Myrick: "The only thing I thought I knew for certain was that Sherry hated me more than anyone else in the world. She had written a few letters to the newspaper and the parole board expressing what she thought about me. I'll just say they were hard to read. Sometimes I'd go back and re-read a couple of the ones I had. Although it was painful, I need to remember what I had done and in turn re-dedicate myself to not be that seventeen-year-old who stole a young man's life."[50]

Prior to meeting with Myrick, Rivera underwent prep sessions with Losalu, which he reported as invaluable: "She asked me questions and prepared me to be able to better articulate my feelings, and she also helped instill a sense of confidence in me."[51] When the time came to meet with Myrick face to face, Rivera described it as the most nervous and fearful moment of his life: "When I finally entered the room, I looked at Sherry and immediately saw the pain in her eyes. The emotion was so raw and powerful that I began to cry before I even reached my seat."[52] Losalu was in the room facilitating the encounter, and she explained that Myrick was given total control over the situation, including the seating arrangement and scheduling of the dialogue sessions. "It was important to give Sherry a voice and control in the process," Losalu recalled.[53] She described the day as having two dialogue sessions, with a break in between. For the first session, Sherry chose to be brought into the meeting first, electing to sit across the room from Rivera. The first session focused on Rivera sharing his version of the murder, with Sherry asking questions to clarify details.

During the break, Losalu recalled that Myrick was "thankful to know Jeremy went with Tommy willingly and to know that Jeremy was able to pray at the end of his life."[54] The second session began with Myrick choosing to sit next to Rivera: "Sherry choosing to sit next to Tommy was a powerful moment in and of itself. It was reflective of the restorative space and deep healing that the VOD process was allowing for both of them."[55] Losalu told me that each VOD she has facilitated was special in its own way and that the healing both Myrick and Rivera experienced was incredible and "only able to occur through the VOD process."[56] Restorative justice may not work for every victim, and some victims may be uninterested, but for many of those who engage in the process, the results have proven to be effective in assisting with the delicate process of moving on.

After the *Miller v. Alabama* decision, other prison staff recognized that Rivera would eventually be released. When the *Miller* opinion was announced, housing manager Janelle Thayer approached Rivera about transferring to a lower security level. At first, he was hesitant to accept a lesser custody assignment, knowing that each reduction in security carries unique circumstances and involves a different caliber of inmate population. Rivera credits Thayer with gradually moving him into less restricted settings, making his journey through the various security levels as smooth as possible.

Rivera was released on parole in May 2022 and returned to live in Cheyenne. Although he left prison without getting a tattoo, Rivera underwent an apprenticeship with accomplished tattoo artist Trinidad Serrano and received his first tattoo from his mentor. He is enrolled in classes at the local community college and is studying pre-law. The lack of self-esteem that plagued Rivera as a teenager has been replaced with confidence and skills in many areas that he developed in prison. His greatest teachers were other inmates, in particular men who had committed criminal homicide. Rivera has developed a talent for drawing and learned to weld, and he has transformed his body through exercise. He has cultivated the qualities he once thought unattainable, and he did all this while he was imprisoned. Now that he has been released on parole, he has been surprised and encouraged by support and compassion from many people, although he has received some

FIGURE 8.2. Tommy Rivera speaking at a conference. Image provided to author by Tommy Rivera.

negative comments on social media. While Rivera does not let the negativity bother him, he feels guilt for his crime on a daily basis, and that will always be with him. "I was young, a juvenile, and very immature, that's all true. But the fact is, I still killed Jeremy and I will live with that forever. But . . ." he added, "I am trying to make amends for it in every way possible."[57]

Tommy Rivera's miracle of life was bestowed by the United States Supreme Court, not the governor or because he went to law school with the governor or because he hired the attorney general's brother to represent him. He was saved by the fact that he was a few months shy of his eighteenth birthday when he murdered Jeremy Kragness. Rivera has a constant awareness of the good fortune he has received, and it translates into a passion for life (figure 8.2). He knows what it is like to wake up every day and face the prospect of never leaving prison. Now that Rivera is free, he is having a substantial and positive impact on his community, and that is one example of why we need to take a second look at the lifers in US prisons.

9

Consequences of Three Strikes

Orland Glenn received his life sentence for attempted first-degree murder, the same crime that sent Mark Farnham to prison. Like Farnham, Glenn shot his victim but did not kill her; in the process, he was shot by law enforcement but survived.[1] In April 1988, Glenn left his ex-wife's residence after an argument during which he physically assaulted her. She reported the beating, and officers responded to her residence to investigate, at which time Glenn returned and crashed his truck into the house and garage. Glenn then fired shots at his ex-wife and wounded her before officers returned fire, shooting Glenn and arresting him in the process.[2] The Wyoming Supreme Court later described Glenn's action as a "murderous assault upon his ex-wife for which he received a life term prison sentence."[3] After he was sent to prison, Glenn conducted himself in admirable fashion, accumulating what Wyoming Governor Mark Gordon called an "exemplary disciplinary record," describing Glenn as "a role model for other inmates."[4]

Due to his impressive work as an inmate, Glenn received a commutation of his life sentence to seventy-five years to life in 2003 from Governor

https://doi.org/10.5876/9781646428557.c009

Dave Freudenthal and another commutation from Governor Matt Mead in 2013, further reducing his sentence to forty-three-and-a-half years to life.[5] Despite acknowledging Glenn's efforts at programming while in prison, "including your completion of substance abuse treatment, victim impact courses, and certifications for trade skills," Gordon denied the board's 2020 commutation recommendation on behalf of Glenn, writing to him that "given the severity of your crime and legislative changes, which accelerate your parole eligibility date, I am denying your request for commutation."[6] The governor noted that Glenn would be eligible for parole in July 2021 and that the parole board had already granted him parole on his eligibility date.[7] Glenn was released from prison on his eligibility date and is living on parole in a Wyoming community. However, questions remain. Should Glenn have been released earlier, given his apparently sincere and sustained efforts at rehabilitation? His crime was severe, but did it justify thirty-three years in prison?

STRIKING OUT AT LIFE

Another inmate who received one of the three commutations granted by Governor Mead is Brad Skinner, who did not shoot or kill anyone when committing his crime. Skinner received a life sentence under Wyoming's version of a "three-strikes law." In Wyoming, the statute is called a "habitual criminal" penalty. Using a baseball analogy to describe these penalties of "three strikes and you're out," such laws are based on the notion that "offenders convicted repeatedly of serious offenses should be removed from society for long periods of time, in many cases for life."[8] Three-strikes laws, like the Wyoming habitual criminal statute, require that the individual has to have been convicted of two or more previous felonies arising out of separate occurrences, in Wyoming or elsewhere, before prosecutors can pursue the penalty.[9] The Wyoming three-strikes law provides that if a "habitual criminal" has three or more previous felony convictions (essentially facing a "fourth strike") and is subsequently convicted of a violent felony, the term of imprisonment is life.[10] Prior to his conviction for aggravated assault and battery in October 1999, Skinner had eight previous felony convictions.[11]

The facts of Brad Skinner's case involve an incident of domestic violence that took place in March 1999.[12] Skinner and his wife had been drinking at a bar in Casper, Wyoming, when Skinner discovered some money his wife had obtained from an unknown source. He wanted to know where the money came from, which precipitated an argument. Skinner began to yell at his wife and asked that she return a hunting knife he had given her. She complied and the couple left the bar, stopping to buy more alcohol at a drive-through window. Skinner's wife later testified that when they arrived home, Skinner grabbed her by the hair and shirt, and she responded by slapping and hitting him and crying for help. Skinner proceeded to place his knee in his wife's stomach and covered her mouth and nose as the couple continued to fight. At one point, when Skinner turned to close the door, his wife called 911 and put the phone down without Skinner noticing, which allowed the dispatcher to hear what was happening in the Skinner residence. The dispatcher overheard a man screaming and a woman crying. The dispatcher could hear the woman being slapped and pleading for the assault to stop and the man replying "I'll kill you now." The dispatcher testified that there was no mention of a knife during the phone call.[13]

Skinner's wife testified that the fighting continued, with Skinner throwing her against the wall, pinning her there, and head-butting her. The record then indicates that she asked for the knife back, which led Skinner to take it out of his pocket with one hand while using the other hand to hold her by the neck.[14] Within a short time, police officers responded and knocked on the door. When they received no response, the officers kicked in the door and arrested Skinner, finding a knife in his front pants pocket. Skinner's wife informed the police that Skinner had held the open knife to her throat. She would later testify at trial that during Skinner's release on bond, he asked her to deny that he had held a knife to her throat and that he had asked to change her statement. Skinner's wife further testified that in another fight over her expected testimony, Skinner had threatened to kill her, held a baseball bat to her throat, and hit her, leaving a black eye.[15] During direct examination at trial, Skinner's wife initially testified that she could not remember whether Skinner had ever held the knife to her throat. On cross-examination, she testified that Skinner "had indeed placed a knife at her throat and threatened to kill her."[16] Skinner never denied that the domestic dispute had occurred; he argued that he had never held a knife to his wife's throat, an essential element of the crime that elevated it to a felony. The jury found Skinner guilty of aggravated assault and battery and found him to be a habitual criminal based on his numerous earlier felony convictions. He was sentenced to life.[17]

Following his conviction as a habitual criminal in October 1999, Skinner served sixteen years in prison before Governor Mead reduced his life sentence to thirty-five to forty-five years on November 3, 2015.[18] Five years later, in a letter dated November 11, 2020, Governor Mark Gordon denied another commutation request from the parole board on behalf of Skinner, which would have further reduced his sentence to a term of twenty-five to thirty-five years.[19]

GROWTH OF THREE STRIKES

As mentioned earlier, clemency (*clementia*) means the "willingness to show benevolence towards others, despite conscious suspicion, belief or knowledge that they do not deserve it."[20] Does Skinner not merit some type of benevolence, even if he may not be completely deserving? Surely our resources can be used for offenders who have demonstrated to be a much higher risk to re-offend than Brad Skinner, even if they were deemed habitual at some point. He has been incarcerated for several decades for a violent crime that did not result in death and arguably never rose to the level of an aggravated assault, if one believes Skinner's version of events. Either way, we will continue to pay for his housing in the Wyoming Department of Corrections for several more years.

To some degree, the concepts of mass incarceration and life sentences have become an integral part of how citizens of the United States view the criminal justice system, particularly when compared with the rest of the world. The system is uniquely punitive, and the American public appears largely accepting of that reality. Law professor Mugambi Jouet has commented that the shift has endured long enough to influence a generation of judges: "Mass incarceration has been such an enduring and extraordinary phenomenon that it has profoundly shaped the notion that justice in the United States is inherently harsher than in Europe, where more humane conceptions of punishment are influential. Because prison population explosion emerged approximately four decades ago, many jurists have known no other penal system in America. The Supreme Court's reasoning only reinforced this image. As Americans faced imprisonment levels on a scale virtually unprecedented in global history, the Court recurrently concluded that the Eighth Amendment's bar on 'cruel and unusual punishment' effectively does not cover draconian prison terms."[21]

The case of *Ewing v. California* is an unfortunate example of the United States Supreme Court's approval of draconian prison sentences for minor crimes, as the Court upheld a twenty-five-year to life sentence for the crime of stealing three golf clubs, as part of California's three-strikes penalty. Justice Sandra Day O'Connor wrote that Gary Ewing's sentence reflected "rational legislative judgement" that was "justified by the State's public safety interest in incapacitating and deterring recidivist felons." The Supreme Court reached this conclusion without empirical evidence that such sentences in fact reduce crime.[22]

The Supreme Court's view that the fear of a three-strikes penalty or a life sentence somehow serves as a deterrent to criminal behavior is unsupported by any evidence and is flatly wrong. Research shows that life sentences have a limited deterrent effect. Daniel S. Nagin, a professor of public policy at Carnegie Mellon University and a national authority on deterrence, wrote: "Research demonstrates that increases in already long prison sentences, say from 20 years to life, do not have material deterrent effects on crime."[23] Research conducted by Paul Robinson, a law professor at the University of Pennsylvania, and Princeton University psychology professor John Darley indicates that long sentences have a limited deterrent effect because most people who commit crimes do not expect to be caught, have no idea what the legal consequences will be, and in the majority of cases are intoxicated and likely suffering from mental health impairment.[24] Federal data also support the notion that those who commit crimes stand a good chance of getting away with it. FBI statistics indicate that fewer than two-thirds of murders are cleared by arrest, and the clearance rate drops to only one-third of reported rapes.[25]

The low clearance rate for these crimes is one of many reasons criminologists now dispel the belief that the severity of a punishment, such as a three-strikes law, is more effective than certainty of punishment. Nagin has claimed that "the evidence in support of the deterrent effect of the certainty of punishment is far more consistent and convincing than [that] for the severity of punishment" and "the effect of certainty rather than severity of punishment reflects a response to the certainty of apprehension."[26] Nagin conducted a survey of deterrence research with University of Chicago Professor Steven N. Durlauf and summarized their findings: "For the general incarceration of aged criminals to be socially efficient, it must have a deterrent effect on younger criminals . . . Simply no reliable evidence is available that such an effect is sufficiently large to justify the costs of long prison sentences."[27]

Senator Tom Cotton, a Republican, believes the low clearance rate is proof that we need to lock up more people in the United States, despite the painfully obvious fact that we have become the world leader in mass incarceration. In 2016, Cotton stated, "The claim that there are too many criminals being jailed, that there is over-incarceration, ignores an unfortunate fact: for the vast majority of crimes, a perpetrator is neither identified or arrested, let alone prosecuted, convicted, and jailed." He continued: "If anything, we have an under-incarceration problem. The truth is, you cannot decrease the severity and certainty of sentences without increasing crime. It's simply impossible."[28] Senator Cotton offered no evidence to support his claim that it is impossible to reduce sentences without increasing crime; further, he seems to be unaware of the research that has developed with regard to the age-crime curve and human brain development or of the simple, humane idea that people change over time.

Senator Cotton's fellow politician from Arkansas, former president Bill Clinton, had more to do with fueling mass incarceration in the United States than any other person in American history, and he is a Democrat. Along with leading the charge to implement three-strikes laws in the 1990s, Clinton helped perpetuate the racial caste system Michelle Alexander discusses in her book *The New Jim Crow*, in which she examines the racial injustices that exist in the criminal justice system. With regard to Clinton's role in mass incarceration, Alexander pulled no punches:

> In 1992, presidential candidate Bill Clinton vowed that he would never permit any Republican to be perceived as tougher on crime than he. True to his word, just weeks before the critical New Hampshire primary, Clinton chose to fly home to Arkansas to oversee the execution of Ricky Ray Rector, a mentally impaired black man who had so little conception of what was about to happen to him that he asked for the dessert from his last meal to be saved for him until the morning. After the execution, Clinton remarked, "I can be nicked a lot, but no one can say I'm soft on crime." Once elected, Clinton endorsed the idea of a federal "three strikes and you're out" law, which he advocated in his 1994 State of the Union address to enthusiastic applause on both sides of the aisle. The $30 billion crime bill that was sent to President Clinton in August

> 1994 was hailed as a victory for the Democrats, who "were able to wrest the crime issue from the Republicans and make it their own." The bill created dozens of new federal capital crimes, mandated life sentences for some "three-strikers," and authorized more than $16 billion for state prison grants and expansion of state and local police forces.[29]

When Bill Clinton ran for president in 1992, I was a Republican living in Wyoming, but like many swing voters at the time, I was caught up in Clinton's charisma. The idea of a three-strikes penalty seemed reasonable on the surface. Reflecting back to that time, the title of the new law was catchy, and I can understand in hindsight how it had mass appeal. Like many things in life, unfortunately, we did not fully prepare ourselves for the adverse side effects of three-strikes laws: that our prisons would begin to swell with cases like *Ewing v. California* and with individuals like Ben Small.

RACISM AND LIFE

Ben Small is another Wyoming inmate serving life as a result of a "three-strikes" penalty. Small was convicted of involuntary manslaughter in December 1983 and was also found to be a habitual offender, mandating a life sentence. Despite commutation recommendations from the board of parole, after more than forty years, Small remains in prison for involuntary manslaughter. Small's crime took place in an area of Cheyenne near Crow Creek, not far from where Tommy Rivera would commit murder roughly thirteen years later. Small and his cousin William Hairston got stuck in the mud along Crow Creek after leaving a bar in Cheyenne. Small's victim, a man named Eddie Vigil, stopped to render aid to Small and his cousin. The three men's combined efforts proved unsuccessful in getting the car out of the mud, and Vigil offered to give Small and his cousin a ride home.[30]

During the failed attempt to free the car, Vigil and Small began to exchange racial slurs. Vigil and Hairston then began fighting, and Vigil was badly beaten. Hairston retreated from the conflict, and Vigil raised himself off the ground to his hands and knees and attempted to blow blood from his nose and mouth. Vigil then approached Small and another fight ensued, during which Small got on top of Vigil, kicking him in the face and head. The two briefly separated, exchanging more insults, and Small threw Vigil to the ground. Vigil hit his head on the pavement and did not regain consciousness. Small placed Vigil in his vehicle and parked it around the corner. Vigil succumbed to his injuries and was later found dead in his car. The Wyoming Supreme Court noted: "Eddie Vigil died as a result of massive head trauma induced by a blunt object. He was a young chicano male about five feet two inches, weighing 130 pounds. Hairston and Small are black, the latter, six feet two inches tall. It was obvious to both Hairston and Small that Vigil was very drunk."[31]

I have read the Wyoming Supreme Court opinion that affirmed Small's life sentence several times, and I am still unsure about the rationale for including the racial demographics of the parties involved in the crime. Perhaps it was to provide context for the referenced racial slurs. I am also uncertain why Ben Small will likely continue to sit in prison after Brad Skinner has been released, both having received life sentences under Wyoming's three-strikes law. Does it have anything to do with the fact that Small is Black and Skinner is white? This is a legitimate question in this instance, given that the race of the involved parties seemed to be a significant consideration for the Wyoming Supreme Court in evaluating Small's appeal.

Small received two commutations from Governor Sullivan, one in April 1994 that reduced his life sentence to ninety to ninety-five years and another in December 1994 that further cut his sentence to eighty-nine years and eight months to ninety-five years.[32] Small received another time cut from Governor Freudenthal in 2003, reducing his sentence to seventy-one to ninety-five years.[33] Despite other recommendations from the parole board, his sentence remains at a seventy-one-year minimum term, making him parole-eligible in 2037. However, during the Mead era, Brad Skinner, Orland Glenn, and Joe Welch—all white men—received commutations.

Wyoming incarcerates a disproportionate number of people of color compared to the incarceration rates for white people. According to a study published by the Vera Institute of Justice in December 2019, "In Wyoming, black people constituted 2% of state residents, but 11% of people in jail and 5% of people in prison."[34] Using 2010 census data, the Prison Policy Initiative has identified that whites are underrepresented in the Wyoming incarcerated population while Blacks, Latinos, and American Indians are all overrepresented in the prisons and jails.[35] Unfortunately, the overrepresentation of Black Americans in the criminal justice system is well documented. While Black men comprise roughly 13 percent of the male population in the United States, they account for about 35 percent of men in prison.[36] The Vera Institute reported: "One in five black people born in

2001 is likely to be incarcerated in their lifetime, compared to one in 10 latinx people and one in 29 white people."[37]

It is not easy to be a Black man in the Wyoming prison system. The Wyoming parole board has the authority to "flatten" an inmate's sentence, which is a colloquial term for removing all of an inmate's good time, meaning they would have to serve the maximum sentence if not paroled.[38] The parole board can flatten an inmate's sentence for disciplinary violations or failure to engage in programming, usually at the request of the Wyoming Department of Corrections. In a few cases, the parole board has been provided with evidence of inmate assaults where race was a motivating factor. In one flattening case when I was on the parole board, we were shown video evidence of a younger white male sucker-punching an oblivious older Black man while standing in line at the chow hall. The video quality was good, and we could also see the signaling between the assailant and another identified white supremacist gang member prior to the unprovoked attack. It was sickening to watch.

Ben Small has experienced similar incidents. Small's nephew, Jerome Hairston, spoke to me about his uncle's time in prison. "When Ben was younger, not many other inmates would mess with him," Hairston told me. "Now that he is getting older, he's been a target of some of the younger white inmates, and it's harder for him to defend himself."[39] Small has kept track of the times he's been attacked in prison. In a letter he told me "there are some white racist groups that have targeted me 5 times in the past 39 years, they have all been one-on-one conflicts."[40] I have never forgotten Ben Small's case because I believe his punishment has been more than what the average white inmate in Wyoming has to endure. I believe he has been punished for killing Eddie Vigil, and now he's punished for being Black—and not just by other inmates.

The aforementioned concept of "American exceptionalism" is often raised in conversations about criminal justice policy decision-making in the United States. According to Kevin R. Reitz, the author of the revisions to the Model Penal Code, American exceptionalism "comes loaded with several different meanings and a number of historical and comparative claims."[41] Mugambi Jouet has called it "an idea often misunderstood or misrepresented as a faith in American superiority."[42] Former Supreme Court Justice Antonin Scalia was an open advocate of American exceptionalism, declaring in a plurality opinion: "Severe, mandatory penalties may be cruel, but they are not unusual in the constitutional sense, having been employed in various forms throughout our nation's history."[43] In expressing his approval of mass incarceration in the United States during oral arguments on an Eighth Amendment case involving excessive punishment, Scalia said, "Modern penology has abandoned that rehabilitation thing, and they no longer call prisons reformatories . . . Punishment is the criterion now. Deserved punishment for crime."[44]

Reliance on American exceptionalism seems to work for conservatives when they want to justify life sentences, but they will quickly liken the United States to other countries when it comes to the issue of abortion. Lindsey Graham, the senior Republican senator from South Carolina, was confronted by women after he proposed a nationwide ban on abortion in the wake of the Supreme Court overturning *Roe v. Wade*. In response to the angry women, he defended his action as merely trying to bring US abortion laws in line with the rest of the international community: "The world has pretty much spoken on this issue. The developed world has said at this stage of the pregnancy, the child feels pain, and we're saying we're going to join the rest of the world and not be like Iran."[45] It would be nice if Senator Graham and other conservatives would adopt the same attitude when it comes to the retributive focus of the criminal justice system in America and begin advocating for a second look at life sentences to bring us in line with the rest of the developed world.

10

Transformative Education and Recommendations

Growing up in Cody, Wyoming, young Alan Simpson was not the type of person many would expect to end up on federal probation. However, the son of then-Wyoming Governor Milward Simpson and his friends once set "out to do damage" by burning down an abandoned World War II relocation building, thereby committing arson on federal property—a crime punishable by up to twenty years in prison if no one is hurt and life if the fire causes death.[1] Simpson and his friends also engaged in reckless juvenile behavior involving guns, shooting at rocks and attempting to hit them as close as possible to another friend.[2] The boys stole their bullets from the local hardware store. In both cases, someone could have easily been killed.

Simpson and his friends continued to act out with guns. In one incident, Simpson and his cohorts fired their rifles at mailboxes, destroying several while killing a cow.[3] They fired their guns at a road grader, and "just raised hell."[4] When Simpson's criminal behavior eventually caught up with him, he was charged with the federal crime of property destruction and pleaded guilty, receiving two years probation and an order to pay restitution.

https://doi.org/10.5876/9781646428557.c010

Simpson was initially resistant to probation. Rather than get a job, he hustled money at the pool hall and told his probation officer that he was attending "choir practice."[5]

Simpson experienced a moment of personal growth after spending a night in the Laramie jail. Simpson was about to enter a Laramie bar that was popular with African Americans when he met a man leaving the bar. The man claimed to have been in a knife fight inside the bar and began uttering racial slurs.[6] Simpson told the man he was in the wrong bar with his racist attitude, and the man attacked Simpson. Simpson responded by pushing the man down, just as the police arrived on the scene. The police separated the two men and noticed the knife wounds on the other man, which led the officers to arrest Simpson. During the arrest, Simpson punched the officer who was holding him, and the officer responded by hitting Simpson in the head with a billy club. Simpson recalled, "I still carry a lovely little crescent above my eyebrow as a reminder of how stupid one can get."[7]

Simpson described the jail that night as a "sea of puke and urine," but it produced a "creeping maturity" in him, and he vowed to change his ways: "The older you get, the more you realize . . . your own attitude is stupefying, and arrogant, and cocky, and a miserable way to live."[8] Simpson's federal probation officer was a man named J. B. Mosley, and Simpson credits Mosley with helping him rehabilitate himself.[9] Simpson served as Wyoming's US senator from 1978 until 1996, was the Republican whip from 1984 to 1994, and was chair of the Senate Veterans Affairs Committee in addition to holding many other positions in the United States Senate.[10] After choosing not to run again in 1996, Simpson taught and later directed the Institute of Politics at Harvard University's John F. Kennedy School of Government. He remains a symbol of equality and courage.[11] Simpson passed away peacefully in March 2025 at age ninety-three.[12]

EDUCATION TRANSFORMING LIVES

For Simpson, his probation officer was a catalyst for change. For many other offenders, education can be the key to transformation. The data demonstrate that education is the single most effective program at reducing recidivism.[13] Research shows that if inmates take some college classes, they are 43 percent less likely to recidivate; that number if 85 percent for those who earn an associate's degree and 95 percent if they earn a bachelor's degree.[14] At one point, it was relatively common for an inmate to obtain a college degree in prison, at least until Bill Clinton's presidency. In attempting to court the elusive swing voter, Clinton not only sought to prove that he was as tough on crime as any Republican, but he also put an end to higher education in US prisons as part of his attack on social welfare.[15] Michelle Alexander observed that Clinton—"more than any other president—created the current racial undercaste."[16] Clinton "ended welfare as we know it" by making felony drug offenders ineligible for services and redirecting that federal funding—which previously supported welfare assistance and public housing—toward prison construction.[17] Clinton also put an end to inmates receiving aid under the federal Pell Grant program, effectively killing college programs in US prisons.[18]

Before Clinton's presidency, hundreds of colleges and universities offered college degrees to inmates. However, as part of the Violent Crime Control and Law Enforcement Act of 1994, inmates became ineligible to receive Pell Grants, and the number of schools that offered degrees to inmates dwindled to only nine or ten colleges.[19] President Barack Obama sought to make the funds available to inmates again, authorizing partial eligibility under the Second Chance Pell experiment, which provided grants to 70 schools to begin offering classes and degrees to prisoners.[20] That number was increased to 200 institutions in 2022–2023, and the University of Wyoming (UW) is one of the universities that has benefited from the Second Chance Pell experiment, creating a new four-year degree program for inmates in 2022.[21]

Northwestern University's Prison Education Program has become a beacon for other programs to follow. The program started in 2018 as a pilot, supported by a $1 million grant from the Andrew W. Mellon Foundation.[22] The Northwestern program began with men at Statesville Prison and has since expanded to the women's prison in Logan, Illinois.[23] Washington University in St. Louis has also created a Prison Education Project, which recently conferred fourteen associate and four bachelor's degrees to inmates at the Missouri Eastern Correctional Center.[24] In the spring of 2022, Georgetown University launched a bachelor's degree program for inmates as part of its Prisons and Justice Initiative.[25] Hamline University in Minnesota has taken higher education in prison to the next level, as the School of Law has admitted Maureen Onyelobi, an inmate in the Minnesota prison system—making Hamline the first American Bar Association–accredited law school in the country to offer a legal education to a currently incarcerated individual.[26] Other universities and colleges around the nation, too numerous to mention, are creating prison education programs again now that the Second Chance Pell experiment is infusing them with optimism and cash.

INMATES AS TEACHERS AND ROLE MODELS

At UW, I have been fortunate to assist with the creation of a bachelor's degree program for inmates. The program is called Pathways from Prison, and it offers a general studies degree, hoping to provide a broad education while allowing students to gear their studies toward a certain discipline if they desire. Like Northwestern, UW piloted its program at one institution, the women's prison, beginning with an initial cohort of twenty women in the fall of 2022. Both Darla Rouse and Amy Doerr were enrolled in that first class, and Rouse has transitioned to parole while she is pursuing her degree. In Doerr's case, unless she receives a commutation in the next four years, she will likely finish her degree as an inmate. In the fall of 2023, the program was expanded to a cohort of twenty men. Through recent grant funding, a full-time staff person has been hired to manage day-to-day operations.[27]

While these developments in prison education are encouraging, it is important to recognize that very few inmates are actually benefiting from these programs at this point. Graduation classes are small, the programs have just begun, and only a few inmates are enrolled. The reality is that many of the best teachers are the inmates themselves, as Tommy Rivera can attest. Many staff members helped Rivera during his incarceration, but he learned the most valuable skills and lessons from other inmates, two in particular: Francisco Sanchez and Martin Gabriel, both of whom are also serving life for murder.

Francisco "Pancho" Sanchez was convicted of second-degree murder and aggravated assault in 1999, when he was nineteen.[28] According to the Wyoming Department of Corrections (WDOC), he is not a big man, standing 5'4" and weighing 120 pounds.[29] The facts from his Wyoming Supreme Court opinion recount that around midnight on June 24, 1999, Sanchez and a friend became involved in a conflict with four other young men that involved an ex-girlfriend of one of the other men.[30] "Some arguing occurred, and Sanchez reached behind his back and pulled out a club," the opinion stated.[31] Sanchez ended up striking his victim in the left temple, causing him to stumble and fall. The victim's friends picked him up and carried him to a nearby house. The victim later objected to being taken to the hospital and asked to be taken home, where he went "straight to bed."[32] Unfortunately, the victim later died from the injury.[33] Similar to Ben Small's case, the facts are clear that Sanchez did not intend to kill his victim, yet he received a life sentence.

When the *Miller v. Alabama* decision was announced, Tommy Rivera knew he might not be in prison much longer. He tried to obtain as many skills as he could before he became eligible for parole. Rivera had befriended Francisco Sanchez and had watched him study and practice art on a daily basis. Rivera recalls, "My friend Pancho was one of the best artists I have ever seen in the Wyoming State Penitentiary. I admired his skill, but I never felt that I had the same ability. Once I knew that I was getting out, I asked him to teach me."[34] Rivera explained that Sanchez spent months teaching him the basics of drawing—first with a pencil, and then later advanced techniques using graphite and pastel (figure 10.1). Now that he is on parole, Rivera has parlayed what Sanchez taught him into an apprenticeship at a respected tattoo studio.

Rivera also credits Martin Gabriel with instilling a pro-social attitude in him while he was incarcerated. Gabriel was convicted of first-degree murder and two counts of attempted second-degree murder in 1996. He shot and killed a man in a jealous rage and also tried to murder his wife. At the time of the incident, Gabriel and his wife had separated when he found her in the company of another man. Gabriel first challenged the other man to a fight. When the man refused, he left the apartment and returned with a pistol, which he used to shoot and kill the man before attempting to shoot his wife.[35] Gabriel's crime is undoubtedly serious, and he deserves a lengthy prison sentence. According to Rivera, however, the Martin Gabriel he knew is nothing like the jealous killer described in the criminal appeal.

"With Gabe, it didn't matter if you were his friend or just a random person, he cared about people in general," Rivera said. Rivera described Gabriel's "epiphany" after being thrown into solitary confinement for disciplinary violations. "Gabe was able to have a phone call with his dad while he was in the 'hole.' Gabe asked his dad for fifty dollars for commissary, and Gabe's dad replied: 'Son, when are you gonna stop destroying your community?' " As Rivera tells the story, it took Gabriel some time to process what his father had said. Gabriel had never looked at the prison as a community, but that question from his father "planted a seed" in Gabriel that would "grow into something unbelievably huge." Martin Gabriel developed

FIGURE 10.1. Tommy Rivera drawing of an angel. Image provided to author by Tommy Rivera.

the concept of a community in prison into the Community Minded Workshop, a prison rehabilitation program that "focuses on life-changing principles such as responsibility, integrity, communication, and empathy."[36] Rivera was fortunate enough to assist Gabriel in developing the Community Minded Workshop. Since 2005, the program has been approved by and sanctioned to be offered throughout the WDOC.

Both Francisco Sanchez and Martin Gabriel have talents they could be sharing with the community. The reality is that neither man may ever leave prison, at least not in the current political climate. I believe strongly that they should both get out of prison someday soon, and I realize that a percentage of people will disagree with my view. As I have stated repeatedly, I am done seeking a pound of flesh and am promoting alternatives to retribution. Retribution has its place and always will, but there is time for redemption and rebirth of the self. I conclude with recommendations and examples specific to the issue of life sentences in the United States, with one recommendation in particular.

RECOMMENDATIONS FOR LIFE SENTENCES IN AMERICA

1. Institute a twenty-year review for all sentences with stakeholder involvement that removes the executive official

Mark Mauer and Ashley Nellis present some alarming life sentence data in a recent book. They determined that "a comprehensive 2016 international analysis of life imprisonment found that the number of people serving life imprisonment in the United States is higher than the combined totals in the other 113 countries surveyed."[37] That statistic is both distressing and disgraceful. Mauer and Nellis argue that prison sentences should be capped at twenty years, and I agree that twenty years is an excellent starting point.[38] I also believe, based on my personal experience, that some inmates are not ready for release after twenty years and a small percentage of inmates will continue to pose a threat to society. However, the vast majority of inmates are like the individuals I have profiled—rehabilitated and ready for release—which is why I recommend a review at twenty years rather than a cap on sentence length.

In terms of structure and operation, I suggest that each state create a review board that would consider inmate petitions for re-sentencing after twenty years. Inmates would have the right to petition for a sentence reduction, which would operate similar to commutation. Requiring inmates to file a petition would not only provide access to a mechanism by which their sentence could potentially be reduced but would also put the initial burden of raising the issue on the inmate rather than adding more duties to the already overworked criminal justice system.

I also have faith that some prosecutors might avail themselves of the option to petition the court for re-sentencing in cases of manifest injustice, such as instances of wrongful convictions. Accordingly, I would add a feature by which prosecutors could seek a sentence reduction from the review board at any time prior to the twenty-year review period. As an example, in 2018, California passed Assembly Bill 2942, which allows district attorneys to reevaluate old cases and request re-sentencing.[39] In commenting on this newfound power of California prosecutors, attorney Roxann Matthews wrote that "prosecutors need to courageously embrace their increased power to rectify excessive sentences that do nothing to promote public safety, waste taxpayer money, exacerbate racial disparities, separate families, and deprive communities of those who would otherwise be productive, law-abiding members."[40] Along with prosecutors, the California law instructs re-sentencing courts to weigh "postconviction factors, including but not limited to, the inmate's disciplinary record and record of rehabilitation while incarcerated, evidence that reflects whether age, time served, and diminished physical condition, if any, have reduced the inmate's risk for future violence, and evidence that reflects that circumstances have changed since the inmate's original sentencing so that inmate's continued incarceration is no longer in the interest of justice."[41]

With the California model, the sentencing court would retain jurisdiction to reduce the sentence. Rather than rely on the sentencing court, though, I am proposing that the review board would have the legal power to hear and grant sentence reduction petitions that can be filed by either the prosecutor or the inmate. The review board would be required to obtain input on re-sentencing from the prosecutor, sentencing judge, and victim. In terms of victim involvement, I would also include a legislative mandate that a restorative justice program be created to supplement the review board, which could be managed by a victim advocate, just as Randi Losalu ran the victim-offender dialogue program described in chapter 8.

While the creation of such a review board would require funding, a drastic reduction in life sentences would eventually fund the restorative justice component of my proposed re-sentencing board. Second look laws have the potential to reduce the "anchor point," a term used by the Model Penal Code to describe a mechanism that places upward pressure on the entire US system of sentencing, which in turn can lead to wide-scale prison population reductions.[42] While not necessary, I would also offer that existing US parole boards could be suitably inserted into the role I have envisioned for the proposed sentence review board.

The American Law Institute (ALI), author of the Model Penal Code, has recommended the creation of "second look" sentence modification mechanisms, finding it "imperative whenever a legal system deprives offenders of their liberty for a substantial portion of their lives."[43] Kevin Reitz, the primary architect of the ALI's recent revisions to the Model Penal Code, has recommended against vesting this re-sentencing power with parole boards, claiming that "states with the highest standing incarceration rates in the early twenty-first century are nearly all indeterminate-sentencing jurisdictions."[44] While Reitz's claim may be true, I believe he overlooked a critical fact: The governor, not the parole board, makes the ultimate decision when it comes to commutations for inmates serving life sentences.

Typically, the most parole boards can do is make recommendations regarding life sentences to the governor, and, as I witnessed in Wyoming, governors are often no longer willing to risk their political image by appearing to be soft on crime. If this power were taken away from governors, I believe parole boards would grant many more sentence reductions than some might expect. The comments to the ALI recommendations "acknowledge that many states will be tempted to place existing parole boards in charge of the sentence-modification process, but recommend that states exercise caution in bestowing this responsibility because of parole boards' susceptibility to political influences."[45] This is a valid point, but I would argue that a parole board is far less susceptible to political influence than a governor is.

While a parole board might make sense in creating a sentencing review entity, that entity does not need to be a parole board, although such a panel should involve the sentencing judge and prosecutor in some fashion. Restorative justice options should also be made available to the victims in cases where the review panel considers a reduction in sentence and possible release of the inmate. Perhaps the most important feature of this proposal is that the board's decision would be final and unalterable by the governor. Another important aspect of this panel would be that each member would have an equal vote, and while the court's and prosecutor's inputs are crucial, those officials would not have the power to veto a decision of the panel. It is hoped that some governors would welcome this proposal, as they would no longer be required to confront the politics involved in making these decisions. Several more recommendations follow, all subsidiary to the first.

2. Restore voting rights and jury service, and end other collateral consequences

This proposal would apply to all former felons, not just those released from a life sentence, as the time has come to abandon the uniquely American practice of stripping convicted felons of their basic rights of citizenship. This would include restoring the right to vote, serve on a jury, and receive social welfare benefits. Granted, there have been advancements in these areas, but more needs to be done.[46] In chapter 8, I referenced Mitch McConnell's remark that felons have violated the social contract and therefore should not be permitted to vote.[47] I prefer the approach Justice Anthony Kennedy voiced to the American Bar Association: "To be sure the prisoner has violated the social contract; to be sure he must be punished to vindicate the law, to acknowledge the suffering of the victim, and to deter future crimes. Still, the prisoner is a person; still, he or she is part of the family of humankind."[48]

There are many ways to approach the restoration of these civil liberties and end the needless practice of imposing a lifetime of collateral consequences upon former felons. As a guiding rule, I believe that anyone who is lawfully working a job, paying taxes, and otherwise living a pro-social and crime-free life should be permitted access to the vote, jury box, and social welfare programs.

3. Reduce obstacles to employment for felons

An abundance of research has proven that similar to education, employment decreases the odds of recidivism, which leads to safer communities.[49] An estimated 70 million people in the United States have criminal records, which can often make it difficult to get a job.[50] A movement is afoot to ease the barriers to employment that felons face. Since 2018, 7 states have enacted "clean slate" laws, which wipe away certain criminal convictions after a period of time; 37 states and more than 150 cities have adopted Ban the Box laws, which eliminate the criminal history question from many job applications.[51] While this book is not the place to discuss these approaches in depth, these efforts need to be sustained and expanded.

4. Provide media education and build coalitions that support reforms

In 2024, the Sentencing Project published a list of crime coverage "dos and don'ts," which is a useful tool in seeking to educate the media on how to responsibly report on crime.[52] The document features ten recommendations, and I will focus on a few that are relevant to examples I used earlier. The first recommendation is to situate crime stories and proposed solutions within their broader historical and geographic context. This proposal references the spike in violent crime in 2020 and the relative lack of historical context the media and politicians have offered in their coverage. Another recommendation is to avoid amplifying false or unsupported claims by police, prosecutors, and legislators—examples of which I have provided. This suggestion also advises the media to be cognizant of the fact that longer prison terms for violent crimes are a major factor in mass incarceration but to be equally aware that long sentences have proven ineffective in a number of aspects, including the lack of a deterrent effect and the fact that people age out of crime, making them a low risk for recidivism if released.[53]

Relatively few groups are advocating for criminal justice reform, whereas very powerful organizations are effectively lobbying for "tough on crime" laws.[54] Rachel E. Barkow observed that "the communities hit hardest by mass incarceration also suffer from organizational shortcomings."[55] However, more groups are springing up that seek justice and reform in the criminal justice system, including conservative groups like Right on Crime, which shares the same goal as the liberal ACLU: reducing mass incarceration.[56]

5. Place limits on executive clemency or abolish altogether, and concluding thoughts

This recommendation is the least important and is likely to have only a minimal impact. Beyond that, it is incredibly difficult to amend the United States Constitution. Doing so requires supermajorities in each chamber of the United States Congress and then ratification by three quarters of state legislatures. However, as history has proven, the power of executive clemency can be abused. Stripping presidents of this power would be consistent with our Founding Fathers' desire to reject a monarchy, and it would also relieve presidents of the political pressure that accompanies clemency decisions. The power of clemency has also been abused at the state level, and if the power of executive clemency were abolished at the presidential level, many states would likely follow suit, for the same reasons.

In terms of the morality of imposing life sentences, we know that the rest of the international community rarely employs them, at least not at the US rate. What we need in the United States is a shift in the way we view prisons; rather than rely on them for a lifetime of retribution, we should view them as places of rehabilitation and education. Mugambi Jouet compared this shift to an earthquake: "My theory evokes a seismograph that regularly swings up or down while moving steadily in a particular fashion. American justice may cyclically oscillate between repressive or humanitarian aspirations and simultaneously converge with other Western democracies in gradually limiting or abolishing the harshest punishments over the long term. On a seismograph, a terrible earthquake may occur. This may be one way to perceive mass incarceration—an intense social shock but not the permanent essence of American punishment."[57]

Back in the 1970s and 1980s, the "tough on crime" and "war on drugs" movements were earthquakes that pushed the needle toward long sentences. It will take a sustained and persistent effort to move the needle in the other direction. Even if the proposals offered here were adopted wholesale by the federal government and all fifty states, crime would persist. As Jouet sagely observed: "In any event, neither of these potential scenarios signifies that utopia awaits. Social injustices abound in modern Europe, despite the absence of mass incarceration, life without parole, and executions."[58] That is true, yet that region incarcerates far fewer people than the US does. It was not always that way in the United States, and things can change.

The change can start in Wyoming, where the constitution states that "the penal code shall be framed on the humane principles of reformation and prevention."[59] Nowhere does the Wyoming Constitution offer retribution as a principle of punishment, which is not the case in other states. For example, while California recently enacted the progressive re-sentencing law discussed earlier, it also adopted a retributive approach to crime decades ago in passing the 1976 Uniform Determinate Sentencing Act. By "emphasizing mandatory penalties and stiff prison sentences," California's overall focus on punishment overshadows that of rehabilitation.[60] The Wyoming Constitution, in contrast, stresses reformation first and prevention second. I challenge the state to live up to the stated goals of its founders and adopt a second look law for life sentences, based on the recent California re-sentencing law. More changes can come later, but I suggest we start by taking a chance on a second look.

Action and Change

Judgment is without mercy to the one who has not shown mercy.
Mercy triumphs over judgment.
–JAMES 2:13

The idea that the US imprisonment rate could take decades to reduce was captured by Keith Humphreys in an article for *The Atlantic* in 2025. "That's why the 2009 peak of US imprisonment came 18 years after the 1991 peak in the violent-crime rate," Humphreys wrote. "The prison system is like a badly overloaded tractor trailer—it takes a long time to stop even after the brakes are hit. That tractor trailer is finally slowing down, decades after the 'great crime decline' began in the 1990s."[1]

Scholars who have studied the great crime decline have concluded that increased incarceration contributed only modestly to the drop. Experts for the National Research Council concluded that "the increase in incarceration may have caused a decrease in crime, but the magnitude of the reduction is highly uncertain and the results of most studies suggest it was unlikely to have been large."[2]

As I was writing this book, I gave a presentation on some of the research and recommendations to another professor's class at the University of Wyoming. When it came to my recommendations, one student asked why

https://doi.org/10.5876/9781646428557.c011

I thought the highly conservative Wyoming State Legislature would ever adopt my proposal to reduce the number of life sentences. My answer at the time was based on an appeal to the Judeo-Christian values of forgiveness and mercy. However, that answer, while persuasive, is too obvious. I also know that the Wyoming State Legislature is more receptive to criminal justice reform than many would think, and I can point to recent examples.

One example is a 2023 Wyoming bill that was sponsored by state senator Eric Barlow, which became law and restores the civil rights to serve on a jury, hold public office, and possess a firearm to nonviolent former felons.[3] "Talk about a cruel and unusual punishment, i.e., losing your rights forever," said Barlow during a floor speech.[4] While that example may be a small step, it is recent progress.

Another example is how quickly the Wyoming State Legislature passed a law in response to the *Miller v. Alabama* decision.[5] That opinion was issued in 2012, and only one year later, the Wyoming State Legislature acted swiftly and smartly by passing statutory amendments providing that juveniles serving life sentences, such as Tommy Rivera, would become parole-eligible after twenty-five years.[6] Wyoming was an example for other states in taking the lead on post-*Miller* legislation. In late 2013, I was contacted by reporters from the *Boston Globe*, who had heard that Wyoming had passed a progressive new law dealing with the mandates outlined by the United States Supreme Court in the *Miller v. Alabama* decision.[7] The reporters wanted to know about our new law, as the Massachusetts legislature was trying to devise its own methods of implementing the decision. At the time, I recall feeling a sense of pride in my home state of Wyoming, in that it was on the cutting edge of a significant shift in the way the US would approach juvenile sentencing for violent crimes.

The Wyoming State Legislature can remain at the vanguard of innovations in the criminal justice system. Just as the State of Massachusetts looked to Wyoming for guidance in the early years following *Miller v. Alabama*, the Massachusetts Supreme Judicial Court has issued a landmark opinion in *Commonwealth v. Mattis* that can serve as a blueprint for Wyoming.[8] In *Mattis*, the Massachusetts high court ruled that individuals ages eighteen through twenty—"emerging adults"—cannot be sentenced to life in prison without the possibility of parole. This decision, based on the Massachusetts Constitution's prohibition against cruel or unusual punishment, effectively extends the protections previously afforded to juveniles to this age group. Different versions of second look laws are at varying stages of the legislative process across the country, and by the time this book is published, it is hoped that there will be other examples to examine and learn from.

A final and convincing reason for reducing the number of life sentences in Wyoming is the money and resources: The state doesn't have enough. The state had to send 240 inmates to a private prison in Mississippi in November 2023, after the Wyoming Department of Corrections (WDOC) announced a 25 percent staff vacancy rate, resulting in a lack of personnel to fully operate the prisons.[9] Two of those individuals moved to Mississippi were James Koester and Pancho Sanchez, who could be out of prison and saving the state millions of dollars over the coming years. "I want these people home as soon as possible," WDOC Director Dan Shannon said. He continued, "Keeping them away from home with no home visits and limited family interaction—they do have access to video conferences and things like that—it does have a negative impact on the rehabilitative mindset."[10] In response to the move of inmates out of state, State Senator Cale Case offered: "I prefer we really drill down on criminal justice reform. I think we have too many people locked up, too many things that are crimes."[11]

To be clear, I'm not an advocate of prison abolition. I don't believe prosecutors should enjoy absolute immunity. I still believe the vast majority of prosecutors have noble intentions, as do most law enforcement professionals. However, I believe strongly that we are currently abusing life sentences in the United States, and the abuse can be stopped. A recent high-profile example of California's second look law occurred in May 2025, when the Menendez brothers were re-sentenced. Lyle and Erik Menendez were originally sentenced to life without the possibility of parole for the 1989 murders of their parents. A Los Angeles judge re-sentenced them to fifty years to life under the new second look law, making them eligible for parole after serving more than thirty-four years—over the objections of the district attorney.[12]

In a sign that the California second chance law is not a "get out of jail free card," both Menendez brothers were denied release at their initial parole hearings in August 2025 as a result of "years of rule-breaking while behind bars."[13] The denial has a silver lining, however, as the California board based the decision on the disciplinary violations and not the seriousness of the underlying crimes. Both brothers will be eligible to see the board again in three years.[14]

Now that we are moving through the Covid era, the US prison population shows signs of inching up again, but Humphreys believes we can continue the "de-prisoning of America," to levels not seen in fifty years. Humphreys suggests that one way to accelerate decarceration is for the United States to "not let its prison system become the most expensive and inhumane of nursing homes. The rate of recidivism among senior citizens is near zero, and compassionate release of sick and aging inmates should be the default rather than the exception, a reversal of current practice."[15]

Despite the evidence that people age out of crime, particularly juvenile offenders, the Republican-controlled United States Congress is attempting to undo the remarkably successful second look law adopted by the District of Columbia, the Incarceration Reduction Amendment Act (IRAA).[16] The IRAA permits individuals who committed crimes before age twenty-five to petition for a sentence reduction after serving at least fifteen years in prison. The IRAA has had a remarkable 97 percent success rate, with less than 3 percent recidivating. In September 2025, Congress introduced the Strong Sentences for Safer DC Streets Act, which will eliminate the DC second look law if passed.[17] On his website, Lindsey Graham touted the Senate version of the bill: "Repealing these foolish, soft-on-crime laws is an important step in Making DC Safe Again. Our work on this legislation would ensure that violent criminals are not set free early solely based on age. This reckless practice needs to end now."[18] With crime rates at historic lows, politicians unfortunately continue to deal in fear-mongering, despite powerful evidence that individuals sentenced to long periods of incarceration rarely re-offend if released.

When I began writing this book in 2021, Darla Rouse, Mark Farnham, and Tommy Rivera were in prison. Since that time, they have all been released and are thriving in their respective Wyoming communities. Each of them has a drive to give back to the community. Their passion has inspired me, and I know their stories will inspire others. They are living proof that second chances work, and we can all use a second chance at some point in life.

Notes

INTRODUCTION: FRAMING THE ISSUE

1. Ashley Nellis, "No End in Sight: America's Enduring Reliance on Life Imprisonment," *Sentencing Project*, February 2021, 19, https://www.sentencingproject.org/wp-content/uploads/2021/02/No-End-in-Sight-Americas-Enduring-Reliance-on-Life-Imprisonment.pdf.
2. Marieke Liem and Nicholas J. Richardson, "The Role of Transformation Narratives in Desistance Among Released Lifers," *Criminal Justice and Behavior* 41, no. 6 (February 2014): 694, https://journals.sagepub.com/doi/10.1177/0093854813515445.
3. Nellis, "No End in Sight," 15–18.

CHAPTER 1: DEALING WITH LIFE

1. *Rouse v. State*, 966 P.2d 967, 969 (Wyo. 1998).
2. *Rouse*, 966 P.2d at 969.
3. *Rouse*, 966 P.2d at 969.
4. *Rouse*, 966 P.2d at 969.
5. *Rouse*, 966 P.2d at 969.
6. *Rouse*, 966 P.2d at 969.
7. *Rouse*, 966 P.2d at 969.

8. *Rouse*, 966 P.2d at 969.
9. Jennifer Kocher, "Gordon Commutes Sentence of Woman Convicted in 1996 Kidnapping," *Cowboy State Daily* (Cheyenne, WY), December 23, 2021, https://cowboystatedaily.com/2021/12/23/gordon-commutes-sentence-of-woman-convicted-in-1996-kidnapping/.
10. Kocher, "Gordon Commutes Sentence."
11. Kocher, "Gordon Commutes Sentence."
12. *Rouse*, 966 P.2d at 969.
13. Kocher, "Gordon Commutes Sentence."
14. *Rouse*, 966 P.2d at 972.
15. Attorney General's Office, memo to Governor Freudenthal, 2009, on file with author.
16. Kocher, "Gordon Commutes Sentence."
17. Kocher, "Gordon Commutes Sentence."
18. Kocher, "Gordon Commutes Sentence."
19. Kocher, "Gordon Commutes Sentence."
20. "Wyoming Offender Locator," Wyoming Department of Corrections, State of Wyoming, 2023, http://wdoc-loc.wyo.gov/Home/Detail/?id=874&dbType=WCIS.
21. Wyo. Stat. §7-18-109 (b) (2022).
22. Meda Chesney-Lind, "Girls' Crime and Woman's Place: Toward a Feminist Model of Female Delinquency," *Crime and Delinquency* 35, no. 1 (January 1989), https://doi.org/10.1177/0011128789035001002.
23. Emily J. Salisbury and Patricia Van Voorhis, "Gendered Pathways: A Quantitive Investigation of Women Probationers' Paths to Incarceration," *Criminal Justice and Behavior* 36, no. 6 (May 2009), https://doi.org/10.1177/0093854809334076.
24. Tim Brennan, Markus Breitenbach, William Dieterich, Emily J. Salisbury, and Patricia van Voorhis, "Women's Pathways to Serious and Habitual Crime: A Person-Centered Analysis Incorporating Gender Responsive Factors," *Criminal Justice and Behavior* 39, no. 11 (October 2012), https://doi.org/10.1177/0093854812456777.
25. Kathleen Daly, "Women's Pathways to Felony Court: Feminist Theories of Lawbreaking and Problems of Representation," *Southern California Review of Law and Women's Studies* 2, no. 1 (January 1992): 27–28, https://www.researchgate.net/publication/284292910_Women%27s_pathways_to_felony_court_Feminist_theories_of_lawbreaking_and_problems_of_representation.
26. Becki Ney, "10 Facts About Women in Jails," *American Jails* 27, no. 6 (January 2014): 8, 9, https://www.libproxy.uwyo.edu/login?url=https://www.proquest.com/trade-journals/10-facts-about-women-jails/docview/1545082771/se-2.
27. Joanne Belknap, *The Invisible Woman: Gender, Crime, and Justice* (Belmont, CA: Wadsworth, 1996), 69–70.
28. Belknap, *Invisible Woman*, 81.
29. Belknap, *Invisible Woman*, 81.
30. "Wyoming Offender Locator."
31. Benjamin N. Cardozo School of Law, *Reevaluating Lineups: Why Witnesses Make Mistakes and How to Reduce the Chances of a Misidentification: An Innocence Project Report* (New York: Innocence Project Inc., 2009), 6, https://www.innocenceproject.org/wp-content/uploads/2016/05/eyewitness_id_report-5.pdf.

32. Daniel S. Nagin and Kenneth C. Land, "Age, Criminal Careers, and Population Heterogeneity: Specification and Estimation of a Nonparametric, Mixed Poisson Model," *Criminology* 31, no. 3 (August 1993): 330–331, https://doi.org/10.1111/j.1745-9125.1993.tb01133.x.
33. Travis Hirschi and Michael R. Gottfredson, "Age and the Explanation of Crime," *American Journal of Sociology* 89, no. 3 (1983): 564, https://troublesofyouth.pbworks.com/f/age+and+the+explanation+of+crime+-+Hirschi+and+Gott.pdf.
34. Hirschi and Gottfredson, "Age and the Explanation of Crime," 554.
35. James Tuttle, "The Age-Crime Curve Is Dead, Long Live the Age-Crime Curve! An Examination of the FBI's 2024 Arrest Data," *Journal of Crime and Justice* (2025): 1–12, doi: 10.1080/0735648X.2025.2571411.
36. *Roper v. Simmons*, 543 U.S. 551, 578 (2005).
37. *Graham v. Florida*, 130 S. Ct. 2011, 2026–2027 (2010).
38. *Miller v. Alabama*, 132 S. Ct. 2455, 2464 (2012).
39. *Miller*, 132 S. Ct. at 2465.
40. *Graham*, 130 S. Ct. at 2026; *Roper*, 543 U.S. at 569; *Miller*, 132 S. Ct. at 2465.
41. *Roper*, 543 U.S. at 569; *Graham*, 130 S. Ct. at 2026; *Miller*, 132 S. Ct. at 2454.
42. *Roper*, 543 U.S. at 570.
43. Aaron White, "Substance Abuse and Adolescent Brain Development: An Overview of Recent Findings with a Focus on Alcohol," Address presented to the New York Academy of Sciences, New York City, NY, 2003.
44. Aaron White, "Substance Abuse and Adolescent Brain Development: An Overview of Recent Findings with a Focus on Alcohol," *Youth Studies Australia* 22, no. 1 (March 2003): 39, https://www.ojp.gov/ncjrs/virtual-library/abstracts/substance-use-adolescent-brain-development-overview-recent-findings.
45. Lee Ellis, "Genes, Criminality, and the Evolutionary Neuroandrogenic Theory," in *Biosocial Criminology: Challenging Environmentalism's Supremacy*, edited by Anthony Walsh and Lee Ellis (Hauppauge, NY: Nova Science Publishers, 2003), 13–34.
46. Raymond E. Collins, "Onset and Desistance in Criminal Careers: Neurobiology and the Age-Crime Relationship," *Journal of Offender Rehabilitation* 39, no. 3 (2004), https://psycnet.apa.org/record/2004-21662-001; Elaine Walker, "Adolescent Neurodevelopment and Psychopathology," *Current Directions in Psychological Science* 11, no. 1 (2002), https://journals.sagepub.com/doi/10.1111/1467-8721.00161.
47. Laurence Steinberg, "Adolescent Brain Science and Juvenile Justice Policymaking," *Psychology, Public Policy, and Law* 23, no. 4 (2017): 414, https://psycnet.apa.org/record/2017-15237-001.
48. Daniel Blonigen, "Explaining the Relationship Between Age and Crime: Contributions from the Developmental Literature on Personality," *Clinical Psychology Review* 30, no. 1 (2010): 89–100, https://pubmed.ncbi.nlm.nih.gov/19892450/.
49. Avshalom Caspi and Terrie E. Moffitt, "The Continuity of Maladaptive Behavior: From Description to Understanding in the Study of Antisocial Behavior," in *Developmental Psychopathology*, edited by Dante Cicchetti and Donald Cohen (Hoboken, NJ: John Wiley and Sons, 1995), https://psycnet.apa.org/record/1995-97697-013.

50. Terrie E. Moffitt, "Adolescence-Limited and Life-Course–Persistent Antisocial Behavior: A Developmental Taxonomy," *Psychological Review* 100, no. 4 (1993), https://psycnet.apa.org/doiLanding?doi=10.1037%2F0033-295X.100.4.674.
51. Moffitt, "Adolescence-Limited and Life-Course-Persistent Antisocial Behavior," 674–701.
52. Terrie E. Moffitt and Anthony Walsh, "The Adolescence-Limited/Life Course–Persistent Theory of Antisocial Behavior: What Have We Learned?" in *Biosocial Criminology: Challenging Environmentalism's Supremacy*, edited by Anthony Walsh and Lee Ellis (Hauppauge, NY: Nova Science Publishers, 2003).
53. Mary Stohr, Anthony Walsh, and Craig Hemmens, *Corrections: A Text/Reader*, 3rd ed. (Los Angeles: Sage, 2018), 486.
54. Stohr et al., *Corrections*, 486.
55. Stohr et al., *Corrections*, 486.
56. Darla Rouse, "Hard Won Lessons," *Wagadu: A Journal of Transnational Women's and Gender Studies* 17, no. 1 (2017): 111–124, https://digitalcommons.cortland.edu/wagadu/vol17/iss1/11.
57. Rouse, "Hard Won Lessons," 123.
58. Rouse, "Hard Won Lessons," 113.
59. Rouse, "Hard Won Lessons," 112.
60. Rouse, "Hard Won Lessons," 124.
61. Darla Rouse, letter to author, August 13, 2022.
62. Rouse, letter to author.
63. Jennifer Kocher, "Wyoming Inmate Convicted in Kidnapping Eligible for Parole in 2025," *Cowboy State Daily* (Cheyenne, WY), January 3, 2022, https://cowboystatedaily.com/2022/01/03/wyoming-woman-convicted-in-kidnapping-eligible-for-parole-in-2025/.
64. Rouse, letter to author.
65. Rouse, letter to author.
66. Rouse, letter to author.

CHAPTER 2: THE MISUNDERSTOOD POWER OF EXECUTIVE CLEMENCY

1. Jeffrey P. Crouch, *The Presidential Pardon Power* (Lawrence: University Press of Kansas, 2009), 10–11.
2. Crouch, *Presidential Pardon Power*, 10–11.
3. Crouch, *Presidential Pardon Power*, 10–11.
4. "The President's Conditional Pardon Power," *Harvard Law Review* 134, no. 8 (2021): 2836.
5. *United States v. Wilson*, 32 U.S. 150, 160 (1833).
6. Paul J. Larkin Jr., "Clemency, Parole, Good-Time Credits, and Crowded Prisons: Reconsidering Early Release," *Georgetown Journal of Law and Public Policy* 11, no. 1 (2013): 5–6, https://papers.ssrn.com/sol3/papers.cfm?abstract_id=2302930.
7. US Const. art. II, §2, cl. 1 (2022).
8. Wyo. Const. art. IV, §5 (2022).
9. Colleen Long and Zeke Miller, "Biden Pardons, Fauci, Milley and the Jan. 6 Panel: It's a Guard Against Potential 'Revenge' by Trump," *Associated Press*, January 20, 2025, https://www.yahoo.com/news/biden-pardons-fauci-milley-effort-121317946.html.

10. Long and Miller, "Biden Pardons."
11. Wyo. Stat. Ann. §6-10-301(c) (2022).
12. *Schick v. Reed*, 419 U.S. 256 (1974).
13. Paul J. Larkin Jr., "Guiding Presidential Clemency Decision Making," *Georgetown Journal of Law and Public Policy* 18, no. 2 (Summer 2020): 466, https://www.law.georgetown.edu/public-policy-journal/wp-content/uploads/sites/23/2020/10/Guiding-Presidential-clemency-18-2.pdf.
14. David Caner, "Clemency, a Neglected Aspect of Early Christian Philanthropy," *Religions* 9, no. 8 (2018): 1, https://www.mdpi.com/2077-1444/9/8/229.
15. "Power of Clemency Taken from the Crown," *Washington Post*, January 14, 1914, 6.
16. Paul J. Larkin Jr., "The Lost Due Process Doctrines," *Catholic University Law Review* 66, no. 2 (2017): 327–332, https://scholarship.law.edu/lawreview/vol66/iss2/7.
17. US Const. art. I, §7, cl. 2.
18. US Const. art. II, §2, cl. 1.
19. US Const. art. II, §2, cl. 2.
20. US Const. art. II, §3.
21. Larkin, "Guiding Presidential Clemency," 453–454.
22. Larkin, "Guiding Presidential Clemency," 454, original emphasis.
23. *Trump v. United States*, 603 U.S. 593 (2024).
24. "Presidential Pardons and Commutations," *Gale Opposing Viewpoints Online Collection*, Gale, 2021, https://go.gale.com/ps/searchTopic?p=OVIC&u=seoblogs&topicId=XURBMX776115486&searchType=ts&sid=bookmark-OVIC&asid=0113ea3b.
25. "Presidential Pardons and Commutations," *Gale Opposing Viewpoints Online Collection*.
26. Rachel E. Barkow, "The Ascent of the Administrative State and the Demise of Mercy," *Harvard Law Review* 121, no. 5 (2008): 1348–1349, https://harvardlawreview.org/2008/03/the-ascent-of-the-administrative-state-and-the-demise-of-mercy/.
27. *Brady v. Maryland*, 373 U.S. 83, 87 (1963); *Argersinger v. Hamlin*, 407 U.S. 25, 37 (1972).
28. Larkin, "Clemency," 34–35.
29. Crouch, *Presidential Pardon Power*, 145.
30. Crouch, *Presidential Pardon Power*, 4–5.
31. Andrea Ringer, "'Purely Personal and Philosophical': Gov. Winthrop Rockefeller's Death Sentence Commutations," *Arkansas Historical Quarterly* 74, no. 2 (Summer 2015): 145, https://www.jstor.org/stable/24477468.
32. Peter Baker, "Bush Made Willie Horton an Issue in 1988, and the Racial Scars Are Still Fresh," *The New York Times*, December 3, 2018, https://www.nytimes.com/2018/12/03/us/politics/bush-willie-horton.html.
33. Baker, "Bush Made Willie Horton an Issue."
34. Rachel E. Barkow, *Prisoners of Politics: Breaking the Cycle of Mass Incarceration* (Cambridge: Belknap, 2019), 6.
35. Ringer, "Purely Personal and Philosophical," 145; Alschuler, "Bill Clinton's Parting Pardon Party," 1133–1135.
36. Alschuler, "Bill Clinton's Parting Pardon Party," 1137, 1138, 1143–1160.
37. Alschuler, "Bill Clinton's Parting Pardon Party," 1158, 1160–1161.

38. Kevin Liptak, Daniella Diaz, and Sophie Tatum, "Trump Pardons Former Sheriff Joe Arpaio," *CNN Politics*, August 25, 2017, updated August 27, 2017, https://www.cnn.com/2017/08/25/politics/sheriff-joe-arpaio-donald-trump-pardon/index.html.
39. John Wagner, "Trump Says He Has 'Absolute Right' to Pardon Himself of Federal Crimes but Denies Any Wrongdoing," *Washington Post*, June 4, 2018, https://www.washingtonpost.com/politics/trump-says-he-has-absolute-right-to-pardon-himself-of-federal-crimes-but-denies-any-wrongdoing/2018/06/04/3d78348c-67dd-11e8-bea7-c8eb28bc52b1_story.html.
40. "Trump Grants Clemency to Former Blackwater Contractors Convicted of War Crimes in Iraq and Associates Prosecuted Following the Mueller Investigation," *American Journal of International Law* 115, no. 2 (2021): 333, https://www.proquest.com/docview/2514261020.
41. "Presidential Pardons and Commutations," *Gale Opposing Viewpoints Online Collection.*
42. Rosalind S. Helderman, Josh Dawsey, and Beth Reinhard, "Trump Grants Clemency to 143 People in Late-Night Pardon Blast," *Washington Post*, January 20, 2021, https://www.washingtonpost.com/politics/trump-pardons/2021/01/20/7653bd12–59a2–11eb-8bcf-3877871c819d_story.html.
43. Matt Viser, "Joe Biden Pardons His Son Hunter," *Washington Post*, December 1, 2024, https://www.washingtonpost.com/politics/2024/12/01/hunter-biden-pardon/?utm_source=TMP-Newsletter&utm_campaign=aa16befa19-EMAIL_CAMPAIGN_2024_12_02_11_39&utm_medium=email; Adam Cancryn, "Biden Granted Clemency to the 'Kids-for-Cash' Judge: The White House Didn't Consider the Case Specifics," *Politico*, December 13, 2024, https://www.politico.com/news/2024/12/13/biden-clemency-judge-michael-conahan-000890.
44. Cancryn, "Biden Granted Clemency to the 'Kids-for-Cash' Judge."
45. Graham Lee Brewer and Curt Anderson, "Leonard Peltier Leaves Prison After Biden Commuted His Sentence in the Killing of Two FBI Agents," *Associated Press*, February 18, 2025, https://apnews.com/article/leonard-peltier-release-fbi-killings-indigenous-rights-8b7da707f4921e974b53ede7d032cf23?utm_source=TMP-Newsletter&utm_campaign=a878f0d232-EMAIL_CAMPAIGN_2025_02_19_11_40&utm_medium=email&utm_term=0_5e02cdad9d-a878f0d232-175040141.
46. Spencer S. Hsu, Tom Jackman, Hannah Knowles, and Clara Ence Morse, "Trump Pardons Almost All Involved in Jan. 6 Riot, Commutes Remaining 14 Sentences," *Washington Post*, January 20, 2025, https://apnews.com/article/leonard-peltier-release-fbi-killings-indigenous-rights-8b7da707f4921e974b53ede7d032cf23?utm_source=TMP-Newsletter&utm_campaign=a878f0d232-EMAIL_CAMPAIGN_2025_02_19_11_40&utm_medium=email&utm_term=0_5e02cdad9d-a878f0d232-175040141; Clair McFarland, "Trump's Sweeping J6 Pardons Include at Least Two from Wyoming," *Cowboy State Daily* (Cheyenne, WY), January 21, 2025, https://cowboystatedaily.com/2025/01/21/trumps-sweeping-j6-pardons-include-at-least-two-from-wyoming/?utm_source=Klaviyo&utm_medium=campaign&_kx=SSKOyqape-XIj9sMr-U5Ul09Q3Qt6y23Sar9Js_TfsY.UXPtrV.
47. Adam Gabbatt, "US Police Union That Backed Trump Says January 6 Pardons Send 'Dangerous Message,'" *Guardian*, January 22, 2025, https://www.theguardian.com/us-news/2025/jan/22/trump-january-6-pardons-police-union.

48. Gabbatt, "US Police Union That Backed Trump Says January 6 Pardons Send 'Dangerous Message.'"
49. "Office of the Pardon Attorney," United States Department of Justice, United States Government, 2022, https://www.justice.gov/pardon.
50. United States Department of Justice, Justice Manual, §9-140.112.
51. US Department of Justice, Justice Manual, §9-140.112.
52. US Department of Justice, Justice Manual, §9-140.113.
53. US Department of Justice, Justice Manual, §9-140.113.
54. US Department of Justice, Justice Manual, §9-140.113; Larkin, "Guiding Presidential Clemency," 464.
55. Wyo. Stat. Ann. §7-13-804 (a), 804 (b), 806 (2022).
56. Wyo. Stat. Ann. §7-13-401 (f) (2022).
57. Megan Cassidy, "Wyoming Fugitive Captured, Released After 31 Years on the Lam," *Casper Star-Tribune*, February 11, 2013, https://trib.com/news/local/casper/wyoming-fugitive-captured-released-after-31-years-on-the-lam/article_ea887ead-6ded-5713-b9a5-e99d2f0d46eb.html.
58. Stefan J. Bing, "Reconsidering State Parole Board Membership Requirements in Light of Model Penal Code Sentencing Revisions," *Kentucky Law Journal* 100, no. 4 (2012): 871, https://uknowledge.uky.edu/klj/vol100/iss4/9.
59. *Marie*, directed by Roger Donaldson, written by Peter Maas, released September 27, 1985, on HBOMAX, https://www.imdb.com/title/tt0089555/.
60. Barack Obama, "The President's Role in Advancing Criminal Justice Reform," *Harvard Law Review* 130, no. 3 (January 2017): 835–837, https://harvardlawreview.org/2017/01/the-presidents-role-in-advancing-criminal-justice-reform/.
61. Obama, "President's Role," 837.
62. Charlie Smart, "Obama Granted Clemency Unlike Any Other President in History," *FiveThirtyEight*, January 19, 2017, https://fivethirtyeight.com/features/obama-granted-clemency-unlike-any-other-president-in-history/.
63. Smart, "Obama Granted Clemency."
64. Smart, "Obama Granted Clemency."
65. Paul J. Larkin Jr., "'A Day Late and a Dollar Short'—President Obama's Clemency Initiative 2014," *Georgetown Journal of Law and Public Policy* 16, no. 1 (Winter 2018): 149, https://www.law.georgetown.edu/public-policy-journal/in-print/volume-16-number-1-winter-2018/a-day-late-and-a-dollar-short-president-obamas-clemency-initiative-2014/.
66. Brittany K. Barnett, *A Knock at Midnight: A Story of Hope, Justice, and Freedom* (New York: Crown, 2020), 260.
67. Barnett, *A Knock at Midnight*, 260.
68. Barnett, *A Knock at Midnight*, 261.
69. Rachel E. Barkow and Mark Osler, "Designed to Fail: The President's Deference to the Department of Justice in Advancing Criminal Justice Reform," *William and Mary Law Review* 59, no. 2 (2017): 437, https://scholarship.law.wm.edu/wmlr/vol59/iss2/2/.
70. "An Analysis of the Implementation of the 2014 Clemency Initiative," United States Sentencing Commission, 2017, 35–36, https://www.ussc.gov/sites/default/files/pdf/research-and-publications/research-publications/2017/20170901_clemency.pdf.

71. "Analysis of the Implementation of the 2014 Clemency Initiative," United States Sentencing Commission, 35–36.
72. Barkow, *Prisoners of Politics*, 84.
73. Jeremy Diamond, "Trump Demands Obama Promise Not to Pardon Clinton," *CNN Politics*, September 30, 2016, https://www.cnn.com/2016/09/30/politics/donald-trump-hillary-clinton-obama-pardon/index.html.
74. Diamond, "Trump Demands Obama Promise."
75. Helderman et al., "Trump Grants Clemency to 143 People."
76. Helderman et al., "Trump Grants Clemency to 143 People."
77. Helderman et al., "Trump Grants Clemency to 143 People."
78. Taijuan Moorman, "DOJ Attorney Fired over Refusing Mel Gibson's Gun Rights Request, She Says: Reports," *USA Today*, March 11, 2025, https://www.usatoday.com/story/entertainment/celebrities/2025/03/11/mel-gibson-gun-pardon-trump-federal-attorney-fired/82262709007/.
79. "Clemency Statistics," United States Department of Justice, United States Government, updated October 5, 2022, https://www.justice.gov/pardon/clemency-statistics.
80. "Analysis of the Implementation of the 2014 Clemency Initiative," United States Sentencing Commission, 35–36.
81. John Eligon and Annie Karni, "Trump's Pardon Process Was a Mix of Mercy and Favoritism," *The New York Times*, January 22, 2021, https://www.nytimes.com/2021/01/22/us/trump-biden-pardons.html.
82. Nicole Lewis, Justin George, and Eli Hager, "Trump's Pardons Show the Process Has Always Been Broken," *Marshall Project*, January 19, 2021, https://www.themarshallproject.org/2021/01/19/trump-s-pardons-show-the-process-has-always-been-broken.
83. Lewis et al., "Trump's Pardons Show the Process Has Always Been Broken."
84. Lewis et al., "Trump's Pardons Show the Process Has Always Been Broken."
85. John Gramlich, "Biden Granted More Acts of Clemency than Any Prior President," *Pew Research Center*, February 7, 2025, https://www.pewresearch.org/short-reads/2025/02/07/biden-granted-more-acts-of-clemency-than-any-prior-president/.
86. Gramlich, "Biden Granted More Acts of Clemency than Any Prior President."
87. Gramlich, "Biden Granted More Acts of Clemency than Any Prior President"; Zoe Richards, "Biden Sets Record for Most Pardons and Commutations with New Round of Clemency for Nonviolent Drug Offenders," *NBC News*, January 17, 2025, https://www.nbcnews.com/politics/white-house/biden-record-most-pardons-commutations-2500-nonviolent-drug-offenses-rcna188081?utm_source=TMP-Newsletter&utm_campaign=5131b51c4b-EMAIL_CAMPAIGN_2025_01_17_11_45&utm_medium=email&utm_term=0_5e02cdad9d-5131b51c4b-175040141.
88. Gramlich, "Biden Granted More Acts of Clemency than Any Prior President."
89. Chandelis Duster, "Who Is Alice Marie Johnson, Trump's Newly Appointed 'Pardon Czar'?," *National Public Radio*, February 25, 2025, https://www.npr.org/2025/02/25/nx-s1-5307330/trump-pardon-czar-who-is-alice-marie-johnson.
90. Duster, "Who Is Alice Marie Johnson, Trump's Newly Appointed 'Pardon Czar'?"
91. Duster, "Who Is Alice Marie Johnson, Trump's Newly Appointed 'Pardon Czar'?"

92. Rachel Looker, "Trump Ally Criticizes Pardons for Violent Jan 6 Offenders," *BBC News*, January 26, 2025, https://www.bbc.com/news/articles/c79dlyzvnvxo.
93. Looker, "Trump Ally Criticizes Pardons for Violent Jan 6 Offenders."
94. Jamiles Lartey, " 'Freedom for Captives!' Trump Puts Clemency Machine into Overdrive for Political Allies," *Closing Argument, Marshall Project*, May 31, 2025, https://www.themarshallproject.org/2025/05/31/trump-pardon-chrisley-larry-hoover-nba-youngboy.
95. Thomas B. Edsall, "The Pardon Power Is Helping Trump Realize His Dreams," *The New York Times*, June 10, 2025, https://www.nytimes.com/2025/06/10/opinion/trump-pardon-immunity-autocracy.html.
96. Melissa Gomez, "Trump Has Pardoned 10 Men: Who Are They?" *Los Angeles Times*, May 23, 2019, https://www.latimes.com/nation/la-na-trump-pardons-20190523-story.html.
97. Edsall, "The Pardon Power Is Helping Trump Realize His Dreams."
98. Edsall, "Pardon Power Is Helping Trump Realize His Dreams."
99. Joseph Neff, "Trump Flouts Pardon Rules—and Costs Victims and Taxpayers More than $1 Billion," *Marshall Project*, July 28, 2005, https://www.themarshallproject.org/2025/07/28/trump-pardons-violate-standards.
100. Neff, "Trump Flouts Pardon Rules."
101. Glenn Thrush and Valerie Crowder, "After Ghislaine Maxwell Interview, Concerns Mount over Possibility of Pardon," *The New York Times*, July 25, 2025, updated July 28, 2025, https://www.nytimes.com/2025/07/25/us/politics/ghislaine-maxwell-trump-pardon.html.
102. Thrush and Crowder, "After Ghislaine Maxwell Interview."
103. Jay Stahl, "Trump Addresses Pardon Decision for Sean 'Diddy' Combs, Says Mogul Was 'Half-Innocent,' " *USA Today*, August 2, 2025, https://www.usatoday.com/story/entertainment/celebrities/2025/08/02/will-trump-pardon-sean-diddy-combs/85488194007/.
104. Michael Gold and Grace Ashford, "Santos Is Released After Trump Commutes His Sentence," *The New York Times*, October 17, 2025, https://www.nytimes.com/2025/10/17/us/politics/trump-george-santos-sentence-commute.html.
105. Gold and Ashford, "Santos Is Released After Trump Commutes His Sentence."
106. Gram Slattery and Chris Prentice, "Trump Pardons Convicted Binance Founder 'CZ' Zhao," *Reuters*, October 23, 2025, https://www.reuters.com/world/us/trump-pardons-convicted-binance-founder-zhao-white-house-says-2025-10-23/.
107. Slattery and Prentice, "Trump Pardons Convicted Binance Founder 'CZ' Zhao."
108. Steve Zeidman, "Governors, Use Your Clemency Powers," *The New York Times*, July 11, 2025, https://www.nytimes.com/2025/07/11/opinion/clemency-pardon-governors-trump.html.
109. "Governors of Wyoming," Wyoming State Archives, State of Wyoming, 2022, *https://wyoarchives.wyo.gov/index.php/governors-of-wyoming*. The author maintains a complete copy of commutations granted by governors beginning with Ed Herschler. The entire record is on file at the Wyoming State Archives and the Secretary of State's Office.
110. "Governors of Wyoming," Wyoming State Archives, State of Wyoming, 2023, *https://wyoarchives.wyo.gov/index.php/governors-of-wyoming*.
111. "Governors of Wyoming," 2023.

112. Nalia Awan and Katie Rose Quandt, "Executive Inaction: States and the Federal Government Fail to Use Commutations as a Release Mechanism," *Prison Policy Initiative*, April 2022, https://www.prisonpolicy.org/reports/commutations.html.
113. David A. Lieb, "Missouri Governor Granting Pardons at Pace Not Seen Since WWII Era," *The Seattle Times*, November 24, 2023, https://www.seattletimes.com/nation-world/nation/missouri-governor-granting-pardons-at-pace-not-seen-since-wwii-era/.
114. ACLU of Oregon, "Governor Brown's Historic Legacy of Commutation Actions," January 23, 2023, https://www.aclu-or.org/en/news/governor-browns-historic-clemency-actions-provide-hopeful-lesson.
115. Brian White, "Tens of Thousands of Marylanders Receive Pardons for Marijuana Convictions," *Associated Press*, June 17, 2024, https://apnews.com/article/marijuana-pardons-gov-wes-moore-003a11d2435eabaa060d2d26da63ce42.
116. Jesse Paul and Sandra Fish, "Colorado Governor Pardons 21 People and Reduces Sentences of 7 Others, Including Man Convicted of Murder," *Colorado Sun*, December 22, 2023, https://coloradosun.com/2023/12/22/jared-polis-pardons-clemency-2023/.
117. Jesse Paul and Olivia Prentzel, "Colorado Governor Issues 22 Pardons and Commutes Sentences of 4 People, Including 2 Men Convicted of Murder" *Colorado Sun*, December 20, 2024, https://coloradosun.com/2024/12/20/jared-polis-2025-clemency-power/.
118. Paul and Fish, "Colorado Governor Pardons 21 People"; Paul and Prentzel, "Colorado Governor Isses 22 Pardons and Commutes Sentences of 4 People."

CHAPTER 3: PROFILES IN POLITICAL COURAGE

1. "Mike Sullivan," Wyoming State Archives, WyoHistory.org: A Project of the Wyoming Historical Society, Cheyenne, November 8, 2014, https://www.wyohistory.org/encyclopedia/mike-sullivan.
2. Michael Sullivan, interview by author, February 2, 2022; *State of Wyoming v. Lindsay*, 317 P.2d 506 (Wyo. 1957); "Report of Convicts Dischaged, Earnest Lindsay," on file with author.
3. *State of Wyoming*, 317 P.2d 506, 507.
4. "All Because of the Food," Police Heritage Museum, Hershey, PA, February 21, 2022, https://policeheritagemuseum.com/case003.html.
5. *State of Wyoming*, 317 P.2d 506, 507.
6. *State of Wyoming*, 317 P.2d 506, 507.
7. *State of Wyoming*, 317 P.2d 506, 507.
8. *State of Wyoming*, 317 P.2d 506, 507.
9. *State of Wyoming*, 317 P.2d 506, 507.
10. *State of Wyoming*, 317 P.2d 506, 507.
11. "Commutation of Sentence," December 17, 1957, on file with author.
12. While Governor Simpson granted Lindsay a commutation, specifying that he not ever be paroled, the Wyoming State Legislature did not officially create a life without parole (LWOP) statute until 1996. Wyo. Stat. Ann. 6-10-301. Thus, the governor's admonishment that Lindsay not be paroled was only advisory, and successive governors were free to ignore that provision, which they did.

13. "All Because of the Food," Police Heritage Museum; "Report of Convicts Dischaged, Earnest Lindsay."
14. J. B. Sullivan, letter to Wyoming Board of Parole, September 5, 1963, on file with author.
15. *State of Wyoming*, 317 P.2d 506.
16. J. B. Sullivan, letter to Wyoming Board of Parole, September 5, 1963.
17. "Report of Convicts Dischaged, Earnest Lindsay."
18. "Ernest Lynn Lindsay," Find a Grave, https://www.findagrave.com/memorial/54469572/ernest-lynn-lindsay.
19. Michael Sullivan, interview by author.
20. Michael Sullivan, interview by author.
21. "Wyoming Gov. Michael J. Sullivan," National Governors Association, 2022, https://www.nga.org/governor/michael-j-sullivan/; "Michael Sullivan," Institute of Politics, John F. Kennedy School of Government, Harvard University, 2022, https://iop.harvard.edu/fellows/michael-sullivan.
22. Michael Sullivan, interview by author.
23. Michael Sullivan, interview by author.
24. Michael Sullivan, interview by author.
25. Michael Sullivan, interview by author.
26. "Wyoming Gov. Dave Freudenthal," National Governors Association, 2022, https://www.nga.org/governor/dave-freudenthal/.
27. Michael Sullivan, interview by author.
28. "Wyoming Gov. Michael J. Sullivan," 2022; "Michael Sullivan," Institute of Politics.
29. Michael Sullivan, interview by author.
30. Marion McMillan Huseas, *Legacy of Fear: Mark Hopkinson and the Bridger Valley Murders* (Cheyenne: Marimac Publishing, 2006), 280.
31. Huseas, *Legacy of Fear*, 279.
32. Huseas, *Legacy of Fear*, 289.
33. "State and Federal Info: Wyoming," Death Penalty Information Center, 2022, *https://deathpenaltyinfo.org/state-and-federal-info/state-by-state/wyoming*.
34. "Ed Herschler," Wyoming State Archives, WyoHistory.org: A Project of the Wyoming Historical Society, Cheyenne, November 8, 2014, https://www.wyohistory.org/encyclopedia/ed-herschler.
35. Michael Sullivan, interview by author.
36. Michael Sullivan, interview by author.
37. "Wyoming Gov. Dave Freudenthal," 2022; "Wyoming Gov. Matthew Mead," National Governors Association, 2022, https://www.nga.org/governor/matthew-mead/.
38. Michael Sullivan, interview by author.
39. Ellen Gerst, "Wyoming Governors Rarely Reduce Prison Sentences Anymore, Data Shows," *Casper Star-Tribune*, October 7, 2022, https://trib.com/news/state-and-regional/crime-and-courts/wyoming-governors-rarely-reduce-prison-sentences-anymore-data-shows/article_79cfe94e-4680-11ed-b6e0-9745be6d11c3.html.
40. Michael Sullivan, interview by author.
41. Wendy Sawyer and Peter Wagner, "Mass Incarceration: The Whole Pie 2022," *Prison Policy Initiative*, March 14, 2022, https://www.prisonpolicy.org/reports/pie2022.html.

42. James Austin, Vincent Schiraldi, Bruce Western, and Anamika Dwivedi, "Reconsidering the 'Violent Offender,'" *Square One Project: Reimagine Justice*, May 2019, 14, https://www.prisonpolicy.org/scans/square_one_project/executive-session-pdf-Reconsidering-the-violent-offender-report-ONLINE_FINAL.pdf.
43. Austin et al., "Reconsidering the 'Violent Offender,'" 8.
44. Austin et al., "Reconsidering the 'Violent Offender,'" 7.
45. "Recidivism," National Institute of Justice, Office of Justice Programs, United States Department of Justice, Washington, DC, 2022, https://nij.ojp.gov/topics/corrections/recidivism.
46. "Recidivism," National Institute of Justice.
47. "Measuring Recidivism," National Institute of Justice, Office of Justice Programs, United States Department of Justice, Washington, DC, February 20, 2008, https://nij.ojp.gov/topics/articles/measuring-recidivism.
48. Austin et al., "Reconsidering the 'Violent Offender,'" 24.
49. Sawyer and Wagner, "Mass Incarceration"; Leonardo Antenangeli and Matthew Durose, "Recidivism of Prisoners Released in 24 States in 2008," Bureau of Justice Statistics, United States Department of Justice, September 2021, 1.
50. Sawyer and Wagner, "Mass Incarceration"; Antenangeli and Durose, "Recidivism of Prisoners Released in 24 States in 2008," 5, 10.
51. Delbert Elliott, David Huzinga, and Barbara Morse, "Self-Reported Violent Offending: A Descriptive Analysis of Juvenile Violent Offenders and Their Offending Careers," *Journal of Interpersonal Violence* 1, no. 4 (1986): 506, https://journals.sagepub.com/doi/abs/10.1177/088626086001004006; Terrie E. Moffitt, "Adolescence-Limited and Life-Course–Persistent Antisocial Behavior: A Developmental Taxonomy," *Psychological Review* 100, no. 4 (1993), https://psycnet.apa.org/doiLanding?doi=10.1037%2F0033-295X.100.4.674.
52. Moffitt, "Adolescence-Limited and Life-Course-Persistent"; Marvin E. Wolfgang, Robert M. Figlio, and Thorsten Sellin, *Delinquency in a Birth Cohort* (Chicago: University of Chicago Press, 1972).
53. John H. Laub and Robert J. Sampson, *Shared Beginnings, Divergent Lives: Delinquent Boys to Age 70* (Cambridge, MA: Harvard University Press, 2003), 275–282; Robert J. Sampson and John H. Laub, "Life-Course Desisters? Trajectories of Crime Among Delinquent Boys Followed to Age 70," *Criminology* 41, no. 3 (2003), https://scholar.harvard.edu/files/sampson/files/2003_crim_laub_1.pdf.
54. Alex R. Piquero, Wesley G. Jennings, and J. C. Barnes, "Violence in Criminal Careers: A Review of the Literature from a Developmental Life-Course Perspective," *Aggression and Violent Behavior* 17, no. 3 (May–June 2012): 171–179, https://www.ojp.gov/ncjrs/virtual-library/abstracts/violence-criminal-careers-review-literature-developmental-life.
55. Piquero et al., "Violence in Criminal Careers," 177.
56. Moffitt, "Adolescence-Limited and Life-Course-Persistent," 674–701.
57. Moffitt, "Adolescence-Limited and Life-Course-Persistent," 674–701.
58. Bill McCarthy, "Micheli in Race for Governor: Who Will Join Him?" *Wyoming Tribune Eagle* (Cheyenne, WY), October 4, 2009, https://www.wyomingnews.com/news

/micheli-in-race-for-governor-who-will-join-him/article_6b28c5e0-9e38-5ca5-b49f-01541a207f45.html.

59. Ed Kilgore, "2022 Won't Be Another 1994 Republican Tidal Wave," *Intelligencer*, July 27, 2021, https://nymag.com/intelligencer/2021/07/no-lindsey-graham-2022-wont-be-another-1994-landslide.html.

CHAPTER 4: PLEADING FOR LIFE

1. Exodus 20:13.
2. *The Shawshank Redemption*, directed by Frank Darabont, produced by Niki Marvin, Beverly Hills, CA: Castle Rock Entertainment, 1994; Stephen King, *The Shawshank Redemption* (New York: Viking, 1982).
3. *The Shawshank Redemption*, directed by Frank Darabont, produced by Niki Marvin.
4. Wyo. Stat. Ann. §6-10-301(c) (2022).
5. Peter Enns, *Incarceration Nation: How the United States Became the Most Punitive Democracy in the World* (Cambridge: Cambridge University Press, 2006), 3.
6. Ashley Nellis, "Still Life: America's Increasing Use of Life and Long-Term Sentences," Sentencing Project, May 2017, 5, https://www.prisonlegalnews.org/media/publications/Sentencing%20Project%20-%20Still%20Life%2C%20Life%20Sentences%2C%202017.pdf.
7. Nellis, "Still Life," 5.
8. Ashley Nellis and Celeste Barry, "A Matter of Life: The Scope and Impact of Life and Long Term Imprisonment in the United States," Sentencing Project, January 8, 2025, 2, https://www.sentencingproject.org/app/uploads/2025/01/A-Matter-of-Life-The-Scope-and-Impact-of-Life-and-Long-Term-Imprisonment-in-the-United-States.pdf.
9. Nellis, "Still Life," 5.
10. Nellis, "Still Life," 5.
11. Information provided by the Wyoming Department of Corrections, on file with author.
12. Nellis, "Still Life," 5.
13. Jenna Scafuri, "Low Recidivism Rates Reported Among Convicted Offenders," *Corrections Today*, February 2011, 14, https://www.thefreelibrary.com/Low+recidivism+rates+reported+among+convicted+murderers.-a0253538752.
14. John L. Anderson, "Recidivism of Paroled Murderers as a Factor in the Utility of Life Imprisonment," *Current Issues in Criminal Justice* 17, no. 2 (2019): 255–268, https://www.tandfonline.com/doi/full/10.1080/10345329.2019.1605870?scroll=top&needAccess=true.
15. Barack Obama, "The President's Role in Advancing Criminal Justice Reform," *Harvard Law Review* 130, no. 3 (January 2017): 812, https://harvardlawreview.org/2017/01/the-presidents-role-in-advancing-criminal-justice-reform/.
16. Gregg D. Caruso, *Rejecting Retributivism: Free Will, Punishment, and Criminal Justice* (Cambridge: Cambridge University Press, 2021), 5.
17. Caruso, *Rejecting Retributivism*, 7.
18. Sonja Starr, "On Prisoners, Politics, and the Administration of Criminal Justice: Professor Rachel Barkow," *University of Chicago Law Review* 88, no. 7 (2021): 1775–1789, https://chicagounbound.uchicago.edu/uclrev/vol88/iss7/16/; Sanford H. Kadish, Stephen J.

Schulfhofer, and Rachel E. Barkow, *Crimial Law and Its Processes: Cases and Materials*, 10th ed. (Boston: Aspen, 2016).

19. Rachel E. Barkow, *Prisoners of Politics: Breaking the Cycle of Mass Incarceration* (Cambridge: Belknap, 2019), 19.
20. Barkow, *Prisoners of Politics*, 39.
21. Barkow, *Prisoners of Politics*, 40.
22. Barkow, *Prisoners of Politics*, 40–41.
23. Caruso, *Rejecting Retributivism*, 19.
24. James M. Binnall, *Twenty Million Angry Men: The Case for Including Convicted Felons in Our Jury System* (Oakland: University of California Press, 2021), 19.
25. Barkow, *Prisoners of Politics*, 89–90.
26. Barkow, *Prisoners of Politics*, 91–92, 95.
27. Naomi Murakawa, *The First Civil Right: How Liberals Built Prison America* (Oxford: Oxford University Press, 2014), 130.
28. Murakawa, *The First Civil Right*, 105–106; Daniel M. Fetsco, "Early Release from Prison in Wyoming: An Overview of Parole in Wyoming and Elsewhere and an Examination of Current and Future Trends," *Wyoming Law Review* 11, no. 1 (2011): 99–102, 110–111, https://scholarship.law.uwyo.edu/wlr/vol11/iss1/4.
29. Enns, *Incarceration Nation*, 60–64.
30. Daniel M. Fetsco, "No Credit for Time Served: The Fiscal and Equitable Problems with Wyoming's Parole Statutes," *Wyoming Law Review* 22, no. 1 (2022): 142–143, https://scholarship.law.uwyo.edu/wlr/vol22/iss1/5.
31. Barkow, *Prisoners of Politics*, 106; Francis T. Cullen, Bonnie S. Fisher, and Brandon K. Applegate, "Public Opinion About Punishment and Corrections," *Crime and Justice* 27, no. 1 (2019): 27, https://scholarcommons.sc.edu/cgi/viewcontent.cgi?article=1011&context=crim_facpub.
32. Willard M. Oliver, "The Power to Persuade: Presidential Influence over Congress on Crime Control Policy," *Criminal Justice Review* 28, no. 1 (2003): 120, https://journals.sagepub.com/doi/10.1177/073401680302800107.
33. James Kilgore, *Understanding Mass Incarceration: A People's Guide to the Key Civil Rights Struggle of Our Time* (New York: New Press, 2015), 113.
34. Mason Walker and Katerina Eva Matsa, "News Consumption Across Social Media in 2021," Pew Research Center, September 20, 2021, https://www.pewresearch.org/journalism/2021/09/20/news-consumption-across-social-media-in-2021/#:~:text=A%20little%20under%20half%20%2848%25%29%20of%20U.S.%20adults,Center%20survey%20conducted%20July%2026-Aug.%208%2C%202021.%201.
35. Nikki Goth Itoi, "How Social Media Shapes Our Perceptions About Crime," *Stanford University Human-Centered Artificial Intelligence*, February 27, 2023, https://hai.stanford.edu/news/how-social-media-shapes-our-perceptions-about-crime.
36. Barkow, *Prisoners of Politics*, 107; Marc Mauer, "Why Are Tough on Crime Policies So Popular," *Stanford Law and Policy Review* 11, no. 1 (1999): 15, https://heinonline.org/HOL/LandingPage?handle=hein.journals/stanlp11&div=9&id=&page=.
37. Barkow, *Prisoners of Politics*, 107; Mauer, "Tough on Crime Policies," 15.
38. Barkow, *Prisoners of Politics*, 107; Mauer, "Tough on Crime Policies," 15.

39. Barkow, *Prisoners of Politics*, 107; Mauer, "Tough on Crime Policies," 15.
40. Barkow, *Prisoners of Politics*, 107.
41. Alex Altman, "No President Has Spread Fear Like Donald Trump," *Time*, February 9, 2017, https://time.com/4665755/donald-trump-fear/.
42. Karen Tumulty and David Nakamara, "Trump's Rallying Cry: Fear Itself," *Washington Post*, February 3, 2017, https://www.washingtonpost.com/politics/trumps-rallying-cry-fear-itself/2017/02/03/7d2a0432-ea4a-11e6-bf6f-301b6b443624_story.html.
43. Barkow, *Prisoners of Politics*, 107.
44. Barkow, *Prisoners of Politics*, 107.
45. John Gramlich, "Voters' Perceptions of Crime Continue to Conflict with Reality," Pew Research Center, November 16, 2016, https://www.pewresearch.org/fact-tank/2016/11/16/voters-perceptions-of-crime-continue-to-conflict-with-reality/.
46. John Gramlich, "What We Know About the Increase in U.S. Murders in 2020," Pew Research Center, October 27, 2021, https://www.pewresearch.org/fact-tank/2021/10/27/what-we-know-about-the-increase-in-u-s-murders-in-2020/.
47. Gramlich, "Increase in U.S. Murders" (emphasis added).
48. Gramlich, "Increase in U.S. Murders."
49. Ethan Corey, "Ask the Appeal: Why Do Americans Think the U.S. Is Too 'Soft' On Crime?" *The Appeal*, February 13, 2024, https://theappeal.org/why-do-voters-think-the-us-soft-on-crime/.
50. David Moye, "Trump's Latest Claim About Crime Is a Real Doozy," *Huffington Post*, August 20, 2024, https://www.huffpost.com/entry/trumps-claim-about-crime-loaf-of-bread_n_66c50a75e4b0e284ae54f786.
51. Arianne Keegan, Roberta Meyers Douglas, and Victoria Palacio Carr, "Politicans Push Failed 'Tough-on-Crime' Measures as Crime Rates Near Record Lows," *The Appeal*, June 13, 2024, https://theappeal.org/tough-on-crime-rates-record-low/.
52. Beneson Strategy Group, "New Polling Shows Criminal Justice Reform Is a Winning Issue for 2024 Election," October 2024, https://www.fwd.us/wp-content/uploads/2024/10/New-Polling-Shows-Criminal-Justice-Reform-is-a-Winning-Issue-for-2024-Election-1.pdf.
53. Ashley Wu and Tim Arango, "After Surge During Pandemic, Homicides Fall Significantly," *The New York Times*, July 24, 2025, https://www.nytimes.com/2025/07/24/us/murders-crime-us-covid-19.html.
54. Jeff Asher, "It's Not Just Murder That's Likely Historic Lows," *Jeff-alytics*, June 23, 2025, https://jasher.substack.com/p/its-not-just-murder-thats-likely.
55. Gelb quoted in Wu and Arango, "After Surge During Pandemic, Homicides Fall Significantly."
56. Quoted in Wu and Arango, "After Surge During Pandemic, Homicides Fall Significantly."
57. Mollie Reilly, "Tom Cotton Thinks America Isn't Locking Enough People Up," *Huffington Post*, May 19, 2016, https://www.huffpost.com/entry/tom-cotton-criminal-justice_n_573e3305e4b00e09e89e8cad.
58. David Moye, "Tom Cotton Blamed Democrats for a Trump Crime Bill and Twitter Users Had a Lot to Say," *Huffington Post*, February 16, 2022, https://www.yahoo.com/news/tom-cotton-blamed-democrats-trump-235225597.html.

59. Moye, "Tom Cotton Blamed Democrats."
60. Moye, "Tom Cotton Blamed Democrats."
61. Moye, "Tom Cotton Blamed Democrats."
62. Meredith McGraw, "Trump's Criminal Justice Reform Bill Becomes Persona Non Grata Among GOPers," *Politico*, May 1, 2022, https://www.politico.com/news/2022/05/01/trump-republicans-first-step-act-00029104.
63. McGraw, "Trump's Criminal Justice Reform Bill."
64. Carl Hulse, "As Jackson Faces Senators, Her Criminal Defense Record Is a Target," *The New York Times*, March 16, 2022, https://www.nytimes.com/2022/03/16/us/politics/ketanji-brown-jackson-criminal-defense.html.
65. Hulse, "Jackson Faces Senators."
66. Hulse, "Jackson Faces Senators."
67. Harriet Alexander, "Republicans Tear into Biden's Pro-Police Reform Judicial Nominee and Say HER Policies Have Caused Skyrocketing Crime, Homicide and Carjacking Rates," *Daily Mail*, February 16, 2022, https://www.dailymail.co.uk/news/article-10521835/Republicans-tear-Bidens-pro-police-reform-judicial-nominee-say-policies-increased-crime.html.
68. Jennifer Bendery, "Chuck Schumer Recommends 3 Progressive Women for Federal Judgeships," *Huffington Post*, September 1, 2021, https://www.huffpost.com/entry/chuck-schumer-judicial-nominees-biden_n_612f8a5fe4b05f53eda226f0.
69. Alexander, "Biden's Pro-Police Reform Judicial Nominee."
70. Associated Press, "Fact Check: Judge Ketanji Brown Jackson Child Porn Sentences 'Pretty Mainstream,'" ABC News, March 21, 2022, https://www.msn.com/en-us/news/crime/fact-check-judge-ketanji-brown-jackson-child-porn-sentences-pretty-mainstream/ar-AAViNcR?li=BBnb7Kz.
71. Christopher Wilson, "Greene Revives QAnon Smear in Attack on GOP Senators Backing Jackson's SCOTUS Nomination," *Yahoo News*, April 5, 2022, https://www.yahoo.com/news/greene-revives-q-anon-smear-in-attack-on-gop-senators-backing-jacksons-scotus-nomination-140627286.html.
72. Associated Press, "Fact Check."
73. Associated Press, "Fact Check."
74. Associated Press, "Fact Check."
75. Amber Phillips, "Five Takeaways from Day 2 of Judge Jackson's Confirmation Hearing," *Washington Post*, March 22, 2022, https://www.msn.com/en-us/news/politics/five-takeaways-from-day-2-of-judge-jacksons-confirmation-hearing/ar-AAVn3FA?li=BBnb7Kz.
76. Brent Griffiths, "Durbin Swats Back at Josh Hawley over Attacks on Ketanji Brown Jackson's Record on Sex Offenders, Even Using the National Review to Make His Point," *Business Insider*, March 21, 2022, https://www.msn.com/en-us/news/politics/durbin-swats-back-at-josh-hawley-over-attacks-on-ketanji-brown-jackson-s-record-on-sex-offenders-even-using-the-national-review-to-make-his-point/ar-AAVklD8.
77. Hulse, "Jackson Faces Senators."
78. Kylie Murdock and Jim Kessler, "The Red State Murder Problem," Third Way, March 15, 2022, https://www.thirdway.org/report/the-red-state-murder-problem.

79. Associated Press, "U.S. Presidential Election Results 2020: Biden Wins," NBC News, November 22, 2022, https://www.nbcnews.com/politics/2020-elections/president-results; Associated Press, "2024 Presidential Election Results," updated February 21, 2025, https://apnews.com/projects/election-results-2024/?office=P.
80. Murdock and Kessler, "Red State Murder Problem."
81. Priya Krishnakumar, Emma Tucker, Ryan Young, and Pamela Kirkland, "Fueled by Gun Violence, Cities Across the US Are Breaking All-Time Homicide Records This Year," CNN, December 12, 2021, https://www.cnn.com/2021/12/12/us/homicides-major-cities-increase-end-of-year-2021/index.html; German Lopez, "A Violent Crisis: The Brooklyn Shooting and Other Headline-Making Violence Are Part of Broader Trend," *The New York Times*, April 17, 2022, https://www.nytimes.com/2022/04/17/briefing/violent-crime-ukraine-war-week-ahead.html.
82. McGraw, "Trump's Criminal Justice Reform Bill."
83. Barry Latzer, *The Myth of Overpunishment* (Washington, DC: Republic Book Publisher, 2022), 83.
84. Latzer, *Myth of Overpunishment*, 120.
85. Rafael A. Mangual, *Criminal Injustice: What the Push for Decarceration and Depolicing Gets Wrong and Who It Hurts the Most* (New York: Hachette Book Group, 2022), 48.
86. Rafael A. Mangual, "The Anti-Crime Election: What Some State and Local Results Say About the Future of Public Safety in America," *City Journal* (New York), November 6, 2024, https://www.city-journal.org/article/the-anti-crime-election.
87. Charles Fain Lehman, "Build More Prisons: The Case for Incarceration," *City Journal* (New York), Autumn 2024, https://www.city-journal.org/article/build-more-prisons.
88. John Pfaff, "What Democrats Get Wrong About Prison Reform," *Politico Magazine*, August 14, 2019, https://www.politico.com/magazine/story/2019/08/14/what-democrats-get-wrong-about-prison-reform-227623/.
89. Pfaff, "What Democrats Get Wrong About Prison Reform."
90. Tolman quoted in McGraw, "Trump's Criminal Justice Reform Bill."; "Brett Tolman," Our Team, Right on Crime, 2022, https://rightoncrime.com/about/team/brett-tolman/.
91. Roday quoted in McGraw, "Trump's Criminal Justice Reform Bill."
92. Lila Kazemian and Jeremy Travis, "Imperative for Inclusion of Long Termers and Lifers in Research and Policy," *Criminology and Public Policy* 14, no. 2 (May 2015), https://doi.org/10.1111/1745-9133.12126.
93. Nellis, "Still Life," 7.
94. Nellis, "Still Life," 7; Alfred Blumstein, Jacqueline Cohen, and Paul Hsieh, *The Duration of Adult Criminal Careers: Final Report to the National Institute of Justice* (Pittsburgh: Carnegie-Mellon University, 1982), https://www.ojp.gov/pdffiles1/Digitization/89569NCJRS.pdf; Alfred Blumstein and Kiminori Nakamura, "Redemption in the Presence of Widespread Criminal Background Checks," *Criminology: An Interdisciplinary Journal* 47, no. 2 (2009), https://psycnet.apa.org/record/2009-08151-002.
95. Nellis, "Still Life," 7.
96. Nellis, "Still Life," 7.
97. David Ansley, "Casper Man Admits Killing His Ex-Wife," *Casper Star-Tribune*, January 14, 1981.

CHAPTER 5: A POUND OF FLESH

1. Larry DeGraw, interview by author, August 2022.
2. Larry DeGraw, interview by author.
3. Larry DeGraw, "Affidavit," State of Wyoming, County of Natrona, June 6, 1988, on file with author; Larry DeGraw, interview by author.
4. James Koester, interview by author, June 2022.
5. Rea, "Casper Man Pleads Guilty."
6. *Bd. of Prof'l Responsibility v. Meenan*, 464 P.3d 232 (Wyo. 2011).
7. Ben Neary, "Gov. Freudenthal Pardons Former Casper Prosecutor Kevin Meenan," *Casper Star-Tribune*, September 1, 2010, https://trib.com/news/state-and-regional/gov-freudenthal-pardons-former-casper-prosecutor-kevin-meenan/article_2f33a732-b5eb-11df-9ebf-001cc4c03286.html.
8. Wyoming judge, letter to Wyoming Board of Parole, April 22, 2009, photocopy in author's possession.
9. *Mattern v. State*, 151 P.3d 1116, 1129–1130 (Wyo. 2007).
10. *Murray v. State*, 713 P.2d 202, 206 (Wyo. 1986).
11. *Bouwkamp v. State*, 833 P.2d 486, 494–495 (Wyo. 1992).
12. Wyo. Stat. Ann. §6-2-101 (b) (2022); Wyo. Stat. Ann. §6-2-104 (2022).
13. Larry DeGraw, interview by author.
14. *County 10* staff, "Fremont County Coroner Died Monday Morning," *County 10*, October 17, 2022, https://county10.com/fremont-county-coroner-died-monday-morning/.
15. "Wyoming Gov. Dave Freudenthal," *National Governor's Association*, 2005, https://www.nga.org/governor/dave-freudenthal/.
16. Davis quoted in Emily Bazelon, *Charged: The New Movement to Transform American Prosecution and End Mass Incarceration* (New York: Random House, 2019), xxvi, 17.
17. Keith A. Findley and Michael S. Scott, "Multiple Dimensions of Tunnel Vision," *Wisconsin Law Review* 2 (2006): 291–371, https://repository.law.wisc.edu/s/uwlaw/media/39349.
18. Findley and Scott, "Multiple Dimensions of Tunnel Vision," 309.
19. Bazelon, *Charged*, 17–18.
20. George T. Felkenes, "The Prosecutor: A Look at Reality," *Southwestern University Law Review* 7, no. 1 (Spring 1975): 110, https://heinonline.org/HOL/LandingPage?handle=hein.journals/swulr7&div=10&id=&page=.
21. Felkenes, "The Prosecutor," 100.
22. Felkenes, "The Prosecutor," 121.
23. Diane Lozano, email to author, February 10, 2022.
24. Felkenes, "The Prosecutor," 121.
25. Daniel S. Medwed, "The Prosecutor as Minister of Justice: Preaching to the Unconverted from the Post-Conviction Pulpit," *Washington Law Review* 84, no. 1 (2009): 36, https://www.proquest.com/docview/213149700/fulltextPDF/B4E0E6E0DE943D7PQ/1?accountid=14793.
26. Ronald F. Wright and Kay L. Levine, "The Cure for Young Prosecutors' Syndrome," *Arizona Law Review* 56, no. 4 (2014): 1068, 1081, 1082–1085, https://arizonalawreview.org/wright-levine/.

27. Angela J. Davis, *Arbitrary Justice: The Power of the American Prosecutor* (Oxford: Oxford University Press, 2009), 4.
28. Davis, *Arbitrary Justice*, 5.
29. Bruce A. Green, "Why Should Prosecutors 'Seek Justice?'" *Fordham Urban Law Journal* 26 (1999): 607–644, 616.
30. Somil Trivedi and Jared Keenan, "Coerced Out of Justice: How Prosecutors Abuse Their Power to Secure Guilt Pleas," *ACLU of Arizona: News and Commentary*, July 8, 2021, https://www.acluaz.org/en/news/coerced-out-justice-how-prosecutors-abuse-their-power-secure-guilty-pleas.
31. *Garcetti v. Ceballos*, 547 U.S. 410 (2006).
32. Jocelyn M. Pollock, *Ethical Dilemmas and Decisions in Criminal Justice*, 11th ed. (Boston: Cengage Learning, 2022), 251–252.
33. *Lane v. Franks*, 573 U.S. 228 (2014).
34. *Franks*, 573 U.S. 228, 240–241.
35. Thomas P. Sullivan and Maurice Possley, "The Chronic Failure to Discipline Prosecutors for Misconduct: Proposals for Reform," *Journal of Criminal Law and Criminology* 105, no. 4 (Fall 2015): 909–910, https://scholarlycommons.law.northwestern.edu/cgi/viewcontent.cgi?referer=&httpsredir=1&article=7573&context=jclc.
36. Jim Dwyer, Peter Neufeld, and Barry Sheck, *Actual Innocence: Five Days to Execution and Other Dispatches from the Wrongly Convicted* (New York: Doubleday, 2000), 175, 229.
37. *Imbler v. Pachtman*, 424 U.S. 409, 424 (1976).
38. *Chapman v. California*, 386 U.S. 18, 22 (1967).
39. Steve Weinberg, "Breaking the Rules," Center for Public Integrity, June 26, 2003, https://publicintegrity.org/politics/state-politics/harmful-error/breaking-the-rules/.
40. Sullivan and Possley, "Failure to Discipline Prosecutors," 909, 922–923.
41. *Beagle v. State*, 86 P.3d 1271, 1274 (Wyo. 2004).
42. Sullivan and Possley, "Failure to Discipline Prosecutors," 912.
43. *United States v. Hastings*, 461 U.S. 499, 506 n.5 (1983).
44. Hon. D. Brooks Smith, "Policing Prosecutors: What Role Can Appellate Courts Play," *Hofstra Law Review* 38, no. 3 (2010): 842, https://law.hofstra.edu/pdf/academics/journals/lawreview/lrv_issues_v38n03_cc1_smith_final.pdf.
45. Sullivan and Possley, "Failure to Discipline Prosecutors," 913.
46. *Imbler v. Pachtman*, 424 U.S. 409, 427 (1976).
47. *Connick v. Thompson*, 563 U.S. 51, 66–68 (2011).
48. *Connick*, 563 U.S. 51, 66.
49. Sullivan and Possley, "Failure to Discipline Prosecutors," 925.
50. Margaret Z. Johns, "Unsupportable and Unjustified: A Critique of Absolute Prosecutorial Immunity," *Fordham Law Review* 80, no. 2 (November 2011): 521, https://ir.lawnet.fordham.edu/cgi/viewcontent.cgi?article=4662&context=flr.
51. *Kalina v. Fletcher*, 522 U.S. 118, 127–129 (1997); *Buckley v. Fitzsimmons*, 509 U.S. 259, 268–269 (1993).
52. *Kalina*, 522 U.S. 118, 124; *Imbler*, 424 U.S. 409, 427.
53. *Buckley*, 509 U.S. 529, 268–270.

54. Johns, "Unsupportable and Unjustified," 527, 534.
55. Frederic Block, "Let's Put an End to Prosecutorial Immunity," Marshall Project, March 13, 2018, https://www.themarshallproject.org/2018/03/13/let-s-put-an-end-to-prosecutorial-immunity.
56. Kate Levine and Joanna Schwartz, "Hold Prosecutors Accountable, Too," *Boston Review*, June 22, 2020, https://www.bostonreview.net/articles/kate-levine-joanna-schwartz-against-prosecutorial-immunity/.
57. Alexa Van Brunt, "Prosecutors Shouldn't Have Immunity from Their Unethical—or Unlawful—Acts," *Guardian*, February 5, 2015, https://www.theguardian.com/commentisfree/2015/feb/05/prosecutors-immunity-unethical-unlawful-acts.
58. Van Brunt, "Prosecutors Shouldn't Have Immunity"; Melinda S. McCorkle, "The Prosecutor's Post-Conviction Duties," *Wyoming Lawyer*, February 2022, 12–13, http://digitaleditions.walsworthprintgroup.com/publication/?i=736874&article_id=4204737&view=articleBrowser.
59. Martin A. Schwartz, "Prosecutorial Immunity Developments," *New York Law Journal*, September 2, 2022, https://www.law.com/newyorklawjournal/2022/09/02/prosecutorial-immunity-developments/.
60. Schwartz, "Prosecutorial Immunity Developments."
61. Nazgol Ghandnoosh, "A Second Look at Injustice," Sentencing Project, May 12, 2021, 1–2, https://www.sentencingproject.org/publications/a-second-look-at-injustice/.
62. Becky Feldman, "The Second Look Movement: A Review of the Nation's Sentence Review Laws," Sentencing Project, May 2024, 4–5, https://www.sentencingproject.org/app/uploads/2024/05/Second-Look-Movement.pdf.
63. Ghandnoosh, "Second Look at Injustice," 6–7.
64. Ghandnoosh, "Second Look at Injustice," 7.
65. John F. Pfaff, "The Micro and Macro Causes of Prison Growth," *Georgia State University Law Review* 28, no. 4 (April 2013), https://readingroom.law.gsu.edu/cgi/viewcontent.cgi?article=2700&context=gsulr; John Pfaff, "A Mockery of Justice for the Poor," *The New York Times*, April 29, 2016, https://www.nytimes.com/2016/04/30/opinion/a-mockery-of-justice-for-the-poor.html.
66. Ghandnoosh, "Second Look at Injustice," 7.
67. Laura M. Maruschak and Todd D. Minton, "Correctional Populations in the United States, 2017–2018," Bureau of Justice Statistics, US Department of Justice, https://bjs.ojp.gov/library/publications/correctional-populations-united-states-2017-2018.
68. Ghandnoosh, "Second Look at Injustice," 7.
69. Ghandnoosh, "Second Look at Injustice," 7.
70. Nazgol Ghandnoosh, "America's Incarceration Crossroads: Reversing Progress amid Record-Low Crime Rates," Sentencing Project, November 12, 2025, 1, https://www.sentencingproject.org/policy-brief/americas-incarceration-crossroads-reversing-progress-amid-record-low-crime-rates/.
71. Ames Grawert and Tim Lau, "How the First Step Act Became Law—and What Happens Next," Brennan Center for Justice, January 4, 2019, https://www.brennancenter.org/our-work/analysis-opinion/how-first-step-act-became-law-and-what-happens-next.

72. Shon Hopwood, "Second Looks and Second Chances," *Cardozo Law Review* 41, no. 1 (October 2019): 104, http://cardozolawreview.com/second-looks-second-chances/.
73. Erik Ortiz, "Thousands of Federal Inmates Still Await Early Release Under Trump-Era First Step Act," NBC News, July 3, 2022, https://www.nbcnews.com/news/us-news/thousands-federal-inmates-still-await-early-release-trump-era-first-st-rcna35162.
74. Ortiz, "Thousands of Federal Inmates Still Await Early Release."
75. Kelsey Vlamis, "Trump Called on Lawmakers to Institute the 'Death Penalty for Drug Dealers' Despite the Fact That He Pardoned People Convicted of Selling Drugs," *Business Insider*, September 4, 2022, https://www.businessinsider.com/trump-calls-for-death-penalty-drug-dealers-despite-pardoning-some-2022-9.
76. Vlamis, "Trump Called on Lawmakers."
77. "Model Penal Code: Sentencing," American Law Institute, updated 2022, 802, https://www.ali.org/publications/show/sentencing/.
78. "Model Penal Code: Sentencing," American Law Institute, 338, 797.
79. Edward E. Rhine, Joan Petersilia, and Kevin R. Reitz, "The Future of Parole Release," *Crime and Justice* 46, no. 1 (2017): 294, https://www.researchgate.net/publication/309750438_The_Future_of_Parole_Release.
80. Celeste Fremon, "New Poll Shows U.S. Voters Favor 'Second Look' Policies to Reduce Excessive Prison Terms," *WitnessLA*, March 1, 2020, https://witnessla.com/new-poll-shows-u-s-voters-favor-second-look-policies-to-reduce-excessive-prison-terms/.
81. *County 10* staff, "Fremont County Coroner Died."
82. University of Wyoming student, email to author, November 8, 2022.

CHAPTER 6: ROADS TO FORGIVENESS

1. Jeanne Flavin, *Our Bodies, Our Crimes: The Policing of Women's Reproduction in America* (New York: New York University Press, 2008), 74.
2. Ann R. Bumbak, *Profiling Cop-Killers* (New York: Taylor and Francis Group, 2014), 219.
3. Bernadette Stewart, John Cochran, M. Dwayne Smith, Beth Bjerregaard, and Sondra J. Fogel, "Cop Killers and the Death Penalty: An Exploratory Mixed Method Analysis," *Journal of Crime and Justice* 43, no. 1 (2019): 66, https://www.researchgate.net/publication/331367438_Cop_killers_and_the_death_penalty_an_exploratory_mixed_methods_analysis_North_Carolina_1977-2009.
4. Mark Farnham, "Convict Who Has Served 32 Years Says He's a Million Dollar Man," *WyoFile: People, Places, and Policy*, February 24, 2015, https://wyofile.com/hope-edmonds-gets-lecture-wyoming-discrimination-2/.
5. Farnham, "Convict Who Has Served 32 Years."
6. William Browning, "Two Men, Introduced in a Gruesome Scene Almost Three Decades Ago, Still Search for Answers and Plead for Forgiveness," *Casper Star-Tribune*, January 16, 2011, *https://trib.com/news/local/two-men-introduced-in-a-gruesome-scene-almost-three-decades-ago-still-search-for-answers/article_8ae5e2aa-c8c8-51d2-803e-e309d81a4a4a.html.*
7. Rachel E. Barkow, "The Ascent of the Administrative State and the Demise of Mercy," *Harvard Law Review* 121, no. 5 (2008), https://harvardlawreview.org/2008/03/the-ascent-of-the-administrative-state-and-the-demise-of-mercy/.

8. Farnham, "Convict Who Has Served 32 Years."
9. Wyo. Stat. Ann. §7-13-402 (b)(i)(ii) (2022).
10. Farnham, "Convict Who Has Served 32 Years."
11. Amy Reid, "Steve Watt: Forgiving the Fugitive," *CBN*, 2022, https://www1.cbn.com/700club/steve-watt-forgiving-fugitive.
12. Associated Press, "Prison Guard Killed, Three Inmates Injured in Botched Escape," *AP News*, June 26, 1997, https://apnews.com/article/71ab81d8a2828267e836630fce2d7a65.
13. Browning, "Two Men."
14. Reid, "Steve Watt."
15. Reid, "Steve Watt."
16. Reid, "Steve Watt."
17. Browning, "Two Men."
18. Reid, "Steve Watt."
19. Browning, "Two Men."
20. Lee Benson, "Pardon Is Already Granted," *Deseret News* (Salt Lake City, UT), September 1, 2002, https://www.deseret.com/2002/9/1/19675015/pardon-is-already-granted.
21. Reid, "Steve Watt."
22. Reid, "Steve Watt."
23. Browning, "Two Men."
24. Browning, "Two Men."
25. Browning, "Two Men."
26. Steve Watt, interview by author, September 2022.
27. Steve Watt, interview by author.
28. Steve Watt, interview by author.
29. Steve Watt, interview by author.
30. Steve Watt, interview by author.
31. Steve Watt, interview by author.
32. Sofia Saric, "Despite Board's Recommendation, Man's Attempt at Sentence Reduction Denied," *Casper Star-Tribune*, January 6, 2023, https://trib.com/news/state-regional/despite-boards-recommendation-mans-attempt-at-sentence-reduction-denied/article_1249938c-86f5-11ed-992b-9f87d69afaa5.html.
33. Mark Farnham, letter to author, August 2022.
34. Carl P. Malmquist, "Infanticide/Neonaticide: The Outlier Situation in the United States," *Aggression and Violent Behavior* 18, no. 3 (2013): 400, https://www.sciencedirect.com/science/article/abs/pii/S1359178913000268.
35. Malmquist, "Infanticide/Neonaticide," 400.
36. Susan Hatters Friedman and Phillip J. Resnick, "Child Murder by Mothers: Patterns and Prevention," *World Psychiatry* 6, no. 3 (October 2007): 137, https://www.ncbi.nlm.nih.gov/pmc/articles/PMC2174580/.
37. Deirdre Stoelzle, "Amy Doerr Pleads Guilty: Receives Life in Prison for Death of Infant Son," *Casper Star-Tribune*, December 7, 1995, https://www.newspapers.com/newspage/446539545/.
38. Stoelzle, "Amy Doerr Pleads Guilty."

39. Stoelzle, "Amy Doerr Pleads Guilty"; Ben Neary, "Gov. Freudenthal Pardons Former Casper Prosecutor Kevin Meenan," *Casper Star-Tribune*, September 1, 2010, https://trib.com/news/state-and-regional/gov-freudenthal-pardons-former-casper-prosecutor-kevin-meenan/article_2f33a732-b5eb-11df-9ebf-001cc4c03286.html; Associated Press, "Former Natrona County Prosecutor Kevin Meenan Disbarred," *Billings (MT) Gazette*, February 23, 2004, https://billingsgazette.com/news/state-and-regional/wyoming/former-natrona-county-prosecutor-kevin-meenan-disbarred/article_50d104fd-eb22-5007-b3b4-3980a0759ae2.html.
40. Stoelzle, "Amy Doerr Pleads Guilty."
41. Stoelzle, "Amy Doerr Pleads Guilty."
42. Stoelzle, "Amy Doerr Pleads Guilty."
43. Friedman and Resnick, "Child Murder by Mothers," 137.
44. Flavin, *Our Bodies, Our Crimes*, 83.
45. Flavin, *Our Bodies, Our Crimes*, 83.
46. Malmquist, "Infanticide/Neonaticide," 400.
47. Malmquist, "Infanticide/Neonaticide," 403.
48. Malmquist, "Infanticide/Neonaticide," 403.
49. Michael Sullivan, interview by author, February 2, 2022.
50. David Garland, "The Concept of American Exceptionalism and the Case of Capital Punishment," in *American Exceptionalism in Crime and Punishment*, edited by Kevin R. Reitz (New York: Oxford University Press, 2017), 109–110; Malmquist, "Infanticide/Neonaticide," 403.
51. Antonin Scalia, "Keynote Address: Foreign Legal Authority in the Federal Courts," *Proceedings of the Annual Meeting* (American Society of International Law) 98, no. 1 (2004): 305–310, https://www.jstor.org/stable/25659941.
52. Stephen Jimenez, *The Book of Matt: Hidden Truths About the Murder of Matthew Shepard* (Hanover, NH: Steerforth, 2013); Associated Press, "23 Years Later: How Matthew Shepard's Story Sparked a Movement Against Hate," *10 Tampa Bay*, October 11, 2021, https://www.wtsp.com/article/news/history/23-years-matthew-shepard-lgbtq-legacy/67-067da2df-6e7b-4adf-bb8e-faf9b8742f46.
53. Jimenez, *Book of Matt*, 1, 11.
54. Associated Press, "New Details Emerge in Matthew Shepard Murder," ABC News, November 26, 2004, https://abcnews.go.com/2020/story?id=277685&page=1.
55. Associated Press, "New Details Emerge."
56. *Nicodemus v. Lampert*, 336 P.3d 671, 672–673 (Wyo. 2014).
57. *Nicodemus*, 336 P.3d 671, 675.
58. *Nicodemus*, 336 P.3d 671, 676.
59. Associated Press, "New Details Emerge."
60. Associated Press, "New Details Emerge."
61. Associated Press, "Matthew Shepard's Murder Still Haunts Wyoming 20 Years Later," *Los Angeles Times*, October 13, 2018, https://www.latimes.com/nation/nationnow/la-na-wyoming-matthew-shepard-20181013-story.html.
62. Associated Press, "Matthew Shepard's Murder."

63. Dennis and Judy Shepard, "Matthew Shepard's Parents Talk 25th Anniversary of His Death," interview with Katie Couric, *The Today Show*, October 12, 2023, https://www.today.com/video/matthew-shepard-s-parents-talk-25th-anniversary-of-his-death-194973253887?search=shepard.
64. Dennis and Judy Shepard, "Matthew Shepard's Parents Talk," interview with Katie Couric.
65. Dennis and Judy Shepard, "Matthew Shepard's Parents Talk," interview with Katie Couric.
66. Steve Dow, "'There's No Forgiveness in Us': 25 Years After Matthew Shepard's Murder, His Parents Want the World to Remember," *Guardian*, May 9, 2024, https://www.theguardian.com/stage/article/2024/may/10/laramie-project-matthew-shepard-murder-gay-hate-crime-wymoning.
67. Clair McFarland, "Matthew Shepard's Killer Commutation Request Denied," *Cowboy State Daily*, September 19, 2024, https://cowboystatedaily.com/2024/09/19/matthew-shepard-killer-commutation-request-denied/?utm_source=Klaviyo&utm_medium=campaign&_kx=SSKOyqape-XIj9sMr-U5Ulo9Q3Qt6y23Sar9Js_TfsY.UXPtrV.
68. McFarland, "Matthew Shepard's Killer Commutation Request Denied"; Stephen Jimenez, *The Book of Matt: Hidden Truths About the Murder of Matthew Shepard* (Lebanon, NH: Steerforth Press, 2020).
69. McFarland, "Matthew Shepard's Killer Commutation Request Denied."
70. *Nicodemus*, 336 P.3d 671, 673. I do not speak for Mr. Nicodemus but wish him the best in earning his eventual release.
71. Jimenez, *The Book of Matt*.
72. Alan K. Simpson, "A Sentence Too Cruel for Children," *Washington Post*, October 23, 2009, https://www.washingtonpost.com/archive/national/2009/10/23/a-sentence-too-cruel-for-children/60fe1508-81fa-450b-9309-8a42ee1496d2/.

CHAPTER 7: MERCY AS A VIRTUE

1. Randi Losalu, interview by author, September 2022.
2. Randi Losalu, interview by author.
3. Ian M. Borton, "Effects of Race, Sex, and Victims' Reason for Victim-Offender Dialogue," *Conflict Resolution Quarterly* 27, no. 2 (2009): 215, https://doi.org/10.1002/crq.256.
4. Jon Wilson, "Jon Wilson Curriculum Vitae: Victim-Centered VOD Facilitator and Trainer," *Just Alternatives*, 2022, https://justalternatives.org/about-us/jon-wilson-cv-training-experience-in-victimsurvivor-offender-and-vod-issues/.
5. Randi Losalu, interview by author.
6. William Shakespeare, *The Merchant of Venice*, act 4, scene 1.
7. William Shakespeare, *The Merchant of Venice*, act 4, scene 1.
8. Jeffrie G. Murphy and Jean Hampton, *Forgiveness and Mercy* (Cambridge: Cambridge University Press, 1988), 174.
9. Dan Markel, "Against Mercy," *Minnesota Law Review* 88, no. 6 (2004): 1480, https://scholarship.law.umn.edu/mlr/734/.
10. Stephen J. Morse, "Review: Justice, Mercy, and Craziness," review of *Madness and the Criminal Law*, by Norval Morris, *Stanford Law Review* 36, no. 6 (July 1984): 1507, https://www.jstor.org/stable/1228675?origin=crossref.
11. Friedrich Nietzsche, *On the Genealogy of Morals* (London: Penguin Classics, 2014), 48–59.

12. Nietzsche, *On the Genealogy of Morals*, 48–49.
13. Nietzsche, *On the Genealogy of Morals*, 49.
14. Nietzsche, *On the Genealogy of Morals*, 51.
15. Nietzsche, *On the Genealogy of Morals*, 58–59.
16. Carol S. Steiker, "Murphy on Mercy: A Prudential Reconsideration," *Criminal Justice Ethics* 27, no. 2 (June 2008): 45, https://heinonline.org/HOL/LandingPage?handle=hein.journals/crimjeth27&div=25&id=&page=; Paul Larkin, "Guiding Presidential Clemency Decision Making," *Georgetown Journal of Law and Public Policy* 18, no. 1 (Summer 2020): 451, https://www.law.georgetown.edu/public-policy-journal/wp-content/uploads/sites/23/2020/10/Guiding-Presidential-Clemency-18-2.pdf.
17. Larkin, "Presidential Clemency Decision Making," 493.
18. Steiker, "Murphy on Mercy," 16, 23.
19. Jeffrie G. Murphy, "Remorse, Apology, and Mercy," in *Criminal Law Conversations*, edited by Paul H. Robinson, Stephen Garvey, and Kimberly Kessler Ferzan (Oxford: Oxford University Press, 2011), 190–191.
20. Murphy and Hampton, *Forgiveness and Mercy*, 173.
21. Smart, "Mercy," 345, 348.
22. Smart, "Mercy," 349, 353–355.
23. Smart, "Mercy," 350–351.
24. Claudia Card, "On Mercy," *Philosophical Review* 81, no. 2 (1972): 182, 188, https://philpapers.org/rec/CAROM.
25. Card, "On Mercy," 184.
26. Card, "On Mercy," 190.
27. Card, "On Mercy," 191.
28. Nigel Walker, "The Quiddity of Mercy," *Philosophy* 70, no. 271 (1995): 27, 32–34, https://www.jstor.org/stable/3751584.
29. Andrea Ringer, "'Purely Personal and Philosophical': Gov. Winthrop Rockefeller's Death Sentence Commutations," *Arkansas Historical Quarterly* 74, no. 2 (Summer 2015): 130, https://www.jstor.org/stable/24477468.
30. Ringer, "Purely Personal and Philosophical," 130.
31. Ringer, "Purely Personal and Philosophical," 131.
32. Ringer, "Purely Personal and Philosophical," 145–146; Jenna Scafuri, "Low Recidivism Rates Reported Among Convicted Offenders," *Corrections Today*, February 2011, 14, https://www.thefreelibrary.com/Low+recidivism+rates+reported+among+convicted+murderers.-a0253538752.
33. Jocelyn M. Pollock, *Ethical Dilemmas and Decisions in Criminal Justice*, 11th ed. (Boston: Cengage Learning, 2022), 2–3.
34. Scott Powers, "Rick Scott Yanks Cop-Killer Case from Aramis Ayala, Reassigns It," *Florida Politics*, March 16, 2017, https://floridapolitics.com/archives/234092-rick-scott-yanks-cop-killer-case-aramis-ayala-reassigns/.
35. Pollock, *Ethical Dilemmas and Decisions*, 3.
36. Marion McMillan Huseas, *Legacy of Fear: Mark Hopkinson and the Bridger Valley Murders* (Cheyenne, WY: Marimac, 2006), 271.
37. Huseas, *Legacy of Fear*, 279.

38. Randi Losalu, interview by author.
39. Randi Losalu, interview by author.
40. "Our Team," Specialty Counseling and Consulting, Cheyenne, WY, accessed January 25, 2026, https://www.specialtycounseling.com/team/.

CHAPTER 8: THE POWER OF RESTORATIVE JUSTICE

1. *Graham v. Florida*, 130 S.Ct. 2011, at 2026 (2010); *Roper v. Simmons*, 543 U.S. 551, at 569 (2005); *Miller v. Alabama*, 132 S.Ct. 2455, at 2465 (2012).
2. Associated Press, "Weapon in Cheyenne Homicide May Have Been Police Chief's," *Casper Star-Tribune*, January 25, 1996.
3. Affidavit of Probable Cause, January 21, 1996, on file with the Laramie County District Court, Wyoming, and maintained by the author.
4. Affidavit of Probable Cause, January 21, 1996.
5. Affidavit of Probable Cause, January 21, 1996.
6. Associated Press, "Weapon in Cheyenne Homicide."
7. Thomas Rivera, interview by author, September 2022.
8. Megan Cassidy, "Wyoming Is One of the Toughest States for Ex-Felon Voting Rights," *Casper Star-Tribune*, September 22, 2012, https://trib.com/news/state-and-regional/wyoming-is-one-of-toughest-states-for-ex-felon-voting-rights/article_45b90f9c-b6b7-5229-800a-ebfe34dac548.html; Bridgett A. King and Laura Erickson, "Disenfranchising the Enfranchised: Exploring the Relationship Between Felony Disenfranchisement and African American Voter Turnout," *Journal of Black Studies* 47, no. 8 (2016): 801, https://journals.sagepub.com/doi/full/10.1177/0021934716659195.
9. Marc Mauer, "Confronting Felony Disenfranchisement: Toward a Movement for Full Citizenship," *Social Justice* 45, no. 1 (2018): 16, https://web.p.ebscohost.com/abstract?direct=true&profile=ehost&scope=site&authtype=crawler&jrnl=10431578&AN=134789138&h=IUn1UrhT3FfWsVFNG3rftKoUIoiq6XQdsAedyojcc8qjZnQMCG5vcqX2rUAkJTwTVXXEUl4fU%2bKNPB%2bgYulxsQ%3d%3d&crl=c&resultNs=AdminWebAuth&resultLocal=ErrCrlNotAuth&crlhashurl=login.aspx%3fdirect%3dtrue%26profile%3dehost%26scope%3dsite%26authtype%3dcrawler%26jrnl%3d10431578%26AN%3d134789138.
10. Cassidy, "Wyoming Is One of the Toughest States."
11. Joshua Wolfson, "Wyoming Lawmakers Rebuff Changes to Juvenile Life Sentences," *Casper Star-Tribune*, October 26, 2012, https://trib.com/news/state-and-regional/wyoming-lawmakers-rebuff-changes-to-juvenile-life-sentences/article_b8e4f74c-7ba3-596a-ae32-4aa6f4be8bcd.html#tncms-source=login.
12. Jeff Manza and Christopher Uggen, *Locked Out: Felon Disenfranchisement and American Democracy* (Oxford: Oxford University Press, 2006), 12.
13. Mauer, "Confronting Felony Disenfranchisement," 14.
14. Manza and Uggen, *Locked Out*, 26.
15. Lara Bazelon, *Rectify: The Power of Restorative Justice After Wrongful Conviction* (Boston: Beacon, 2018), 113.

16. John Braithwaite, "Restorative Justice: Assessing Optimistic and Pessimistic Accounts," *Crime and Justice* 25, no. 1 (1999): 1.
17. Bazelon, *Rectify*, 112.
18. Braithwaite, "Restorative Justice," 2.
19. Malcolm David Eckel, "A Buddhist Approach to Repentance," in *Repentance: A Comparative Perspective*, edited by Amitai Etzioni and David E. Carney (New York: Rowman and Littlefield, 1997), 135.
20. Braithwaite, "Restorative Justice," 4.
21. Daniel W. Van Ness and Karen Heetderks Strong, *Restoring Justice: An Introduction to Restorative Justice*, 5th ed. (Cincinnati: Anderson, 2014), 25.
22. Howard Zehr, *Changing Lenses: A New Focus for Crime and Justice* (Independence, MO: Herald Press, 1990), 227.
23. Howard Zehr, "Commentary: Restorative Justice: Beyond Victim-Offender Mediation," *Conflict Resolution Quarterly* 22, no. 1 (2004), https://onlinelibrary.wiley.com/doi/10.1002/crq.103.
24. Zehr, "Commentary," 306.
25. Zehr, "Commentary," 306.
26. Zehr, "Commentary," 306.
27. Zehr quoted in Bazelon, *Rectify*, 113.
28. Shadd Maruna, "Desistance and Restorative Justice: It's Now or Never," *Restorative Justice* 4, no. 3 (2016): 290, https://www.tandfonline.com/doi/full/10.1080/20504721.2016.1243853.
29. Maruna, "Desistance and Restorative Justice," 295.
30. Maruna, "Desistance and Restorative Justice," 296.
31. Maruna, "Desistance and Restorative Justice," 296; John Braithwaite, *Crime, Shame, and Reintegration* (Cambridge: Cambridge University Press, 1989); Dennis Sullivan and Larry Tifft, *Restorative Justice: Healing the Foundations of Our Everyday Lives* (St. Louis: Willow Tree, 2001).
32. Elizabeth Lightfoot and Mark Umbreit, "An Analysis of State Statutory Provisions for Victim-Offender Mediation," *Criminal Justice Policy Review* 15, no. 4 (2004), https://www.ojp.gov/ncjrs/virtual-library/abstracts/analysis-state-statutory-provisions-victim-offender-mediation.
33. Shannon M. Silva and Carolyn G. Lambert, "Restorative Justice Legislation in the American States: A Statutory Analysis of Emerging Legal Doctrine," *Journal of Policy Practice* 14, no. 2 (2015), https://www.researchgate.net/publication/275246984_Restorative_Justice_Legislation_in_the_American_States_A_Statutory_Analysis_of_Emerging_Legal_Doctrine.
34. Silva and Lambert, "Restorative Justice Legislation."
35. Albert Dzur and Alan Wertheimer, "Forgiveness and Public Deliberation: The Practice of Restorative Justice," *Criminal Justice Ethics* 21, no. 1 (Winter–Spring 2002), https://www.ojp.gov/ncjrs/virtual-library/abstracts/forgiveness-and-public-deliberation-practice-restorative-justice.
36. Jocelyn Pollock, *Ethical Dilemmas and Decisions in Criminal Justice*, 11th ed. (Boston: Cengage, 2022), 341.

37. Braithwaite, "Restorative Justice," 79–84.
38. Sherry Myrick, interview by author, September 2022.
39. William P. Young, *The Shack: Where Tragedy Confronts Eternity* (London: Hodder and Stoughton, 2008).
40. Sherry Myrick, interview by author.
41. Sherry Myrick, interview by author.
42. Thomas Rivera, interview by author.
43. Thomas Rivera, interview by author.
44. Thomas Rivera, interview by author.
45. Thomas Rivera, interview by author.
46. Thomas Rivera, interview by author.
47. Associated Press, "Inmates Map Out Hispanic History, State for School Kids," *Gillette (WY) News Record*, May 27, 2003.
48. Kathy Johnson, "Inmates Give $2500 in Aid," *Rawlins (WY) Times*, October 7, 2005.
49. *Miller v. Alabama*, 132 S.Ct. 2455, 2464 (2012).
50. Thomas Rivera, interview by author.
51. Thomas Rivera, interview by author.
52. Thomas Rivera, interview by author.
53. Randi Losalu, interview by author, September 2022.
54. Randi Losalu, interview by author.
55. Randi Losalu, interview by author.
56. Randi Losalu, interview by author.
57. Thomas Rivera, interview by author.

CHAPTER 9: CONSEQUENCES OF THREE STRIKES

1. "Moorcroft Woman Stable After Shooting," *Casper Star-Tribune*, April 12, 1988.
2. "Moorcroft Woman Stable After Shooting."
3. *Glenn v. Glenn*, 848 P.2d 819, 823 (Wyo. 1993).
4. Mark Gordon, letter to Orland Glenn, November 11, 2020, on file with author.
5. Grants of commutation, October 12, 2003, and March 13, 2013, on file with author.
6. Mark Gordon, letter to Orland Glenn, November 11, 2020, on file with author.
7. Gordon letter.
8. John Clark, James Austin, and D. Alan Henry, "'Three Strikes and You're Out': A Review of State Legislation," *National Institute of Justice*, September 1997, https://www.ojp.gov/pdffiles/165369.pdf; Wyo. Stat. Ann. §6-10-201 (2022).
9. Clark et al., "Three Strikes and You're Out"; Wyo. Stat. Ann. §6-10-201 (a)(ii) (2022).
10. Wyo. Stat. Ann. §6-10-201 (b)(ii) (2022).
11. *Skinner v. State*, 33 P.3d 758, 762 (Wyo. 2001).
12. *Skinner*, 33 P.3d 758.
13. *Skinner*, 33 P.3d 758, 761.
14. *Skinner*, 33 P.3d 758, 761.
15. *Skinner*, 33 P.3d 758, 761–762.
16. *Skinner*, 33 P.3d 758, 762.

17. *Skinner*, 33 P.3d 758, 762.
18. Grant of commutation, November 3, 2015, on file with author.
19. Mark Gordon, letter to Brad Skinner, November 11, 2020, on file with author.
20. David Caner, "Clemency, a Neglected Aspect of Early Christian Philanthropy," *Religions* 9, no. 8 (2018): 1, https://www.mdpi.com/2077-1444/9/8/229.
21. Mugambi Jouet, "Mass Incarceration Paradigm Shift? Convergence in an Age of Divergence," *Journal of Criminal Law and Criminology* 109, no. 4 (Fall 2019): 705, https://papers.ssrn.com/sol3/papers.cfm?abstract_id=3319069.
22. *Ewing v. California*, 538 U.S. 11, 12, 25 (2003).
23. Daniel S. Nagin, "Guest Post: Reduce Prison Populations by Reducing Life Sentences," *Washington Post*, March 21, 2019, https://www.washingtonpost.com/crime-law/2019/03/21/guest-post-reduce-prison-populations-by-reducing-life-sentences/.
24. Paul Robinson and John Darley, "Does Criminal Law Deter? A Behavioral Science Investigation," *Oxford Journal of Legal Studies* 24, no. 2 (Summer 2004), https://academic.oup.com/ojls/article-abstract/24/2/173/1488620?redirectedFrom=fulltext.
25. "Crime in the United States, 2019: Percent of Offenses Cleared by Arrest or Exceptional Means by Population Group," United States Department of Justice, Federal Bureau of Investigation, https://ucr.fbi.gov/crime-in-the-u.s/2019/crime-in-the-u.s.-2019.
26. Daniel S. Nagin, "Deterrence in the Twenty-First Century: A Review of the Evidence," *Crime and Justice* 42, no. 1 (August 2013): 199, 207, https://www.jstor.org/stable/10.1086/670398.
27. Daniel S. Nagin and Steven N. Durlauf, "Imprisonment and Crime: Can Both Be Reduced?" *Criminology and Public Policy* 10, no. 1 (2011): 38, https://www.ojp.gov/ncjrs/virtual-library/abstracts/imprisonment-and-crime-can-both-be-reduced.
28. Mollie Reilly, "Tom Cotton Thinks America Isn't Locking Enough People Up," *Huffington Post*, May 19, 2016, https://www.huffpost.com/entry/tom-cotton-criminal-justice_n_573e3305e4b00e09e89e8cad.
29. Michelle Alexander, *The New Jim Crow: Mass Incarceration in the Age of Colorblindness* (New York: New Press, 2020), 71.
30. *Small v. State*, 689 P.2d 420–421 (Wyo. 1984).
31. *Small*, 689 P.2d 420, 422.
32. Grants of commutation, April 25, 1994, and December 27, 1994, on file with author.
33. Grant of commutation, October 12, 2003, on file with author.
34. "Incarceration Trends in Wyoming," Vera Institute of Justice, December 2019, https://www.vera.org/downloads/pdfdownloads/state-incarceration-trends-wyoming.pdf.
35. "Wyoming Profile," Prison Policy Initiative, 2025, https://www.prisonpolicy.org/profiles/WY.html.
36. "Incarceration Trends in Wyoming," Vera Institute of Justice.
37. "Incarceration Trends in Wyoming," Vera Institute of Justice.
38. Daniel M. Fetsco, "No Credit for Time Served: The Fiscal and Equitable Problems with Wyoming's Parole Statutes," *Wyoming Law Review* 22, no. 1 (2022): 139–140, https://scholarship.law.uwyo.edu/wlr/vol22/iss1/5.
39. Jerome Hairston, interview with author.
40. Ben Small, letter to author, November 15, 2022.

41. Kevin R. Reitz, *American Exceptionalism in Crime and Punishment* (Oxford: Oxford University Press, 2017), 103.
42. Jouet, "Mass Incarceration Paradigm Shift," 714.
43. Jouet, "Mass Incarceration Paradigm Shift," 719.
44. Jouet, "Mass Incarceration Paradigm Shift," 715.
45. Gino Spocchia, "Lindsey Graham Confronted at Anti-Abortion Event by Woman Whose Unborn Child Had Fatal Abnormality," *Independent* (London, UK), September 14, 2022, https://www.msn.com/en-us/news/politics/lindsey-graham-confronted-at-anti-abortion-event-by-woman-whose-unborn-child-had-fatal-abnormality/ar-AA11P2Op?li=BBnbfcL.

CHAPTER 10: TRANSFORMATIVE EDUCATION AND RECOMMENDATIONS

1. *Graham v. Florida*, 130 S.Ct. 2011 (2010), Brief of former juvenile offenders, 11.
2. *Graham v. Florida*, Brief of former juvenile offenders, 12.
3. *Graham v. Florida*, Brief of former juvenile offenders, 12.
4. *Graham v. Florida*, Brief of former juvenile offenders, 12.
5. *Graham v. Florida*, Brief of former juvenile offenders, 12.
6. *Graham v. Florida*, Brief of former juvenile offenders, 12–13.
7. *Graham v. Florida*, Brief of former juvenile offenders, 13.
8. *Graham v. Florida*, Brief of former juvenile offenders, 13.
9. *Graham v. Florida*, Brief of former juvenile offenders, 11–13.
10. *Graham v. Florida*, Brief of former juvenile offenders, 14.
11. *Graham v. Florida*, Brief of former juvenile offenders, 14.
12. Leo Wolfson, "Former Wyoming U.S. Sen. Al Simpson Dies At 93, Remembered as Gentle Giant," *Cowboy State Daily*, March 14, 2025, https://cowboystatedaily.com/2025/03/14/former-wyoming-u-s-sen-al-simpson-dies-at-93-remembered-as-gentle-giant/.
13. Robin LaBarbera, "The Higher the Degree, the Lower the Recidivism Rate," *Impact Blog, LaBarbera Learning Solutions*, April 18, 2022, https://www.labarberalearning.com/the-higher-the-degree-the-lower-the-recidivism-rate.
14. LaBarbera, "The Higher the Degree."
15. LaBarbera, "The Higher the Degree."
16. Michelle Alexander, *The New Jim Crow: Mass Incarceration in the Age of Colorblindness*, 10th ed. (New York: New Press, 2020), 72.
17. Alexander, *The New Jim Crow*, 72.
18. Sarah Wood, "Prison Education Programs: What to Know," *U.S. News*, March 8, 2022, https://www.usnews.com/education/articles/prison-education-programs-what-to-know.
19. Wood, "Prison Education Programs."
20. Wood, "Prison Education Programs."
21. Wood, "Prison Education Programs"; Maya Shimizu Harris, "UW to Offer Inmate Degrees," *Casper Star-Tribune*, May 3, 2022, https://www.wyomingnews.com/news/local_news/uw-to-offer-inmate-degrees/article_6e4488c4-7562-56e7-acff-952af535d83c.html.

22. Anna Savchenko, "These Women Are Getting College Degrees in Prison, Thanks to a Northwestern Program," *Chicago Sun Times*, September 5, 2022, https://chicago.suntimes.com/education/2022/9/5/23333538/northwestern-university-logan-correctional-center-womens-prison-college-degree-education.
23. Savchenko, "These Women Are Getting College Degrees in Prison."
24. Liam Otten, "'This Program Changes People Celebrating Commencement at the Missouri Eastern Correctional Center," *Newsroom*, June 8, 2022, https://source.wustl.edu/2022/06/this-program-changes-people/.
25. Kate Colwell, "Prisons and Justice Initiative Launches Bachelor's Degree Program," *Georgetown Magazine*, April 26, 2022, https://today.advancement.georgetown.edu/georgetown-magazine/2022/prisons-and-justice-initiative-launches-bachelors-degree-program/.
26. "First Student to Attend Law School from Prison Will Attend Mitchell Hamline," *News and Events*, Mitchell Hamline School of Law, June 13, 2022, https://mitchellhamline.edu/news/2022/06/13/first-student-to-attend-law-school-from-prison-will-attend-mitchell-hamline/.
27. Jen Kocher, "For Some Wyoming Inmates, Prison Is Their Best Shot at Education," *Cowboy State Daily*, July 28, 2024, https://cowboystatedaily.com/2024/07/28/for-some-wyoming-inmates-prison-is-their-best-shot-at-education/.
28. *Sanchez v. State*, 41 P.3d 531 (Wyo. 2002).
29. "Wyoming Offender Locator," Wyoming Department of Corrections, State of Wyoming, 2022, http://wdoc-loc.wyo.gov/Home/Detail/?id=20304&dbType=WCIS.
30. *Sanchez*, 41 P.3d 531, 533.
31. *Sanchez*, 41 P.3d 531, 533.
32. *Sanchez*, 41 P.3d 531, 533.
33. *Sanchez*, 41 P.3d 531, 533.
34. Thomas Rivera, interview by author, September 2022.
35. *Gabriel v. State*, 925 P.2d 234, 236 (Wyo. 1996).
36. Thomas Rivera, interview by author.
37. Marc Mauer and Ashley Nellis, *The Meaning of Life: The Case for Abolishing Life Sentences* (New York: New Press, 2018), 9.
38. Mauer and Nellis, *Meaning of Life*, 145–146.
39. Nazgol Ghandnoosh, "A Second Look at Injustice," *Sentencing Project*, May 12, 2021, 18, https://www.sentencingproject.org/publications/a-second-look-at-injustice/.
40. Roxann Matthews, "Resentencing in California: Prosecutors Have the Tools—Will They Demonstrate the Required Bravery?" *UC Davis Social Justice Law Review* 26, no. 1 (Winter 2022), https://sjlr.law.ucdavis.edu/issues/.
41. Ghandnoosh, "Second Look at Injustice," 18.
42. Ghandnoosh, "Second Look at Injustice," 18.
43. Stefan J. Bing, "Reconsidering State Parole Board Membership Requirements in Light of Model Penal Code Sentencing Revisions," *Kentucky Law Journal* 100, no. 4 (2012): 885, https://uknowledge.uky.edu/klj/vol100/iss4/9.
44. Reitz quoted in Ghandnoosh, "Second Look at Injustice," 16.
45. Bing, "Reconsidering State Parole Board Membership," 886–887.

46. Nazgol Ghandnoosh, "The Next Step: Ending Excessive Punishment for Violent Crimes," *Sentencing Project*, July 19, 2019, 36–37, https://www.sentencingproject.org/publications/the-next-step-ending-excessive-punishment-for-violent-crimes/.
47. Jeff Manza and Christopher Uggen, *Locked Out: Felon Disenfranchisement and American Democracy* (Oxford: Oxford University Press, 2006), 12.
48. Kennedy quoted in Gabriel J. Chin, "Felon Disenfranchisement and Democracy in the Late Jim Crow Era," *Ohio State Journal of Criminal Law* 5, no. 1 (2007): 334, https://kb.osu.edu/bitstream/handle/1811/73294/OSJCL_V5N1_329.pdf?sequence=1&isAllowed=y.
49. Nazish Dholakia, "Hiring People with Conviction Histories Benefits Everyone," Vera Institute of Justice, September 7, 2022, https://www.vera.org/news/hiring-people-with-conviction-histories-benefits-everyone.
50. Dholakia, "Hiring People with Conviction Histories."
51. Dholakia, "Hiring People with Conviction Histories."
52. Nazgol Ghandnoosh, "Media Guide: 10 Crime Coverage Do's and Dont's," *Sentencing Project*, July 9, 2024, https://www.sentencingproject.org/app/uploads/2024/07/Media-Guide.pdf.
53. Ghandnoosh, "Media Guide."
54. Rachel E. Barkow, *Prisoners of Politics: Breaking the Cycle of Mass Incarceration* (Cambridge: Belknap, 2019), 115.
55. Barkow, *Prisoners of Politics*, 116.
56. Barkow, *Prisoners of Politics*, 118.
57. Mugambi Jouet, "Mass Incarceration Paradigm Shift? Convergence in an Age of Divergence," *Journal of Criminal Law and Criminology* 109, no. 4 (Fall 2019): 764, https://papers.ssrn.com/sol3/papers.cfm?abstract_id=3319069.
58. Jouet, "Mass Incarceration Paradigm Shift," 764.
59. Wyo. Const., art. 1 §15.
60. Vanessa Barker, "The Politics of Punishing: Building a State Governance Theory of American Imprisonment Variation," *Punishment and Society* 8, no. 1 (August 2016): 12, https://journals.sagepub.com/doi/10.1177/1462474506059138.

EPILOGUE: ACTION AND CHANGE

1. Keith Humphreys, "America's Incarceration Rate Is About to Fall Off a Cliff," *The Atlantic*, June 25, 2025, https://www.theatlantic.com/ideas/archive/2025/06/prisoner-populations-are-plummeting/683310/.
2. Jeremy Travis, Bruce Western, and Steve Redburn, "The Growth of Incarceration in the United States: Exploring Causes and Consequences," *National Academy of Sciences, Engineering, and Medicine* (2014): 4, https://nap.nationalacademies.org/catalog/18613/the-growth-of-incarceration-in-the-united-states-exploring-causes.
3. Clair McFarland, "Gordon Signs Bill Giving Guns Rights Back to Non-Violent Felons," *Cowboy State Daily*, March 17, 2023, https://cowboystatedaily.com/2023/03/17/gordon-signs-bill-giving-guns-rights-back-to-non-violent-felons/.
4. Sofia Saric, "Nonviolent Felons Could Regain Civil Rights in Wyoming," *Casper Star-Tribune*, January 30, 2023, https://trib.com/news/state-regional/nonviolent-felons

-could-regain-civil-rights-in-wyoming/article_ad688c86-9e85-11ed-a1c8-5fdb6eb3d6f3.html.

5. *Miller v. Alabama*, 132 S.Ct. 2455 (2012).
6. Wyo. Stat. Ann. §§6-10-301 (c) and 7-13-402 (a) (2022).
7. Milton J. Valencia and John R. Ellement, "SJC Decision Could Change Handling of Juvenile Offenders," *The Boston Globe*, December 27, 2013, https://www.bostonglobe.com/metro/2013/12/27/sjc-decision-could-change-state-handling-juvenile-offenders/Q1Yo6ZEhn8609diRkSbRfL/story.html.
8. *Commonwealth v. Mattis*, 493 Mass. 216, 221–22 (2024).
9. Maggie Mullen, "Why Wyoming Sent 240 Inmates to a Mississippi Prison," *Wyofile*, December 11, 2023, https://wyofile.com/why-wyoming-sent-240-inmates-to-a-mississippi-prison/.
10. Mullen, "Why Wyoming Sent 240 Inmates."
11. Mullen, "Why Wyoming Sent 240 Inmates."
12. Dean Fioresi, Chelsea Hylton, and Matthew Rodriguez, "Menedez Brothers Eligible for Parole After Resentencing: One Huge Step Closer to Bringing the Boys Home," CBS News Los Angeles, May 14, 2025, https://www.cbsnews.com/losangeles/news/menendez-brothers-resentencing-hearing-los-angeles/.
13. Jeanine Santucci, "Menedez Brothers' Parole Hopes Shattered After 'Rule-Breaking': What Now?" *USA Today*, August 23, 2025, https://www.usatoday.com/story/news/nation/2025/08/23/menendez-brothers-parole-denied-prison/85796163007/.
14. Jaimie Ding, "California Parole Board Denies Release for Erik Menendez Due to Misbehavior in Prison," Associated Press, August 21, 2025, https://apnews.com/article/menendez-brothers-freedom-murder-parole-erik-lyle-483fee4506e2ea7acb7ce846e844bb8b; Santucci, "Menedez Brothers' Parole Hopes Shattered."
15. Humphreys, "America's Incarceration Rate."
16. Sentencing Project, "Criminal Justice Experts: Congress' Pro-Prison Crime Bills Will Make DC Less Safe," September 8, 2025, https://www.sentencingproject.org/press-releases/criminal-justice-experts-congress-pro-prison-crime-bills-will-make-dc-less-safe/.
17. Sentencing Project, "Criminal Justice Experts."
18. Lindsey Graham, "Graham, Cornyn, Budd and Blackburn Introduce Bill to Eliminate D.C.'s Soft-on-Crime Laws," September 16, 2025, https://www.lgraham.senate.gov/public/index.cfm/2025/9/graham-cornyn-budd-and-blackburn-introduce-bill-to-eliminate-d-c-s-soft-on-crime-laws.

Acknowledgments

Many people have helped me with this book, but none has been as important as my wife, Mollie Hand. From reading early drafts, to creating spreadsheets and graphs, to giving advice on the cover or keeping our kids and dogs out of my hair so I could edit, she was as important to this book getting done as I was. Thank you so much, dear.

I'd like to thank Nina McConigley, who gave me the idea and confidence to write this book, and Governor Mike Sullivan for agreeing to work with me on the project. Nina's suggestion and Governor Sullivan's timely call planted the seed that became this manuscript.

To Mark Corbett, Darla Rouse, and Tommy Rivera, thank you for sharing your story with me and also with my students and the world. Your lived experience and positivity have changed hearts and minds. Thank you to Russell Henderson, Martin Gabriel, Francisco "Pancho" Sanchez, Amy Doerr, Ben Small, Brad Skinner, and James Koester for sharing your stories—I am grateful and will continue this work to help bring you home.

https://doi.org/10.5876/9781646428557.c012

A special thank you to the late, legendary Alan Simpson. While I didn't interview him for this book, his contributions to the second chance movement are significant and motivated me.

Thank you to Larry DeGraw for his willingness to speak with me before he suddenly left us. I hope this book is a small testament to his humanity.

I owe a debt of gratitude to Eric Wodahl, Kipp Coddington, Bernard Phelan, and Ray Hunkins, a diverse group of extraordinary gentlemen who read my entire book—in some cases on extremely short notice—and provided invaluable feedback.

Thank you to Randi Losalu, Sherry Myrick, and Steve Watt for helping me promote the idea of restorative justice by sharing their actions of forgiveness and resilience and for the victim advocacy they have engaged in.

I owe a special thank you to Robin Everett at the Wyoming State Archives, who not only supplied critical research for this book but also provided guidance and friendship, for which I am eternally grateful.

I would like to thank Governor Mark Gordon and his staff for their timely responses to my record requests and to Director Dan Shannon and the hard-working staff at the Wyoming Department of Corrections. Dan was one of the first people I told about this book, and he was consistently supportive. Director Margy White and Lori Garrison from the Wyoming Board of Parole were also incredibly helpful in reviewing my research and manuscript.

To my students—thank you for your help with this process. Your contributions were critical as I tried out early versions of chapter narratives, sharing my research and opinions with you. A few of you did research for me or reviewed my citations and provided encouragement throughout. There are too many of you to mention here, but you are the future and the reason why I teach and do this work.

Finally, I would like to thank my editor, Darrin Pratt, and the staff at the University Press of Colorado for believing in this project years ago. It has taken a few years, but the support from the publication team was constant. The book would not have been possible without their investment of time and effort.

Index

About the Author

Dan Fetsco is an attorney, a professor, and an author. As an attorney, he has served as a public defender, a trial prosecutor, and an appellate prosecutor; he also represented the Wyoming Board of Parole and the Wyoming Department of Corrections. He served as deputy and executive director for the Wyoming Board of Parole for a combined ten years. Since 2017, Dan has been a lecturer in the Criminal Justice and Sociology Department at the University of Wyoming. He has published several law review articles on parole and reentry. Dan also serves as secretary of the board of directors for Compassion Wyoming, an advocacy group that pursues second chance legislation and life sentence reform in Wyoming.